MASTER POINT PRESS
TORONTO • ONTARIO

# ROMAN

# KEYCARD

# BLACKWOOD

## SLAM BIDDING FOR THE 21ST CENTURY

# EDDIE KANTAR

**Master Point Press**
331 Douglas Ave.
Toronto, Ontario, Canada
M5M 1H2
(416) 781-0351
Website:        http://www.masterpointpress.com
Email:          info@masterpointpress.com


**National Library of Canada Cataloguing in Publication**

Kantar, Edwin B., 1932-
        Roman Keycard Blackwood: slam bidding in the 21st century /
Eddie Kantar

ISBN 1-894154-88-6

        1. Contract bridge — Bidding  I. Title.

GV1282.43K36 2004   795.41'52        C2004-902172-9


Editor                          Ray Lee
Cover and interior design       Olena S. Sullivan/New Mediatrix


1 2 3 4 5 6 7   09 08 07 06 05 04
Printed in Canada.

# CONTENTS

# INTRODUCTION

This is my fourth effort at trying to corral RKB (Roman Keycard Blackwood). You'd think by now I'd have a handle on it. Well each time out I think my latest version is the best and so it is with this one. Even so I have misgivings.

The reasons for the misgivings deal with the expertise level of the reader. Some of you may be reading about this convention for the first time (although it's been around long enough for most people at least to have experimented). Others play RKB but only in a skeletal form and may not want to go much beyond that. Still others are experienced and want to learn the finer points of the convention, and finally there are the experts who may want to see if I have actually come up with something they can graft onto their methods. Can one book cater to all these different readers?

My fear is mostly for the first two groups. I feel strongly that they should experiment with using two RKB asks instead of one, a major departure from 'standard', plus the queen-ask, plus the Specific King Ask, plus determining what the agreed suit is (most important of all!). If you fall into these categories, stay with the first four chapters until you feel comfortable before going on.

The bad new is that several chapters in this book are not for everyone; the good news is that you can live without these chapters without losing all that much. But I don't want anyone throwing up their hands up in despair. In particular, the section on the minors (starting with Chapter 10) should be taken slowly, saving the non-agreement chapters until the bitter end. As for the more experienced players, those who are willing to go out on a limb and give some of this a try, my suggestion is that you and your favorite partner each have a book (always building up sales) and go over the recommendations to determine which ones you want to use and initial them — in blood! Also, if you decide not to go along with some of these asks, you should come to terms with what you are going to do when such and such a situation comes up. They don't go away. And remember, what was mentioned in the other three versions applies here (in spades): even a bad agreement is better than no agreement.

If you can get a handle on even some of this, your slam bidding should improve more than you can imagine!

Good luck.

*Eddie Kantar*

# THE
# BASICS

## PART ONE

# C H A P T E R  1

## TWICE THE FUN!

You and your partner have agreed upon a trump suit and someone wants to ask for aces. First of all, forget aces. From now on you will asking for Keycards. What is a Keycard? The four aces and the king of the agreed suit are Keycards. Suddenly there are five Keycards. And let's not forget the queen of the agreed suit, but we'll save that for the next chapter.

So now that you have five Keycards to deal with, how do you answer a Roman Keycard Blackwood (RKB) ask? Assume that the ask is 4NT, which is what it will be after major-suit agreement. After minor-suit agreement, you don't want to know what the ask is just yet. (There is still time to give up on this book.)

And I'm sure you will be overjoyed to hear that in this book we are going to use two sets of responses to RKB

(1) when the strong hand asks the weak hand;
(2) when the weak hand asks the strong hand.

Hello? Are you still there?

## WHEN THE STRONG HAND ASKS THE WEAK HAND, THINK 1430 ('FOURTEEN THIRTY') RESPONSES

When the stronger of the two hands does the asking, the usual case, the ideal case, 1430 responses are in play. Assuming the ask is 4NT, (4♠ 'Kickback' is discussed in the next chapter) these are the responses by steps. Keep in mind that the king of the agreed suit is included in the response. All numbers refer to Keycards.

| | | |
|---|---|---|
| 5♣, the 1st step | = | 1 or 4 (the 14) |
| 5♢, the 2nd step | = | 3 or 0 (the 30) |
| 5♡, the 3rd step | = | 2 or 5 without the queen of the agreed suit |
| 5♠, the 4th step | = | 2 or 5 with the queen of the agreed suit |

**Note:** A '5' Keycard response is so rare (it means the asker didn't have a single Keycard) that it will not be included in any further listing. Also '2' without the queen or '2' with the queen will be referred to as '2 with' or '2 without'.

Because the difference between the two possible numbers of Keycards indicated by each of the 5♣ and 5♢ responses is three, it is assumed that the asker *will know* from the previous bidding whether, for example, responder has

1 or 4 Keycards. When the difference is three and you have trouble knowing which it is from partner's bidding, get a partner who bids better or consider taking up gin rummy.

## WHEN THE WEAK HAND ASKS THE STRONG HAND, THINK 3014 ('THIRTY-FOURTEEN') RESPONSES

When the weak hand asks the strong hand, which is less often, 3014 responses are in play:

| | | |
|---|---|---|
| 5♣, the 1st step | = | 3 or 0 (assume 3) |
| 5♢, the 2nd step | = | 1 or 4 (assume 4) |
| 5♡, the 3rd step | = | 2 without |
| 5♠, the 4th step | = | 2 with |

The difference between 1430 and 3014 responses is that steps 1 and 2 are reversed. Which method is better, and why bother? The method that produces a 1st step response of 5♣ more often is better because it allows the asker more room for the rest of the auction, such as the queen-ask. Patience.

When *strong asks weak*, the most likely response is '1'. If you are playing 1430 that is the 5♣ response. However, when *weak asks strong*, the most likely response is '3', again the 5♣ response. If you are playing 3014, 5♣ is what you will get most of the time.

The obvious conclusion is to play 1430 responses when strong asks weak and 3014 responses when weak asks strong. Why not have the best of both worlds? Indeed, why not? This book champions both sets of responses.

Before we go any further, we have to have rules to decide who is the 'strong' and who is the 'weak' hand. These rules had better be simple (unless I want to end up with no readers!) — and they are.

## WHEN OPENER DOES THE ASKING

When opener asks for Keycards, opener is presumed to be the strong hand, so 1430 responses. However, if responder has made a strong jump shift and opener winds up asking for Keycards, it is a 3014 situation. Don't hold your breath.

| Opener | Responder | |
|---|---|---|
| 1♡ | 2♣ | 1. Game-forcing splinter(slam try). |
| 2♡ | 3♠[1] | 2. Cuebid. |
| 4♣[2] | 4♢[3] | 3. RKB(1430) — opener asking |
| 4NT[4] | ? | (whenever opener asks, 1430). |

| Opener | Responder | |
|--------|-----------|---|
| 1♣ | 1♠ | 1. Two-suited slam try; some play it as a splinter. |
| 2♠ | 4♡[1] | 2. RKB (1430) — opener asking. It actually doesn't matter what 4♡ means, opener is the one asking so 1430 responses apply. |
| 4NT[2] | ? | |

| Opener | Responder | |
|--------|-----------|---|
| 1♡ | 2♠[1] | 1. Strong. |
| 3♠ | 4♣[2] | 2. Cubeid. |
| 4NT[3] | ? | 3. RKB, 3014 responses. The exception — opener asks after a jump shift. At all other times when opener asks, 1430 responses apply. |

## WHEN RESPONDER ASKS FOR KEYCARDS

When responder asks for Keycards, responder is considered the strong hand (1430) *unless* opener has shown extras by:

1. Opening 1NT(strong) or 2NT(even stronger).
2. Opening 1♣ or 2♣, strong and artificial.
3. Reversing.
4. Making a strength-showing jump.
5. Making a game-forcing cuebid in competition.

If opener has done any of the above (usually jumping or reversing), and responder asks for Keycards, it is a 3014 ask. Why? Because opener has shown extra strength and the 5♣ ('3') response becomes very likely. And we love '3' responses, remember. When I refer to this situation throughout the book, I mean to imply all the possibilities, even though they may not be spelled out each time. The bottom line is that the responses will be 1430 about 80%-85% of the time.

**Add on:** You must accept certain inequities in this scenario. For example, if the opening bid is 1NT (15-17), opener is considered the strong hand regardless. This may seem strange to a responder who is looking at 19+ HCP and is still considered the weak hand. It happens.

Let's look at a few sequences to see how simple this is:

| Opener | Responder |
|--------|-----------|
| 1♢ | 1♡ |
| 2♡ | 4NT ? |

Responder is asking and opener hasn't jumped or reversed, so it is strong asking weak (1430).

| Opener | Responder |
|--------|-----------|
| 1◇ | 1♡ |
| 3♡ | 4NT ? |

3014: opener has jumped, so now a 5♣ ('3') response is very likely.

| Opener | Responder |
|--------|-----------|
| 1◇ | 1♡ |
| 1♠ | 4♠ |
| 4NT ? | |

Opener is asking; even though responder has jumped, as long as it wasn't a jump shift, 1430 applies.

| Opener | Oppt. | Responder | Oppt. |
|--------|-------|-----------|-------|
| 1◇ | 2♡¹ | 2♠ | pass |
| 3♡² | pass | 3♠ | pass |
| 4♠ | pass | 4NT? | |

1. Weak.    2. Game-forcing cuebid.

3014: opener has made a game-forcing cuebid which is easily the equivalent of jumping or reversing.

| Opener | Responder | |
|--------|-----------|---|
| 1♡ | 2♠¹ | 1. Strong jump-shift. |
| 4♠ | 4NT ? | |

1430: when a player who has made a strong jump shift asks for Keycards, it is an automatic 1430 ask.

| Opener | Responder |
|--------|-----------|
| 1♠ | 2♣ |
| 3♠ | 4NT ? |

3014: opener has jumped.

| Opener | Responder |
|--------|-----------|
| 1♣ | 1◇ |
| 1♡ | 1♠ |
| 3♠ | 4NT ? |

3014: opener has jumped.

| Opener | Responder |
|--------|-----------|
| 1◇ | 1♠ |
| 2♡ | 4♡ |
| 4NT ? | |

1430: opener is asking.

| Opener | Responder |        |
|--------|-----------|--------|
| 1♢     | 1♠[1]     | 1. Forcing. |
| 2♡     | 3♡        |        |
| 4♡     | 4NT ?     |        |

3014: opener has reversed.

| Opener | Responder |
|--------|-----------|
| 1♠     | 2♢        |
| 2♡     | 3♠        |
| 4♣     | 4NT ?     |

1430: opener hasn't jumped or reversed.

Now you try it. Before looking at the explanation below each sequence, decide whether the Keycard ask requires 1430 or 3014 responses.

| Opener | Responder |        |
|--------|-----------|--------|
| 1♣     | 2♡[1]     | 1. Strong. |
| 3♡     | 4NT ?     |        |

1430: jump-shifter asking.

| Opener | Responder |        |
|--------|-----------|--------|
| 1♣     | 2♡[1]     | 1. Strong. |
| 3♡     | 3♠        |        |
| 4NT ?  |           |        |

3014: the exception. Responder has made a strong jump shift; otherwise if opener asks, 1430.

| Opener | Responder |
|--------|-----------|
| 1♣     | 1♠        |
| 2♠     | 4NT ?     |

1430: opener hasn't jumped or reversed.

| Opener | Responder |
|--------|-----------|
| 1♠     | 2♡        |
| 3♡     | 4NT ?     |

1430: responder is asking and opener has neither jumped nor reversed.

| Opener | Responder |        |
|--------|-----------|--------|
| 1♣     | 1♡        |        |
| 1♠     | 2♢[1]     | 1. Fourth suit. |
| 2♡     | 4NT ?     |        |

1430: opener has shown a minimum (no jump, no reverse) and responder is asking.

| Opener | Responder | |
|--------|-----------|---|
| 1NT[1] | 3♡[2] | 1. 15-17. |
| 4♡ | 4NT ? | 2. Slam try in hearts. |

3014: when the opening bid is 1NT (strong) or 2NT (stronger) and responder asks, it is 3014. Live with it.

| Opener | Responder | |
|--------|-----------|---|
| 1♠ | 2NT[1] | 1. Forcing spade raise. |
| 3♢[2] | 4NT ? | 2. Shortness. |

1430: opener hasn't jumped or reversed. Note: If opener had jumped to 4♠ over 2NT, systemically showing a minimum hand, he would not be considered to have made a strength-showing jump. A jump must show *extras* for responder's ask to become 3014. If the jump to 4♠ shows a minimum, 4NT by responder remains a 1430 ask. *Don't you dare go away!*

| Opener | Responder |
|--------|-----------|
| 1♣ | 1♡ |
| 3♡ | 4NT ? |

3014: opener has jumped (a 'real' jump!).

| Opener | Responder |
|--------|-----------|
| 1♣ | 1♡ |
| 1♠ | 4NT ? |

1430: opener hasn't jumped or reversed.

Now let's look at some 13-card hands. Finally!:

| Opener | Responder | |
|--------|-----------|---|
| ♠ K Q 5 | ♠ A J 7 4 3 | 1 RKB(1430): opener hasn't |
| ♡ A K 8 6 3 2 | ♡ 5 4 | jumped or reversed. |
| ♢ 4 2 | ♢ K Q J 6 3 | 2. '2 with'. |
| ♣ Q 8 4 | ♣ A | 3. One Keycard missing. |
| | | |
| 1♡ | 1♠ | |
| 2♠ | 4NT[1] | |
| 5♠[2] | 6♠[3] | |
| pass | | |

| Opener | Responder | |
|---|---|---|
| ♠ J 10 4 2 | ♠ Q 7 6 5 3 | 1. RKB (3014) — opener has |
| ♡ A K Q | ♡ 6 | jumped. |
| ◇ A Q J 4 | ◇ 2 | 2. '2 without'. |
| ♣ Q 5 | ♣ A K J 7 | 3. 2 Keycards missing. |
| 1◇ | 1♠ | |
| 4♠ | 4NT¹ | |
| 5♡² | 5♠³ | |
| pass | | |

## TAKEOUT DOUBLES

If a takeout double is followed by a Keycard ask, the doubler is the strong hand (no kidding) and 1430 responses are in play. If the partner of the doubler asks, then it's 3014.

## OVERCALLS

If an overcall is followed by a Keycard auction, the partner of the overcaller (called the 'advancer')is considered the strong hand so it's 1430 if he asks, 3014 if the overcaller asks.

## THE BOTTOM LINE

Is it really worth all of this trouble to save one eensy teensy step? Yes! You will see how important that one little step can be in future chapters. It's one of the keys to better slam bidding. You can handle it!

Assuming you are willing to try two sets of asks, and agree with 'strong hand — weak hand' asks to maximize the chances for a 5♣ response, this is what you have to remember:

1) If opener asks, it is 1430 unless partner has jump-shifted — then 3014.

2) If responder asks, it is also 1430 unless opener has jumped or reversed etc., — then it is 3014.

These 'weak hand — strong hand' rules are arbitrary. If you and your partner can come up with a better version, go for it, but keep in mind that the more first-step responses you get to RKB asks, the better placed you are.

That's all there is to it. Hang in there.

# MAJOR -SUIT AUCTIONS

## PART TWO

# CHAPTER 2

# THE TRUMP QUEEN-ASK

Before we discuss the queen-ask itself, let's digress for a moment. After major-suit agreement, 4NT is the standard Keycard ask. However, some players like to use a variation called Kickback. In this version of RKB, 4♠ is RKB when hearts is the agreed suit. Is this better than using 4NT all the time?

Most players who use Kickback also play 3014 responses. They argue that when using 4NT to ask for Keycards a 5◇ '1' response takes away the space for a queen-ask when hearts is the agreed suit. A 4♠ Keycard-ask leaves room for the queen-ask because the '1' response is 5♣, so that 5◇ can be used as the queen-ask.

Sounds good, but if you play two sets of responses to 4NT as suggested, it is not necessary. With 1430 (the stronger hand asking), the '1' response to 4NT is 5♣ and (as we shall see shortly) 5◇ is the queen-ask, so no problem there. A 5◇ response shows '0' or '3', usually '0'. After a 5◇ response, with hearts agreed, a rebid of 5♡ is to play facing '0' and the queen-ask facing '3'. To ask for the queen opposite a '0' response, 5♠ is the queen-ask. So no problem there.

If weak is asking strong, the most likely 3014 response is 5♣('3'), once again allowing for a 5◇ queen-ask. If the response is 5◇ showing '1' or '4' (you will assume '4' when the strong hand is being asked), 5♡ is the queen-ask facing '4' and to play facing '1'. Who signs off after a '4' response? Please.

The bottom line is that if you play both 1430 and 3014 as I suggest, you lose little by using 4NT as RKB in all major-suit agreement auctions. If you play Kickback you have to have solid agreements on when 4♠ is RKB for hearts if spades is a previously-bid suit. Here's another problem:

| Opener | Responder |
|--------|-----------|
| 1♡     | 2◇        |
| 3♡     | 4♠        |

Playing Kickback this is clearly RKB for hearts. Fine. But what if responder wants to splinter in spades? In order to splinter in spades, he is supposed to rebid 4NT (what 4♠ would normally have meant). Okay, so say he bids 4NT to show a spade splinter. Now what if opener wants to ask responder for Keycards? I'm sure Kickback players have this all worked out. Many years ago I asked Paul Soloway about this as he and the late Bobby Goldman were playing Kickback at the time. He told me that he and Bobby had pages of copious notes dealing with this problem. That was enough for me. From here on in, after major-suit agreement, 4NT is RKB with two sets of responses.

## THE TRUMP QUEEN-ASK FOLLOWING A 5♣ RESPONSE TO 4NT (1430 OR 3014)

After a 5♣ response to RKB, 5◇ is the trump queen-ask. The denial response is a return to the five-level of the agreed major. (The denial response to all asks is a minimum return to the agreed suit — with the two exceptions mentioned below to the queen-ask.)

COMING UP SHORT

| Opener | Responder | |
|---|---|---|
| ♠ A 8 4 3 | ♠ K 7 6 5 2 | |
| ♡ A 9 | ♡ K Q 4 | 1. RKB (3014 — opener has |
| ◇ 5 2 | ◇ K Q J 6 | jumped). |
| ♣ A K Q 6 3 | ♣ 2 | 2. '3'. |
| | | 3. Queen-ask. |
| 1♣ | 1♠ | 4. Negative. |
| 4♠ | 4NT[1] | 5. Once responder discovers the |
| 5♣[2] | 5◇[3] | hand is off the ♠Q and an ace, |
| 5♠[4] | pass[5] | he opts out. |

These are the good news queen-showing responses:

### 1. A jump to the six-level of the agreed suit

This jump denies a side-suit king or a side-suit 'extra' (coming up). When responding to the queen-ask holding the queen of the agreed suit plus a side-suit king, bid the king-suit. With two kings, bid the king-suit that can be shown at the lower level. If both kings can be shown at the same level, show the lower-ranking king first.

RIGHT IN THE HEART OF TEXAS

| Opener | Responder |
|---|---|
| ♠ A Q 5 2 | ♠ K J 8 6 3 |
| ♡ A 7 | ♡ K 5 4 |
| ◇ A 9 7 3 2 | ◇ 5 |
| ♣ K 4 | ♣ A Q 5 2 |

| Opener | Responder | |
|---|---|---|
| 1◇ | 1♠ | 1. 3014 — opener has jumped. |
| 4♠ | 4NT[1] | 2. '3'. The most common response |
| 5♣[2] | 5◇[3] | to a 3014 ask. |
| 6♣[4] | 7♠[5] | 3. Queen-ask. |
| | | 4. Yes, with the ♣K, but no ♡K (would have bid 5♡, the king that could have been shown at a lower level). |
| | | 5. Just what the doctor ordered. |

## 2. *The 5NT response to the queen-ask*

If you have the queen without a side-suit king, but do have an 'extra', respond 5NT. In order of importance, these are considered 'extras'

1. The queen of partner's first-bid side suit.
2. Third-round control in partner's second-bid side suit (the queen or a doubleton). This is done when partner's first-bid suit is the trump suit.
3. Extra trump length if you are the long trump hand
4. If no side suits have been bid, third-round control in any unbid suit.

I JUST MIGHT HAVE SOMETHING FOR YOU

| Opener | Responder | |
|---|---|---|
| ♠ K 6 4 2 | ♠ A Q J 7 3 | 1. Splinter for spades. |
| ♡ 6 | ♡ 8 7 4 | 2. Strong spades, little else. |
| ◇ A K J 9 3 | ◇ Q 7 | 3. RKB (1430) — opener asking. |
| ♣ A 10 4 | ♣ 6 5 2 | 4. '1'. |
| | | 5. Queen-ask. |
| 1◇ | 1♠ | 6. Yes, with a non-king extra – here |
| 3♡[1] | 4♠[2] | the ◇Q, the queen of the asker's |
| 4NT[3] | 5♣[4] | first-bid suit. Responder has |
| 5◇[5] | 5NT[6] | shown strong spades so the fifth |
| 6♠[7] | | spade is not really an extra. |
| | | 7. Glad you remembered the system, but we're off an ace! |

*Note:* If the responder to a queen-ask knows of at least ten trumps between the two hands (equivalent of the queen) he answers as if he has the queen.

## TEN IS WHEN

| Opener | Responder | |
|---|---|---|
| ♠ A K 4 | ♠ Q 6 | 1. Limit raise. |
| ♡ A K 10 7 3 | ♡ J 8 6 4 2 | 2. RKB (1430) — opener asking. |
| ◊ 5 | ◊ A J 7 4 | 3. '1'. |
| ♣ K Q J 5 | ♣ 7 3 | 4. Queen-ask. |
| | | 5. Yes, knowing of a ten-card heart |
| 1♡ | 3♡[1] | fit. The jump also denies a |
| 4NT[2] | 5♣[3] | side-suit king or a side-suit |
| 5◊[4] | 6♡[5] | 'extra'. |
| pass | | |

## TEN, AGAIN THE MAGIC NUMBER

| Opener | Responder | |
|---|---|---|
| ♠ A K 9 3 2 | ♠ 8 7 6 5 4 | 1. Strong and artificial. |
| ♡ A K Q 5 4 | ♡ 6 | 2. Waiting. |
| ◊ K Q | ◊ 9 8 2 | 3. Splinter agreeing spades. |
| ♣ 3 | ♣ A J 6 5 | 4. RKB (1430 — opener asking). |
| | | 5. '1'. |
| 2♣[1] | 2◊[2] | 6. Queen-ask. |
| 2♠ | 4♡[3] | 7. Yes, knows of a ten-card spade |
| 4NT[4] | 5♣[5] | fit. Additionally, the leap to six of |
| 5◊[6] | 6♠[7] | the agreed suit denies a side-suit |
| pass | | king or a significant extra. Give |

responder four small spades and responder denies the queen by retreating to 5♠. Opener passes fearing a spade loser as well as a minor-suit ace missing.

Basically the idea is to stay out of a small slam missing an ace and the queen of the agreed suit if you have an eight-card fit. If you have a nine-card trump fit missing the queen and are looking at the jack, you are a slight favorite not to lose a trump trick. If you have both the jack and the ten, you become more of a favorite not to lose a trick. These are the numbers:

| | | | | |
|---|---|---|---|---|
| AKxxx | facing | xxxx | 40% | (No queen, no jack) |
| AKxxx | facing | Jxxx | 53% | (No queen, but jack) |
| AKJxx | facing | xxxx | 53% | (No queen, but jack) |
| AKJ10x | facing | xxxx | 58% | (AKJ10 bunched) |

However, if you are off an ace plus the queen of trumps and you know you have an eight-card trump fit, your percentage move is to give up on slam unless you are looking at the J10 of trumps.

## THE 5♡ QUEEN-ASK FOLLOWING A 5◇ RESPONSE TO RKB (1430)

Playing 1430 (strong asking weak), a 5◇ response shows '3 or 0'. Every so often it will be '3' (when opener or a two-level responder is responding); more often than not it is '0'. In any case, you will know which it is from the bidding and from the number of Keycards you have. *You will know.*

*With hearts agreed,* after a 5◇ response showing '3' or '0', a return to 5♡ is to play facing '0' (partner will pass), but the queen-ask facing '3'. To ask for the queen facing a known '0' (far out to say the least) bid 5♠, a grand slam try. Why a grand slam try? Because if responder doesn't have the queen, the hand is committed to the six-level. Therefore, if responder has the queen, he is supposed to jump to seven!

NICE SUPPORT

| Opener | Responder |
|--------|-----------|
| ♠ 8 6 2 | ♠ A K |
| ♡ A K Q | ♡ J 9 7 6 4 3 |
| ◇ 5 4 | ◇ A K 9 |
| ♣ A 8 7 4 3 | ♣ K 2 |
| | |
| 1♣ | 1♡ |
| 2♡ | 4NT[1] |
| 5◇[2] | 5♡[3] |
| 7♡[4] | pass |

1. RKB (1430). Opener hasn't jumped or reversed.
2. '3' or '0' (guess which).
3. Queen-ask facing '3', to play facing '0'.
4. Shows the ♡Q, denies a side-suit king or a side-suit extra.

DANCING IN THE TULIPS

*With spades agreed,* things are simpler:

| Opener | Responder |
|--------|-----------|
| ♠ A 8 6 3 | ♠ K 7 5 2 |
| ♡ 9 | ♡ A J 7 6 4 |
| ◇ A K Q J 7 2 | ◇ 5 |
| ♣ K 5 | ♣ A 8 3 |
| | |
| 1◇ | 1♡ |
| 1♠ | 4♠ |
| 4NT[1] | 5◇[2] |
| 5♡[3] | 5♠[4] |
| 6◇[5] | pass[6] |

1. RKB (1430) — opener asking.
2. '3' or '0' — must be '3' given the leap to 4♠.
3. Queen-ask facing '3'.
4. Sorry, don't have it.
5. To play (let's hope you've read this book!). When the RKB bidder returns to his first suit at the six-level, it is to play — even if there has been jump agreement in a secondary suit; all this is coming up in the chapter entitled 'Second Suit Options'. I know, you can hardly wait.
6. Yes, I read the stupid book.

# THE QUEEN-ASK FOLLOWING A 5◇ RESPONSE TO RKB (3014)

*When hearts are the agreed suit,* then after a 5◇ response to a 3014 ask showing '1' or '4', 5♡ is the queen-ask facing '4', but to play facing '1'. I'll let you in on a little secret: when the 'strong' hand responds 5◇ to a 3014 ask, the strong hand has '1' once or twice a year — max. The queen-ask facing '4' is 5♡ to save bidding space. There is no such animal as a sign-off after a '4' response.

The negative response to a 5♡ queen-ask is 6♣! What can the poor devil do? The queen-ask is a grand slam try and the asker is willing to play a small slam even if the responder doesn't have the queen. Positive responses to a 5♡ queen-ask, a grand slam try, are king-showing responses or 5NT to show a non-king extra or a leap to 7♡ with the queen and no extra. The 5NT and king-showing responses allow the asker to consider playing 7NT.

*When spades is the agreed suit,* a 5♡ queen-ask is not necessarily a grand slam try because the ask is below five of the agreed suit. However, to repeat: a queen-ask at or above five of the agreed suit is a grand slam try. The asker must be willing to play a grand if the queen is in the facing hand.

## ONCE IN A BLUE MOON

| Opener | Responder |
|---|---|
| ♠ A K 8 7 | ♠ 10 9 4 3 2 |
| ♡ 6 3 | ♡ K Q J 8 |
| ◇ A 4 | ◇ K Q |
| ♣ A Q J 7 3 | ♣ K 4 |
| 1♣ | 1♠ |
| 4♠ | 4NT[1] |
| 5◇[2] | 5♡[3] |
| 5♠[4] | pass |

1. RKB (3014). One of the odd times that the asker actually has '0' Keycards! If he does, he should have the missing kings from here to eternity and be facing a partner who has made some truly deafening aggressive sounds.
2. '4'.
3. Queen-ask.
4. Negative.

## THE SLEUTH

| Opener | Responder |
|---|---|
| ♠ A K Q 5 | ♠ 10 9 4 3 2 |
| ♡ 6 3 | ♡ K Q J 8 |
| ◇ A 4 | ◇ K Q |
| ♣ A J 7 3 2 | ♣ K 4 |
| 1♣ | 1♠ |
| 4♠ | 4NT[1] |
| 5◇[2] | 5♡[3] |
| 6♠[4] | pass[5] |

1. RKB (3014). Again, the asker actually has '0' Keycards!
2. '4'.
3. Queen-ask.
4. I've got it, but, sorry, no king.
5. I know you don't have a king, I've got em' all!

When the weaker hand uses RKB, he figures to have one or two Keycards. To ask without a Keycard is not only rare, but very brave. If you are thinking of doing this, check to see if you can handle all the responses.

AN INFERENCE

| Opener | Responder | |
|---|---|---|
| ♠ 5 2 | ♠ A Q 7 4 | 1. RKB (1430) — opener hasn't jumped or reversed. |
| ♡ Q 10 6 5 | ♡ A K J 7 2 | 2. '1'. |
| ◇ A K 8 7 | ◇ 6 | 3. Queen-ask. |
| ♣ K 4 3 | ♣ A Q 5 | 4. Yes, plus the ♣K but no ♠K. With both black kings, opener bids 5♠ first, the king that can be shown at the lower level. However the 6♣ response does not deny the ◇K. Keep the faith. |
| 1◇ | 1♡ | |
| 2♡ | 4NT[1] | |
| 5♣[2] | 5◇[3] | |
| 6♣[4] | 6♡[5] | |
| pass | | 5. Missing the ♠K, responder settles for a small slam. |

## THE 5NT RESPONSE TO THE QUEEN-ASK

The reasons for showing an 'extra' have already been listed. What wasn't listed was how the asker finds out what that extra is. Keep in mind, if a Keycard is missing, the asker doesn't ask about the extra because there is no chance for a grand. Asking for the extra is a mega-grand slam try.

Assuming the asker is interested in a grand slam, he bids the suit where he needs the extra. When responding to an 'extra' ask, responder bids the grand holding the desired third-round control in the ask suit (the queen in partner's first-bid suit, the queen or a doubleton in partner's second-bid suit). But if responder's extra was trump length, the other possibility, he returns to the trump suit at a minimum-level.

A 'WHO CARES?' EXTRA

| Opener | Responder | |
|---|---|---|
| ♠ A 10 4 | ♠ 6 | |
| ♡ A Q J 10 7 5 4 | ♡ K 3 | 1. RKB for hearts — 3014 as opener has jumped. |
| ◇ 5 | ◇ A K 9 7 6 3 2 | 2. '3'. |
| ♣ A 4 | ♣ K 7 3 | 3. Queen-ask. |
| 1♡ | 2◇ | 4. Shows the queen, denies a side-suit king, but shows an extra — either the ◇Q or an extra heart. |
| 3♡ | 4NT[1] | |
| 5♣[2] | 5◇[3] | |
| 5NT[4] | 7♡[5] | 5. Doesn't care which it is, wants to play a grand. |
| pass | | |

In this auction, if responder wants to know whether the extra is the ◇Q or a seventh heart, he bids 6◇. If the extra is the ◇Q, responder bids 7♡. If the extra is a seventh heart, responder signs off in 6♡.

One more example:

GREAT FIND

| Opener | Responder | |
|---|---|---|
| ♠ A 6 2 | ♠ K | 1. Transfer. |
| ♡ A K Q 10 | ♡ 8 7 6 4 3 | 2. Good hand for hearts with four |
| ◇ Q J 8 3 | ◇ A K 6 5 2 | trumps. |
| ♣ A 10 | ♣ Q 2 | 3. RKB – 3014, weak asking strong. |
| | | 4. '4'. |
| 2NT | 3◇[1] | 5. Queen-ask. |
| 4♡[2] | 4NT[3] | 6. Yes, no side-suit king but maybe |
| 5◇[4] | 5♡[5] | a valuable third-round control. |
| 5NT[6] | 6◇[7] | 7. Is that third-round extra in dia- |
| 7◇[8] | 7NT[9] | monds? |
| | | 8. Yes. The raise of the ask suit shows QJ(x). |
| | | 9. Well, la di da; another commercial and this is only Chapter 2. |

When the only 'real' suit that has been bid is the trump suit, any side-suit third-round control is considered an extra. The previous hand was played in the 2001 World Championships in a match between USA I and USA II. Neither pair arrived at the cold grand.

It's over!

# THE BOTTOM LINE:

- After a 5♣ response to RKB, hearts or spades agreed, 5◇ is the queen-ask, and a return to the agreed suit is to play.
- After a 5◇ (1430) response, hearts agreed, 5♡ is the queen-ask facing '3', to play facing '0'. Facing '0', 5♠ is the queen-ask. (Not going to happen.)
- After a 5◇ (1430 response), spades agreed, 5♡ is the queen-ask and 5♠ is to play.
- After a 5◇ response to a 3014 ask, showing '4', 5♡ is the queen-ask regardless of the agreed suit. The hand must reach slam when the strong hand has '4'. It's a major upset for the strong hand to have only '1'.

The denial response to the queen-ask is a return to the trump suit at the cheapest possible-level. Thus if the queen-ask is 5♡, hearts agreed, the denial response is 6♡! A five-level queen-ask in the agreed suit is a grand slam try. Responder cannot pass a queen-ask with '4' Keycards. Give me a break.

When holding the queen, or knowing that there are at least ten trumps between the two hands, make a positive response to the queen-ask. There are three responses to a queen-ask that show the queen:

1. A jump to six of the agreed suit, which denies a side-suit king or a side-suit extra; the weakest acceptance.
2. Bidding a side-suit king. With two kings, bid the cheaper king-suit first.
3. Bidding 5NT to deny a side-suit king, but showing an extra, typically the queen of partner's first-bid side suit.

# CHAPTER 3

# THE SPECIFIC KING ASK
# AND LATER ASKS

## THE SKA

After a 4NT RKB ask, a follow up bid of 5NT asks for specific kings in ascending order: clubs before diamonds, diamonds before hearts, etc. The king of the agreed suit is not included as it has already been accounted for. The 5NT bid, called the Specific King Ask (SKA), promises joint possession of the four aces as well as the king and queen of the agreed suit. It is a grand slam try.

In response to a SKA, a return to the agreed suit denies a king. If the responder has one king, he bids that suit. With two kings, the cheaper king is shown first. With three kings, responder jumps to 6NT (or bids a grand in the agreed suit knowing of a 9-card or longer trump fit). Any time the responder can count thirteen tricks, he need not respond specific kings: responder is allowed, even encouraged, to leap to a grand. Just do it! Showing a specific king denies the ability to count thirteen tricks — and also denies three kings.

In the world of tournament bridge, playing matchpoints, some partnerships use 5NT in an effort to find a specific king in order to land in 6NT instead of six of the agreed suit. They do not promise all four aces and the king-queen of the agreed suit, so 5NT is not necessarily a grand slam try. We are going the other route: 5NT after 4NT does promise joint possession of the four aces as well as the king-queen of the agreed suit and is a grand slam try.

NOT THIS ONE, THAT ONE

| Opener | Responder | |
|---|---|---|
| ♠ A 8 4 2 | ♠ K Q 7 6 3 | |
| ♡ K 9 5 | ♡ A | 1. RKB (1430) — opener hasn't |
| ◇ 4 3 | ◇ A Q 8 7 2 | jumped or reversed. |
| ♣ A J 5 2 | ♣ K 4 | 2. '2 without'. |
| 1♣ | 1♠ | 3. SKA. |
| 2♠ | 4NT¹ | 4. ♡K, denying a minor-suit king. |
| 5♡² | 5NT³ | 5. Responder knows the ◇K is |
| 6♡⁴ | 6♠⁵ | missing and settles for 6♠. |

GREAT PARTNER

| Opener | Responder | |
|---|---|---|
| ♠ A 8 4 2 | ♠ K Q 7 6 3 | 1. RKB (1430) — opener hasn't |
| ♡ K 9 5 | ♡ A | jumped or reversed. |
| ◇ K 3 | ◇ A Q 8 7 2 | 2. '2 without'. |
| ♣ A 8 5 2 | ♣ K 4 | 3. SKA. |
| 1♣ | 1♠ | 4. ◇K; denies the ♣K but might |
| 2♠ | 4NT[1] | have the ♡K. |
| 5♡[2] | 5NT[3] | |
| 6◇[4] | 7♠ | |

## THE SECOND KING-ASK

Sometimes the SKA bidder hears of one king, but is interested in another. To ask for a second king, the asker bids that suit. Without the king of the ask-suit, responder returns to the agreed suit. This response does not count as a step. Also, if the responder happens to have the ace of the second king-ask suit it should be disregarded: it has already been accounted for.

Holding the king of second king-ask suit, responder can:

- Make a 1st step response, including 6NT, to show Kxx(x).
- Make a 2nd step response to show Kx
- Raise the ask-suit to show KQ(x)

Look at these two examples:

LOOKING FOR MR. RIGHTKINGS

| Opener | Responder | |
|---|---|---|
| ♠ A Q J 9 6 3 | ♠ K 10 5 4 | 1. Jacoby 2NT, a game-forcing balanced raise. After this, the bidding should result in either an immediate or eventual Keycard ask by the opener. |
| ♡ A Q 5 | ♡ K 7 | |
| ◇ A Q 6 | ◇ 8 7 4 2 | |
| ♣ 4 | ♣ A K 5 | |
| 1♠ | 2NT[1] | 2. RKB 1430 — opener asking. |
| 4NT[2] | 5♡[3] | 3. '2 without'. |
| 5NT[4] | 6♣[5] | 4. SKA. |
| 6♠[6] | pass | 5. ♣K — may have the ◇K or the ♡K, but not both. |
| | | 6. Opener signs off in 6♠ knowing responder cannot have both red-suit kings (with three kings the response would have been 7♠). |

| Opener | Responder |
|---|---|
| ♠ A Q J 9 6 3 | ♠ K 10 5 4 |
| ♡ A Q 5 | ♡ K 8 7 4 |
| ◇ A Q 6 | ◇ K 2 |
| ♣ 4 | ♣ A 10 7 |
| | |
| 1♠ | 2NT[1] |
| 4NT[2] | 5♡[3] |
| 5NT[4] | 6◇[5] |
| 6♡[6] | 6NT[7] |
| 7NT[8] | |

1. Jacoby 2NT, a game-forcing balanced raise.
2. RKB 1430 — opener asking.
3. '2 without'.
4. SKA.
5. ◇K — no ♣K, but maybe the ♡K.
6. Looking for a grand if responder has the ♡K.
7. First-step response (excluding 6♠) to show ♡Kxx(x).
8. Able to count 13 top tricks.

# RESPONDING TO A SKA, HEARTS AGREED, HOLDING THE ♠K

When hearts are the agreed suit, the responder to a SKA of 5NT may feel a bit queasy about bidding 6♠ to show the ♠K. A 6♠ response more or less commits the partnership to a grand. Should responder show the ♠K? Yes and no! (Great answer, Kantar.)

If the 5NT bidder is *known* to have spade shortness (has splintered, etc.), the ♠K is not shown. But, if the 5NT bidder is known to have at least two spades (has opened 1NT, etc.), the ♠K is shown. Obviously there are going to be times when the responder will not be able to tell whether the asker has a singleton spade. If the responder can't tell, the ♠K should not be shown. Not a perfect solution, but help is on the way.

NOT HAVING MR. SCARYKING

| Opener | Responder |
|---|---|
| ♠ A | ♠ J 8 2 |
| ♡ K Q 8 7 5 4 | ♡ A 6 2 |
| ◇ A Q J 3 2 | ◇ K 5 |
| ♣ 4 | ♣ A Q J 7 4 |
| | |
| 1♡ | 2♣ |
| 2◇ | 3♡ |
| 4NT[1] | 5♡[2] |
| 5NT[3] | 6◇[4] |
| 7♡ | |

1. RKB 1430 — opener asking.
2. '2 without'.
3. SKA
4. ◇K, may have ♠K
5. At matchpoints opener should bid 7NT, as only an obscene break in either red suit defeats the contract.

## NOT SHOWING MR. SCARYKING

| Opener | Responder | |
|---|---|---|
| ♠ A | ♠ K 8 2 | |
| ♡ K Q 8 7 5 4 | ♡ A 6 2 | |
| ◇ A Q J 3 2 | ◇ 6 5 | 1. RKB 1430 — opener asking. |
| ♣ 4 | ♣ A Q J 7 4 | 2. '2 without'. |
| | | 3. SKA. |
| 1♡ | 2♣ | 4. No minor-suit king; possibly the |
| 2◇ | 3♡ | ♠K. Responder cannot be sure of |
| 4NT¹ | 5♡² | opener's spade length, so the ♠K |
| 5NT³ | 6♡⁴ | is not shown. |
| pass⁵ | | 5. The ◇K is missing. |

# USING THE SPLINTER SUIT WHEN HEARTS IS THE AGREED SUIT

If an RKB ask follows a splinter jump, the splinter suit itself, if it is not a next step queen-ask, can be used to ask for the ♠K (or a singleton spade). The splinter suit can also be used in response to a 5NT SKA to *show* the ♠K. Talk about living in the fast lane; what will they think of next?

## IN NETHER NETHER LAND

| Opener | Responder | |
|---|---|---|
| ♠ 5 4 3 | ♠ A Q 7 2 | |
| ♡ A Q J 4 | ♡ K 10 8 3 2 | 1. Splinter jump agreeing hearts. |
| ◇ A K J 9 6 | ◇ 7 | 2. RKB (3014) — opener has |
| ♣ 5 | ♣ A 6 3 | jumped. |
| | | 3. '2 with'. |
| 1◇ | 1♡ | 4. Do you have the ♠K? (Uses the |
| 4♣¹ | 4NT² | splinter suit to ask for the ♠K.) |
| 5♠³ | 6♣⁴ | 5. No. A return to the agreed suit |
| 6♡⁵ | pass | denies the ♠K. |

## IS THIS FAR OUT, OR WHAT?

| Opener | Responder | |
|---|---|---|
| ♠ K J 3 | ♠ A Q 7 2 | |
| ♡ A Q J 4 | ♡ K 10 8 3 2 | 1. Splinter jump agreeing hearts. |
| ◇ A J 9 6 2 | ◇ 7 | 2. RKB (3014) — opener has |
| ♣ 5 | ♣ A 6 3 | jumped. |
| | | 3. '2 with'. |
| 1◇ | 1♡ | 4. Do you have the ♠K? (Uses the |
| 4♣¹ | 4NT² | splinter suit to ask for the ♠K.) |
| 5♠³ | 6♣⁴ | 5. Yes. A 1st step response shows |
| 6◇⁵ | 7♡ | ♠Kxx(x); a 2nd step response |
| | | (6♠), shows Kx. |

# RESPONDING IN THE SINGLETON SUIT TO SHOW THE ♠K

## I REMEMBER, I REMEMBER!

| Opener | Responder | |
|---|---|---|
| ♠ A Q 4 3 | ♠ K J 6 | |
| ♡ K Q 8 7 2 | ♡ A J 6 4 3 | 1. Singleton diamond (typically |
| ◇ A 4 | ◇ 9 | 11-14 HCP). |
| ♣ A 7 | ♣ Q 10 5 2 | 2. RKB (1430) — opener asking. |
| | | 3. '1'. |
| 1♡ | 4◇¹ | 4. SKA. |
| 4NT² | 5♣³ | 5. Responding in the singleton suit |
| 5NT⁴ | 6◇⁵ | shows the ♠K but denies the ♣K. |
| 6♡⁶ | | 6. Knowing of a club loser. |

## I'VE GOT IT, I'VE GOT IT!

| Opener | Responder | |
|---|---|---|
| ♠ A Q 4 3 | ♠ K 7 6 | |
| ♡ K Q 8 7 2 | ♡ A J 6 4 3 | 1. Splinter. |
| ◇ A 4 | ◇ 9 | 2. RKB (1430) — opener asking. |
| ♣ A 7 | ♣ K 6 5 2 | 3. '1'. |
| | | 4. SKA. |
| 1♡ | 4◇¹ | 5. ♣K, could have the ♠K. |
| 4NT² | 5♣³ | 6. A bid of the singleton suit, to ask |
| 5NT⁴ | 6♣⁵ | for the ♠K! |
| 6◇⁶ | 6♠⁷ | 7. A 1st step response, showing |
| 7♡ | | ♠Kxx(x). |

## DON'T SHOW IT!  FOR GOD'S SAKE, DON'T SHOW IT!

| Opener | Responder | |
|---|---|---|
| ♠ 7 | ♠ A K 4 3 | |
| ♡ A Q J 3 | ♡ K 6 4 2 | |
| ◇ A Q 10 6 2 | ◇ 5 3 | |
| ♣ K Q 5 | ♣ A 7 4 | 1. Splinter. |
| | | 2. Cuebid. |
| 1◇ | 1♡ | 3. RKB (1430) opener asking. |
| 3♠¹ | 4♣² | 4. '3'. |
| 4NT³ | 5◇⁴ | 5. SKA. |
| 5NT⁵ | 6♡⁶ | 6. Does not show the ♠K facing |
| pass | | known shortness. |

# BIDDING RESPONDER'S VOID

After a RKB response, hearts agreed, if the asker bids responder's known void suit he is asking for the ♠K.  What else?

## VOID-SHOWING RESPONSE

| Opener | Responder |
|---|---|
| ♠ A Q 4 3 | ♠ K 7 6 5 |
| ♡ A K Q 8 5 | ♡ J 9 7 6 3 |
| ◇ 7 | ◇ A Q 8 4 |
| ♣ K Q 2 | ♣ — |
| 1♡ | 4♣[1] |
| 4NT[2] | 5♣[3] |
| 6♣[4] | 6◇[5] |
| 7♡ | |

1. Club void, by agreement.
2. RKB (1430) — opener asking.
3. '1'.
4. Using the void suit to ask for the ♠K — more toys.
5. 1st step response showing Kxx(x).

## ANOTHER VOID-SHOWING RESPONSE

| Opener | Responder |
|---|---|
| ♠ A Q 4 3 | ♠ 8 7 6 5 |
| ♡ A K Q 8 5 | ♡ J 9 7 6 3 2 |
| ◇ 7 | ◇ A K 10 |
| ♣ K Q 2 | ♣ — |
| 1♡ | 4♣[1] |
| 4NT[2] | 5♣[3] |
| 6♣[4] | 6♡[5] |
| pass | |

1. Club void, by agreement.
2. RKB (1430) — opener asking.
3. '1'.
4. Using the void suit to ask for the ♠K — more toys.
5. Denies the ♠K — return to agreed suit.

## TO REMEMBER:

### When hearts is the agreed suit:

- After a RKB ask and response (in a splinter sequence), a follow-up bid in either player's known short suit asks for the ♠K. In addition, the response to a king-ask in either player's known short suit shows the ♠K.
- If the RKB bidder is known to have a balanced hand, responder shows the ♠K. However, if there has been no splinter jump and responder cannot tell whether opener has a singleton spade or not, he does not show the ♠K.

## ASKING FOR 3RD-ROUND CONTROL AFTER A SKA

When the response to a 5◇ queen-ask, hearts agreed, is 5♠, this confirms the ♡Q and shows the ♠K. When the response to a 5◇ queen-ask, spades agreed, is 5♡, this confirms the ♠Q and shows the ♡K. In both cases the bidding is still beneath the 5NT-level and responder may still have a minor-suit king, perhaps both minor-suit kings. (Don't hold your breath).

To flush out a minor-suit king, opener bids 5NT. With neither king, responder signs off in the trump suit. With one king, responder bids the king suit. With both kings (meaning he had three) responder bids 6NT. Using 5NT here liberates follow up bids of 6♣ or 6♢ to ask for third-round control (queen or doubleton) in that minor. When partner asks for a third-round control above five of the agreed suit, it must be a grand slam try. Responses are:

1. Lacking third-round control (three small or worse), sign off in the agreed suit, ye olde death response.
2. With a singleton or small doubleton in the ask-suit, bid the grand.
3. With the queen, bid 6NT.
4. With the QJ(x), raise the ask-suit.

The last two steps may allow the partnership to arrive at 7NT, important in matchpoint play, not to mention bragging rights.

### LOOKING FOR A THIRD-ROUND CONTROL

| Opener | Responder |
|---|---|
| ♠ 5 4 | ♠ A K J 7 |
| ♡ A K 8 7 6 5 | ♡ Q J 2 |
| ♢ A K 6 3 | ♢ 7 5 4 |
| ♣ A | ♣ Q 8 4 |
| | |
| 1♡ | 1♠ |
| 3♢ | 4♡ |
| 4NT[1] | 5♣[2] |
| 5♢[3] | 5♠[4] |
| 6♢[5] | 6♡[6] |
| pass | |

1. RKB (1430) — opener asking.
2. '1'.
3. Queen-ask (next step).
4. Yes, with the ♠K.
5. Do you have third-round diamond control? (Would bid 5NT to look for the ♢K.)
6. No — a return to trump suit, the death response, denies third-round control in the ask-suit. It shows xxx(x).

### ANOTHER BYPASS OF SORTS

| Opener | Responder |
|---|---|
| ♠ Q J 3 2 | ♠ A K 8 7 5 4 |
| ♡ Q J | ♡ A K 10 7 6 |
| ♢ A Q J 4 | ♢ 8 |
| ♣ J 9 3 | ♣ A |
| | |
| 1♢ | 1♠ |
| 2♠ | 3♡ |
| 4♢ | 4NT[1] |
| 5♣[2] | 5♢[3] |
| 5NT[4] | 6♡[5] |
| 7♡[6] | 7NT[7] |
| pass[8] | |

1. RKB (1430) — opener minimum.
2. '1'.
3. Queen-ask.
4. No king, but an extra — should be third-round control in the asker's second suit. (Trump length is only considered an extra in the long trump hand.)
5. Third-round heart control?
6. The QJ(x).
7. Notice I was given the ♡10 so we can make 7NT even if hearts are 5-1. It's disgusting.
8. Listen, he wants to sell books.

When a king-showing response to a queen-ask denies a particular king, a follow-up ask in a 'king-denied suit' is by definition a third-round ask:

### LOOKING FOR A THIRD NOT A FOURTH

| Opener | Responder |
|---|---|
| ♠ Q 7 6 3 | ♠ A K J 8 2 |
| ♡ 4 2 | ♡ A K 6 5 3 |
| ◇ A Q 9 4 | ◇ 7 |
| ♣ K J 6 | ♣ A 5 |
| | |
| 1◇ | 1♠ |
| 2♠ | 3♡ |
| 3♠ | 4NT[1] |
| 5♣[2] | 5◇[3] |
| 6♣[4] | 6♡[5] |
| 7♠[6] | pass |

1. RKB (1430) — opener has not jumped or reversed.
2. '1'.
3. Queen-ask.
4. ♣K, denies the ♡K but not the ◇K.
5. Third-round heart control?
6. Yup.

### YOUR CUP RUNNETH OVER

| Opener | Responder |
|---|---|
| ♠ A Q 4 2 | ♠ 6 5 3 |
| ♡ A 10 8 6 4 | ♡ K Q J 3 2 |
| ◇ A 4 | ◇ 9 |
| ♣ A 4 | ♣ K Q 7 5 |
| | |
| 1♡ | 4◇[1] |
| 4NT[2] | 5♣[3] |
| 5◇[4] | 6♣[5] |
| 6♡[6] | |

1. Splinter.
2. RKB (1430) — opener asking.
3. '1'.
4. Queen-ask.
5. ♡Q with the ♣K, but no ♠K (didn't bid 5♠).
6. Missing the ♠K, opener gives up on 7♡ and bids 6♡ hoping to make it. (Notice no ♠J or ♠109x in dummy to make the slam cold. Guilt has set in.)

### SCIENCE IN ACTION

| Opener | Responder |
|---|---|
| ♠ A Q 4 2 | ♠ K 5 3 |
| ♡ A 10 8 6 4 | ♡ K Q 7 3 2 |
| ◇ A 4 | ◇ 9 |
| ♣ A 4 | ♣ K 8 7 5 |
| | |
| 1♡ | 4◇[1] |
| 4NT[2] | 5♣[3] |
| 5◇[4] | 5♠[5] |
| 5NT[6] | 6♣[7] |
| 7♡ | |

1. Splinter.
2. RKB (1430) — opener asking.
3. '1'.
4. Queen-ask.
5. ♡Q with the ♠K, may or may not have another king.
6. Opener needs the ♣K to make a grand, so he tries 5NT after a major-suit king has been shown. Opener must be looking for the ♣K as he can't be looking for the ◇K (responder's singleton suit).
7. Lacking the ♣K, responder signs off in 6♡.

# WHEN A BALANCED HAND FACES A TWO-SUITER

When a *balanced* hand faces a known two-suiter (at least 5-4, or you hope 5-5) and a fit is found and a RKB ask follows, the kings of *both* long suits are counted as Keycards. However, only the queen of the *agreed* suit is included in the RKB response. In these sequences there are 6 Keycards in play, but the responses remain the same. There is no response that shows 6 Keycards! Please. If you have 6 Keycards and partner bids RKB, bid eleven of the agreed suit and expect to make overtricks.

### A SIX-KEYCARD AUCTION

| Opener | Responder |
|--------|-----------|
| ♠ 4 3 | ♠ A Q 10 6 5 |
| ♡ K 8 6 2 | ♡ A Q 10 4 3 |
| ◇ A Q 5 4 | ◇ 7 |
| ♣ A Q J | ♣ K 6 |
| 1NT | 2♡1 |
| 2♠ | 3♡2 |
| 4♣3 | 4NT4 |
| 5♣5 | 6♡6 |

1. Transfer.
2. Five hearts, game force.
3. Presumed cuebid for hearts. With a fit in spades, opener would super-accept the transfer or bid 3♠ over 3♡ to set the trump suit.
4. RKB (3014) — weak asking strong. A 1NT opener, 15-17 or stronger, is the 'strong' hand.
5. '3' including a possible ♠K.
6. Responder (with) 2 Keycards knows a Keycard is missing.

### ALL THE RIGHT CARDS

| Opener | Responder |
|--------|-----------|
| ♠ K 3 | ♠ A Q 10 6 5 |
| ♡ K 8 6 2 | ♡ A Q 10 4 3 |
| ◇ A Q 5 4 | ◇ 7 |
| ♣ A 8 2 | ♣ K 6 |
| 1NT | 2♡1 |
| 2♠ | 3♡2 |
| 4♣3 | 4NT4 |
| 5◇5 | 7♡ |

1. Transfer to spades.
2. Five hearts, game force.
3. Presumed cuebid for hearts.
4. RKB (3014) — weak asking strong.
5. 4 Keycards (don't forget the ♠K).

| Opener | Responder | |
|--------|-----------|---|
| ♠ A K 7 5 3 | ♠ 6 | 1. RKB (1430) — opener hasn't |
| ♡ Q 8 4 2 | ♡ A K 7 6 5 3 |    jumped or reversed. |
| ◇ K 4 | ◇ A 8 3 | 2. '1'. |
| ♣ 6 2 | ♣ A Q J | 3. Queen-ask. |
| | | 4. Yes, plus the ♠K. |
| 1♠ | 2♡ | 5. Have a minor-suit king? |
| 3♡ | 4NT¹ | 6. How does the ◇K grab you? (No |
| 5♣² | 5◇³ |    ♣K). |
| 5♠⁴ | 5NT⁵ | 7. Unless opener has an unlikely |
| 6◇⁶ | 6NT⁷ |    singleton club, the hand figures |
| | |    to play the same in notrump as |
| | |    in hearts. Playing matchpoints, |
| | |    bid 6NT. |

## THE BOTTOM LINE

After a 4NT RKB ask and response, 5NT is the Specific King Ask (SKA). It is a grand slam try confirming joint possession of the four aces as well as the king and queen of the agreed suit. Responder is allowed to waive the response and bid a grand directly if thirteen tricks can be counted.

After a king-showing response to a SKA, a follow-up bid in a suit in which a king has not been denied is a second king-ask. When responding to a second king-ask, a return to the trump suit denies the king. A 1st step response excluding the trump suit shows Kxx(x). A 2nd step response, excluding the trump suit, shows Kx. A raise of the ask suit shows KQ(x).

After a king-showing response to a SKA, a follow-up bid in a suit in which the king has been denied is a grand slam try looking for third-round control in that suit. When hearts is the agreed suit and either player has shown minor-suit shortness, a SKA in the short suit asks for the ♠K. In addition, a response to a SKA in either player's known short suit shows the ♠K. Keep the faith.

# CHAPTER 4

# WHEN THERE IS NO AGREED SUIT

Three chapters in this book are devoted to RKB asks when the last suit bid is a minor and there has been no prior suit agreement. In these auctions, a RKB ask may be possible, but it is seldom 4NT! But what about when the last-bid suit is an unsupported major and partner leaps to 4NT? Is the last-bid major the agreed suit?

| Opener | Responder (you) |
|---|---|
| ♠ K Q 10 6 4 3 | ♠ 7 |
| ♡ 5 | ♡ A K Q 10 6 3 2 |
| ♢ K 6 5 | ♢ A |
| ♣ A 4 2 | ♣ K Q J 8 |
| 1♠ | 2♡ (say) |
| 2♠ | ? |

Sooner or later you are going to want to ask for aces and you don't want partner to think spades is the agreed suit. If he does, he is going to count the king of spades as an ace (a Keycard)! You just want him to count the ace of spades as an ace. How can you ask for Keycards (or just aces) without partner thinking the last-bid suit is the agreed suit?

This is a significant problem and it doesn't go away. What follows are suggestions:

1. If you play strong jump shifts, you can agree that a jump shift followed by 4NT agrees responder's suit.
2. If game-forcing agreement can be made below game in partner's last-bid major and isn't, partner's last-bid major should not be considered the agreed suit. (If you play Two-over-One it is easier to make game-forcing suit agreements below game.)
3. You and partner have to consider methods to allow responder either to agree his own suit or simply to ask for aces without partner thinking his last-bid major is the agreed suit.

| Opener (you) | Responder |
|---|---|
| 1♠ | 2♡ |
| ? | |

Say you want to ask for aces with a hand like this:

♠ A K Q J 7 6 3    ♡ 4    ◇ K Q 5 3    ♣ 7

If you play 'last-bid suit', you can't bid 4NT. You might try 3♠ and then 4NT, but what if partner bids 4♡ over 3♠? You're back to square one. If your system allows you to agree the last-bid major with a forcing three-level raise or a splinter jump (even a fake splinter jump!) below game and this isn't done, the last-bid suit is not the agreed suit. Actually a strong case could be made to make spades the agreed suit if opener jumps to 4NT over 2♡ in this last auction. 'Last-bid suit' works like a charm when you have a fit for the last-bid suit. But if you don't, it's like having an albatross around your neck. And bridge used to be such an easy game.

A 'LAST-BID SUIT' ACCIDENT

| Opener | Responder |
|---|---|
| ♠ K Q J 8 6 3 | ♠ A 2 |
| ♡ K 10 9 4 2 | ♡ J 7 |
| ◇ Q 8 | ◇ A K 5 |
| ♣ — | ♣ A K Q J 10 4 |

| Opener | Responder |
|---|---|
| 1♠ | 2♣ |
| 2♡ | 3◇ |
| 3♡ | 4NT |
| 5♣ | 7NT |
| pass | |

Responder, not playing strong jump shifts, leaped to 4NT to ask for aces. Hah! Opener thought hearts, the last-bid suit, was the agreed suit and showed one Keycard, the ♡K. Responder, not thinking there was an agreed suit, thought opener had the ♡A and bid a grand. Whose fault? The fault was that they lacked a mutual agreement as to what 4NT means when there is no agreed suit. Incidentally, if you play 'last-bid suit' you can usually survive a 4NT ask when you intend to play in your own suit as long as you hold the king of the last-bid suit. At least partner will be forced to answer only aces.

One possibility worth considering is to play that a suit response followed by 4NT agrees *responder's* suit. For example in this sequence:

| Opener | Responder |
|---|---|
| 1♠ | 2♣ |
| 2♡ | 4NT |

If this agreement is in place, 4NT agrees clubs. If responder wanted to agree hearts, and the partnership plays that a raise to 3♡ is forcing, it is easy enough to bid 3♡ and then 4NT. If a raise to 3♡ is not forcing, then a jump to 4◇ agrees hearts and if partner bids 4♡, 4NT can be bid. If responder wants to agree spades, he rebids 2♠ or 3♠, depending upon system, and then bids 4NT.

## OPENER BIDS SPADES AND HEARTS

Say you are the responder with one of these hands:

| Opener | Responder A |
|---|---|
| ♠ A J 8 5 4 | ♠ 3 |
| ♡ K Q 7 3 | ♡ A J 10 5 |
| ◇ Q 6 5 | ◇ A 3 2 |
| ♣ 8 | ♣ A K J 6 4 |

| Opener | Responder B |
|---|---|
| ♠ A J 8 5 4 | ♠ 3 |
| ♡ K Q 7 3 | ♡ 5 |
| ◇ Q 6 5 | ◇ A K 2 |
| ♣ 8 | ♣ A Q J 10 7 6 5 4 |

| | | |
|---|---|---|
| 1♠ | 2♣[1] | 1. Not a game force and not |
| 2♡ | ? | playing strong jump shifts. |

Responder A wants to Keycard in hearts. Responder B wants to Keycard in clubs. If 'last-bid suit' is played, Responder A can bid 4NT, but what about Responder B? The answer is to make Responder A agree hearts either with a forcing raise (3♡) or a jump cuebid (4◇) prior to bidding 4NT. Responder B should be able to jump to 4NT agreeing clubs.

Here are two suggestions for those that don't play 'last-bid suit':

1. A direct jump to 4NT asks for aces, no agreed suit. This is a helpful agreement if strong jump shifts are not in place. If they are, then a jump shift followed by 4NT can be used to agree responder's suit.

2. A suit response followed by a jump to 4NT after a non-jump rebid by opener is Keycard for responder's suit.

| Opener | Responder (you) | |
|--------|-----------------|---|
| ♠ A 9 7 4 3 | ♠ K 2 | 1. Simple ace-asking with a solid suit. |
| ♡ 6 | ♡ A K Q 10 5 4 2 | 2. Two aces. |
| ◇ A J 4 2 | ◇ K Q 7 | 3. To play! The test! Will partner |
| ♣ Q J 6 | ♣ 3 | pass? If firm agreements are in |
| | | place and you are not playing |
| 1♠ | 4NT[1] | 'last-bid suit', he should. However |
| 5♡[2] | 6♡[3] | you may lose a few years of your |
| ? | | life waiting for that 'pass'. |

With decent agreements, the following tragedy could have been avoided:

| Opener | Responder |
|--------|-----------|
| 1♣ | 4NT |
| 5◇ | 5♠ |
| ? | |

4NT was simple Blackwood and 5◇ showed one ace. What is 5♠? Is it to play or is it a conventional request for partner to bid 5NT because two aces are missing? My correspondent bid 5NT. The good news was that the hand was indeed off two aces. The bad news was that the responder had eight spades and converted to 6♠, down one. How could this have been averted?

One way is to have the agreement that a direct jump to 4NT shows an independent suit and asks for aces. Period. Playing that a jump shift followed by 4NT agrees responder's suit is another. Finally, if 'last-bid suit' is being played, and the partner of the 'last-bid suit' wants to ask for Keycards in another suit, the partnership has to work out how to handle this problem. This can be done.

## OPENER MAKES A MINIMUM REBID IN HIS MAJOR

| Opener | Responder (you) |
|--------|-----------------|
| 1♠ | 2◇ |
| 2♠ | 4NT |
| ? | |

Back to the same problem. Is spades the agreed suit or do you have a flock of diamonds?

The problem is easily resolved if 2◇ is a game force. To agree spades you can raise to 3♠ and then bid 4NT. In that case a leap to 4NT should definitely not agree spades. But what if 3♠ is not played as forcing? Again, if you play 'last-bid suit', you can do that, but then you are stuck when you have a flock of diamonds.

Not playing 'last bid-suit' and not playing a raise to 3♠ as forcing, you still have the 'fake splinter' gambit available to agree spades below game with a slam-going spade hand. Jump to 4♣ in this auction, for example, to agree spades whether or not you have a singleton club. Whether partner signs off or cuebids, now you can bid 4NT (1430), with spades agreed.

This agreement liberates a direct jump to 4NT over 2♠ in this auction to be RKB for *diamonds*.

A FAKE SPLINTER IN ACTION

| Opener | Responder | |
|---|---|---|
| ♠ K Q 8 5 3 2 | ♠ A J 6 | 1. Faking a splinter to agree spades |
| ♡ K Q 7 | ♡ A 8 4 | when the partnership is not play- |
| ◇ J 3 | ◇ K 6 | ing 2♣ as a game force, is not |
| ♣ J 2 | ♣ A K Q 5 4 | playing a raise to 3♠ as forcing, |
| | | and is not playing 'last-bid suit'. |
| 1♠ | 2♣ | You're so tricky. |
| 2♠ | 4◇[1] | 2. RKB (1430) — opener minimum. |
| 4♠ | 4NT[2] | 3. '1'. |
| 5♣[3] | 5◇[4] | 4. Queen-ask. |
| 5♡[5] | 6NT[6] | 5. Yes, with the ♡K. |
| | | 6. Protecting the ◇K from a frontal attack. |

Cheer up. You won't have to invent fake splinters if you play strong jump shifts, 'last-bid suit', Two-over-One or a raise to 3♠ as forcing.

# AFTER OPENING A MINOR, OPENER LEAPS TO 4NT OVER RESPONDER'S MAJOR

| Opener | Responder |
|---|---|
| 1♣ or 1◇ | 1♡ or 1♠ |
| 4NT | |

This one seems reasonably clear. Opener figures to have a freak hand with great support for responder's major so 4NT should be treated as RKB (1430), partner's major agreed.

# RKB IN RESPONSE TO OPENER'S PREEMPT

This topic is dealt with at length in Chapter 24.

# OVER OPENER'S JUMP REBID

| Opener | Responder (you) |
|---|---|
| 1♠ | 2♡ |
| 3♠ or 4♠ | 4NT |

Whenever partner has shown a powerful major suit with a jump bid, it is logical to play his suit should be the agreed suit if partner leaps directly to 4NT. With solid hearts and a hand that just wanted to find out about aces, you should have bid 4NT immediately over 1♠ or jump shifted and then bid 4NT.

## A FINAL QUESTION

Finally a confidence builder to end this miserable chapter.
Sitting South, you hold:

♠ K Q J 6    ♡ A Q J 7 2    ◇ J 5    ♣ J 3

| West | North | East | South |
|------|-------|------|-------|
|      |       |      | 1♡ |
| 3♣ | 3◇ | pass | 3♠ |
| pass | 4NT | pass | ? |

What does 4NT mean? Is it Keycard for spades, Keycard for hearts, simple Blackwood with no agreed suit — or is it natural, showing a hand too strong to bid 3NT? Good luck. I'm outta here.

## THE BOTTOM LINE:

You will run into situations where you want to ask for aces or Keycards when no major suit has been explicitly agreed. You can play 'last-bid suit', but it has drawbacks. So:

1. If you play strong jump shifts, you can agree that a jump shift followed by 4NT agrees responder's suit.
2. If game-forcing agreement can be made below game in partner's last-bid major and isn't, partner's last-bid major should not be considered the agreed suit. (If you play Two-over-One it is easier to make game-forcing suit agreements below game.)
3. You and partner have to consider methods to allow responder either to agree his own suit or simply to ask for aces without partner thinking his last-bid major is the agreed suit.

# CHAPTER 5

# HANDLING VOIDS

## ASKING FOR KEYCARDS WITH A VOID

When a void suit enters the mix, bidding slams accurately can present problems. Blackwood seldom works. For example, if you use RKB with two aces and a void and partner shows one ace, you may have to guess which ace it is.

There are several ways to go with slam-going hands that contain a void:

1. Cuebidding. This may or may not lead to a RKB sequence. However, it is dangerous to cuebid a void. Partner may hold the king or king-queen of the void suit and get over-excited.

2. *Use Exclusion Keycard Blackwood (EKB)* — an usual jump in the void suit. In this scenario you ask partner for Keycards outside of the void suit. *Partner doesn't count the ace of the void suit.* In EKB sequences there are only four keycards in play — the three 'working' aces plus the king of the agreed or last-bid suit.

How can you tell whether a jump is EKB (and not a splinter, for example)? EKB jumps are jumps above game in unbid suits (or in a suit bid by an opponent). These jumps are almost always made by the stronger hand and they are always in a void suit. Because these jumps are made at extraordinarily high levels, the asker must be able to handle an 'unlucky' response.

| Opener (you) | Responder A |
|---|---|
| ♠ A K 9 7 5 2 | ♠ Q 10 4 3 |
| ♡ K Q 8 4 3 | ♡ A 2 |
| ◇ K Q | ◇ J 6 4 |
| ♣ — | ♣ K 8 7 3 |

| Opener (you) | Responder B |
|---|---|
| ♠ A K 9 7 5 2 | ♠ Q 10 4 3 |
| ♡ K Q 8 4 3 | ♡ 6 2 |
| ◇ K Q | ◇ 7 6 4 |
| ♣ — | ♣ A Q J 3 |

| | |
|---|---|
| 1♠ | 3♠ |
| 5♣ | |

After a 1♠ opening and a limit 3♠ response, you would like to play in 7♠ facing both red aces, would be pleased to play in 6♠ facing one red ace, and would want out in 5♠ facing neither red ace. The solution is to ask for Keycards outside of clubs, your void suit. You do not want partner to count the ♣A in the response. What you have to do is leap in your void suit *above* the game-level: here you have to leap to 5♣.

Except for a leap to 4♠ after heart agreement (or when hearts is the last-bid suit), EKB leaps when the fit is in a major suit are all made at the five- or six-level. Superman is back.

Responses to EKB are simple and the queen is not included in the response. The first step is '0', the most important step to remember. EKB jumps are neither 1430 nor 3014 asks.

## *Responses to EKB*

| | | |
|---|---|---|
| 1st step | = | 0 |
| 2nd step | = | 1 |
| 3rd step | = | 2 |
| 4th step | = | 3 (a far-out response) |

In the example, Responder A bids 5♡, a 2nd step response, showing '1' Keycard *outside of clubs* and opener bids 6♠. Responder B responds 5◇, a 1st step response, showing '0' Keycards outside of clubs (i.e. the ♣A is not counted); opener signs off in 5♠.

Obviously, you need a whale of a hand to fly off into outer space if you decide to use your new toy.

OUTER SPACE AND THE RIGHT ACE

| **Opener** | **Responder** | |
|---|---|---|
| ♠ A K Q 6 4 3 | ♠ 8 7 5 2 | |
| ♡ — | ♡ K 8 6 5 | |
| ◇ K 3 | ◇ A 8 7 2 | 1. Waiting. |
| ♣ A K Q 7 6 | ♣ 3 | 2. Splinter. |
| | | 3. Exclusion (don't count the ♡A, |
| 2♣ | 2◇[1] | partner). |
| 2♠ | 4♣[2] | 4. '1'. Trust me, for once. |
| 5♡[3] | 5NT[4] | 5. Bingo! It must be the ◇A. |
| 7♠[5] | pass[6] | 6. You're so clever. |

## THE RIGHT TWO ACES

| Opener | Responder (you) | |
|---|---|---|
| ♠ A 8 2 | ♠ K J | 1. Transfer. |
| ♡ J 5 | ♡ AKQ87432 | 2. Exclusion (don't count the ◇A, |
| ◇ K Q J 4 | ◇ — | partner). |
| ♣ A J 7 2 | ♣ K 5 3 | 3. '2' (♣A and ♠A). |
| | | 4. Once you know of both black |
| 1NT | 2◇¹ | aces, 7♡ is the percentage bid. |
| 2♡ | 5◇² | Yes, I see it isn't cold, but it |
| 5NT³ | 7♡⁴ | would be if partner had either |
| pass | | black queen or the ◇A, and is |
| | | easy if you get a spade or a dia- |
| | | mond lead. |

A leap above game after a one- or two-level major-suit response is EKB agreeing responder's major.

## IN THE NICK OF TIME

| Opener | Responder | |
|---|---|---|
| ♠ A K 8 5 3 | ♠ — | |
| ♡ K J 6 4 2 | ♡ Q 8 7 5 3 | |
| ◇ — | ◇ A K Q 5 2 | |
| ♣ K Q 8 | ♣ J 4 3 | |
| | | |
| 1♠ | 2♡ | 1. EKB (don't count the ◇A, |
| 5◇¹ | 5♡² | partner). |
| pass³ | | 2. '0'; I'm not counting anything. |

An EKB ask is also possible after partner bids two suits.

## A MISSED CONNECTION

| Opener | Responder (you) | |
|---|---|---|
| ♠ K 5 4 2 | ♠ A Q J 8 3 | |
| ♡ 6 | ♡ K Q 7 5 4 3 | |
| ◇ A Q 8 | ◇ — | |
| ♣ Q J 7 3 2 | ♣ K 5 | |
| | | |
| 1♣ | 1♡ | 1. A serious EKB leap! |
| 1♠ | 5◇¹ | 2. '1' (excluding ◇A). |
| 5♠² | pass³ | 3. Missing two Keycards. |

This is a rare EKB sequence for two reasons: 1) It comes after a one-level rebid; 2) The asker has only one Keycard. But because the ask comes at such a relatively low-level, even a highly unlikely '0' response will leave you in a playable contract.

| Opener | Responder (you) |
|--------|-----------------|
| ♠ J 10 5 | ♠ A K Q 7 6 3 |
| ♡ 6 3 2 | ♡ K Q J 10 7 4 |
| ◇ K Q J | ◇ 10 |
| ♣ A K Q 7 | ♣ — |
| 1NT | ? |

How can you find out how many red aces partner has? How about this:

| Opener | Responder | |
|--------|-----------|--|
| 1NT | 2◇[1] | 1. Transfer. |
| 2♡ | 5♣[2] | 2. EKB. |
| 5◇[3] | 5♡[4] | 3. The big '0' (outside of clubs). |
| pass | | 4. The hand is off both red aces. |

Why didn't you bid spades on this hand? Well, why would you? Hearts is a playable trump suit even facing two small. What's important is finding out how many usable aces partner has.

## FURTHER ASKS AFTER AN EKB RESPONSE

Nine times out of ten, the EKB bidder places the contract after hearing the first response. However, if the asker has room and is looking for a grand, other asks are available.

### 1. The queen-ask

The next step after an EKB response, including the void suit, but not including 5NT which remains the SKA, is the queen-ask.

| Opener | Responder | |
|--------|-----------|--|
| ♠ — | ♠ A 10 5 | |
| ♡ A K 8 3 2 | ♡ J 7 6 4 | |
| ◇ A K Q 7 3 | ◇ 4 2 | 1. Limit raise. |
| ♣ K Q 5 | ♣ A 8 3 2 | 2. EKB (a leap over game). |
| | | 3. '1' (does not count ♠A). |
| 1♡ | 3♡[1] | 4. Queen-ask (next ranking suit). |
| 4♠[2] | 5♣[3] | 5. Negative. Give responder five |
| 5◇[4] | 5♡[5] | little hearts and he leaps to 6♡ |
| 6♡ | pass | knowing of a ten-card fit. |

## 2. *The specific suit ask (SSA)*

A bid of any new suit that is not the queen-ask bid is a specific suit ask:

| Opener | Responder | |
|--------|-----------|---|
| ♠ A K 8 6 3 2 | ♠ Q J 7 5 | |
| ♡ A K 6 5 4 | ♡ 9 3 2 | |
| ◇ K 6 | ◇ A 8 | 1. Limit. |
| ♣ — | ♣ K 9 7 3 | 2. EKB. |
| | | 3. '1' outside of clubs. |
| 1♠ | 3♠[1] | 4. Specific Suit Ask (SSA) in hearts. |
| 5♣[2] | 5♡[3] | 5. Negative. No second- or third- |
| 6♡[4] | 6♠[5] | round control. |
| pass[6] | | 6. We have a heart loser. |

After the 5♡ response, 5♠ is to play; 5NT is the SKA (Specific King Ask — see the next section) and 6♣, the void suit, the next usable step, is the queen-ask. Finally, 6♡ asks about hearts. Responder shows xxx(x) in hearts by returning to the trump suit. There is a full discussion of the SSA in Chapter 7.

## 3. *The Specific King Ask (5NT) after EKB*

| Opener | Responder | |
|--------|-----------|---|
| ♠ A K 8 6 5 3 | ♠ J 10 4 2 | |
| ♡ A Q J 5 | ♡ K 7 | |
| ◇ K J 4 | ◇ A 6 2 | 1. Limit. |
| ♣ — | ♣ Q 9 5 3 | 2. EKB. |
| | | 3. '1' – must be the ◇A. |
| 1♠ | 3♠[1] | 4. SKA (6♣, the next step excluding |
| 5♣[2] | 5♡[3] | the trump suit and 5NT, is the |
| 5NT[4] | 6♡[5] | queen-ask). |
| 7♠ | | 5. ♡K. |

| Opener | Responder | |
|--------|-----------|---|
| ♠ A K 8 6 5 3 | ♠ J 10 4 2 | |
| ♡ A Q J 5 | ♡ 8 7 | |
| ◇ K J 4 | ◇ A 6 2 | 1. Limit. |
| ♣ — | ♣ K 9 5 3 | 2. EKB. |
| | | 3. '1' – must be the ◇A. |
| 1♠ | 3♠[1] | 4. SKA (6♣, the next step excluding |
| 5♣[2] | 5♡[3] | the trump suit and 5NT, is the |
| 5NT[4] | 6♠[5] | queen-ask). |
| pass | | 5. Denying a side-suit king (the ♣K, |
| | | opener's void, doesn't count). |

In both auctions, there is no need to worry about the ♠Q, as opener is assured of a ten-card trump fit.

## 4. *Rebidding the void suit*

Rebidding the void suit after an EKB response is the queen-ask if it is the next step. But what if it isn't the next step? Rebidding the void suit if not the next step is a SSA in the suit that's needed for the queen-ask. You wouldn't want to lose that ask, would you? Don't answer. I know what you are thinking.

Here's a review of the four follow-up asks after an EKB response:

| Opener | Responder | |
|---|---|---|
| 1♠ | 3♠ | |
| 5◇[1] | 5♠[2] | 1. EKB with a diamond void. |
| ? | | 2. '1' — 5♡, the first step, shows '0'. |

Now opener has the following asks at his disposal:

| | |
|---|---|
| 5NT | SKA (Specific King Ask) |
| 6♣ | Queen-ask (1st step excluding 5NT) |
| 6◇ | SSA in clubs, the queen-ask suit |
| 6♡ | SSA in hearts |

### ANOTHER QUEEN-ASK — JUST WHAT THE DOCTOR ORDERED

| Opener | Responder |
|---|---|
| ♠ — | ♠ Q 8 6 3 2 |
| ♡ A K 9 8 5 | ♡ J 7 6 4 3 |
| ◇ A K 7 | ◇ 2 |
| ♣ K Q 10 5 4 | ♣ A 6 |

| Opener | Responder | |
|---|---|---|
| 1♡ | 4♡ | 1. EKB. |
| 5♠[1] | 6♣[2] | 2. '1'. |
| 6◇[3] | 7♡[4] | 3. Queen-ask — next step. |
| pass | | 4. Knows of a ten-card fit. |

### STAR WARS AGAIN

| Opener | Responder | |
|---|---|---|
| ♠ A K Q | ♠ J 8 7 5 4 2 | 1. Transfer. |
| ♡ A 6 | ♡ K Q J 7 4 3 | 2. Max with three spades, typically |
| ◇ K 6 3 2 | ◇ A |    headed by at least two of the top |
| ♣ J 10 5 4 | ♣ — |    three honors. |
| | | 3. EKB with only '1' Keycard — |
| 1NT | 2♡[1] |    naughty, naughty. |
| 2NT[2] | 5♣[3] | 4. '3' — quite a catch. |
| 5NT[4] | 6♣[5] | 5. The queen-ask (next step). |
| 7♠[6] | pass[7] | 6. Yes, I've got that too. |
| | | 7. Another commercial. |

Even though responder has only one Keycard, the distribution plus partner's strong spade support make the ask reasonable.

## DON'T GO NUTS
Don't get confused by these EKB look-alikes!

| Opener | Responder |
|--------|-----------|
| 1♡ | 4♠ or 5♣ or 5♢ |

First-round jumps by responder to the game-level are natural, not EKB asks.

## LOOKING, LOOKING, LOOKING

| Opener | Responder |
|--------|-----------|
| ♠ A K 8 7 4 3 | ♠ J 6 5 2 |
| ♡ A K 6 4 3 | ♡ Q 2 |
| ♢ — | ♢ Q J 7 4 |
| ♣ K 8 | ♣ A 7 5 |
| 1♠ | 3♠[1] |
| 5♢[2] | 5♠[3] |
| 6♡[4] | 7♠[5] |

1. Limit.
2. EKB (don't count the ♢A, please).
3. '1' — the ♣A.
4. SSA in hearts, probably looking for third-round control (or a singleton) as opener could have bid 5NT to ask for the ♡K.
5. Third-round heart control.

| Opener | Responder |
|--------|-----------|
| ♠ A K 8 7 4 3 | ♠ J 6 5 2 |
| ♡ A K 6 4 3 | ♡ 7 2 |
| ♢ — | ♢ A 9 7 4 |
| ♣ K 8 | ♣ A 7 5 |
| 1♠ | 3♠[1] |
| 5♢[2] | 5♠[3] |
| 6♡[4] | 7♠[5] |

1. Limit.
2. EKB (don't count the ♢A, please).
3. '1' — the ♣A.
4. SSA in hearts, probably looking for third-round control (or a singleton) as opener could have bid 5NT to ask for the ♡K.
5. Third-round heart control.

| Opener | Responder |
|--------|-----------|
| ♠ A K 8 7 4 3 | ♠ J 6 5 2 |
| ♡ A K 6 4 3 | ♡ 8 7 2 |
| ♢ — | ♢ K J 7 4 |
| ♣ K 8 | ♣ A 7 |
| 1♠ | 3♠[1] |
| 5♢[2] | 5♠[3] |
| 6♡[4] | 6♠[5] |
| pass | |

1. Limit.
2. EKB (don't count the ♢A, please).
3. '1' – the ♣A.
4. SSA in hearts, probably looking for third-round control (or a singleton) as opener could have bid 5NT to ask for the ♡K.
5. No third-round heart control.

| Opener (you) | Responder (dealer) | |
|---|---|---|
| ♠ A K 8 7 4 3 | ♠ J 10 5 2 | 1. Drury (three or four spades plus 10-12 support points). |
| ♡ — | ♡ J 10 8 3 | |
| ◇ A Q J 6 4 | ◇ K 3 | 2. Showing a full opening — responder's next bid should tell you the spade count. |
| ♣ K 2 | ♣ A J 7 | |
| | pass | 3. Four spades (a rebid of 2♠ shows three spades). |
| 1♠ | 2♣[1] | |
| 2◇[2] | 3♠[3] | 4. EKB. |
| 5♡[4] | 5NT[5] | 5. '1'. |
| 6◇[6] | 7♠[7] | 6. SSA in diamonds (6♣ is the queen-ask). |
| | | 7. The best possible holding opposite a SSA. |

# WHEN AN EXCLUSION ASK IS DOUBLED (THEY'LL BE SORRY!)

If the opponents are so foolish as to stick in a double over your EKB ask, you can take advantage:

| Opener | | Responder (you) | |
|---|---|---|---|
| ♠ A K 9 7 6 3 | | ♠ Q J 5 2 | |
| ♡ K Q 8 | | ♡ A 4 | |
| ◇ — | | ◇ Q 7 6 4 3 | |
| ♣ K Q J 4 | | ♣ 7 2 | |

| Opener | Oppt. | Responder | Oppt. |
|---|---|---|---|
| 1♠ | pass | 3♠[1] | pass |
| 5◇[2] | dbl[3] | ? | |

1. Limit.
2. EKB.
3. A lunatic double with the doubler on lead. Maybe a self-reminder.

When an EKB ask is doubled, your side has been presented with two extra bids, 'redouble' and 'pass', and you should use them both:

| | | |
|---|---|---|
| redouble | = | 0 Keycards |
| pass | = | 1 Keycard |
| 1st step | = | 2 Keycards |
| 2nd step | = | 3 Keycards |

In the last sequence, responder will pass to show '1', and opener will bid 6♠. With '0', responder would redouble and opener would sign off in 5♠.

# THE BOTTOM LINE

- Exclusion Keycard Blackwood, EKB, is a leap above game in a void suit asking for Keycards in the agreed or last-bid major. The response excludes the ace of the jump suit, but includes the king of the agreed suit. Responses to EKB start with 0 as the first step, and the trump queen is not included.
- After an EKB response, the next step, excluding the agreed suit or 5NT, but including the void suit, is the queen-ask.
- After an EKB response, bidding a new suit that is not the queen-ask suit is a Specific Suit Ask.
- Rebidding the void suit, if not a next-step queen-ask, is a SSA in the queen-ask suit.
- After an EKB response, a rebid of 5NT asks for specific kings.
- If an EKB ask is doubled, 'redouble' = '0', 'pass' = '1', a 1st step response = 2, a 2nd step response = '3'.

---

## RESPONDING TO RKB WITH A VOID

When you use EKB you have a void in the jump suit. If partner, responder, has a void somewhere, he ignores it. But what if the responder (you) to a normal 1430 or 3014 RKB ask has a void? How is it shown? Piece of cake!

*Note:* If you have a void in opener's first-bid suit, it is normally not counted. Also, there are no void-showing responses in double agreement sequences when partner makes a RKB ask (coming up in the next chapter).

### *Responder has an even number of keycards — 5NT*

With '0' or '2' Keycards, plus a void that is not in partner's first-bid suit, respond 5NT. More often than not your response shows '2'. Bidding 5NT with '0' is both risky and optional; it is only done when partner already knows you have a pathetic hand.

### IT DOESN'T TAKE AN EINSTEIN

| Opener | Responder | |
|---|---|---|
| ♠ K J 5 4 3 | ♠ A 10 8 7 | 1. Splinter — played as a singleton |
| ♡ A K Q 10 | ♡ 7 6 4 2 | or void. |
| ◇ Q 5 2 | ◇ — | 2. RKB (1430) opener asking. |
| ♣ 8 | ♣ A Q 6 4 3 | 3. '2' with a void, clearly in dia- |
| | | monds. |
| 1♠ | 4◇[1] | 4. Queen-ask. Next step (see next |
| 4NT[2] | 5NT[3] | hand). |
| 6♣[4] | 6♠[5] | 5. Negative. |
| pass | | |

Opener is prepared to play a grand facing the ♠Q.

## *Responder has an odd number of keycards – more leaping*

With an odd number of Keycards, '1' or '3', responder jumps to six of the void suit. If the void suit is higher-ranking than the trump suit, responder jumps to six of the trump suit. It is assumed that the previous bidding has told partner whether you have '1' or '3'. Although it may kill you, trust your partner to know which you have.

After a six-level leap, if there room, the next step is the queen-ask.

| a) Opener | Responder | b) Opener | Responder |
|-----------|-----------|-----------|-----------|
| 1♡ | 3♡ | 1♠ | 3♠ |
| 4NT | 6♣,6◇,6♡ | 4NT | 6♣,6◇,6♡ |

All of those six-level jumps show voids in the jump suit with 1 or 3 Keycards, surely '1' in this sequence. In (a), leaps to 6♣ or 6◇ show a void in the bid suit, while a leap to 6♡ shows a spade void. In (b) all of the responses show a void in the jump suit.

### REMEMBERING EVERYTHING – SURE!

| Opener | Responder (you) | |
|--------|-----------------|---|
| ♠ A K 10 5 4 2 | ♠ 8 6 3 | 1. 1430. |
| ♡ K Q 7 | ♡ A 4 3 2 | 2. '1' (or '3') Keycard with a dia- |
| ◇ A K J | ◇ — | mond void. |
| ♣ A | ♣ 7 6 5 4 3 2 · | 3. Queen-ask (next step). |
| | | 4. Negative. You figure to have |
| 2♣ | 2◇ | three spades. With four spades |
| 2♠ | 3♠ | and a void, not to mention a |
| 4NT¹ | 6◇² | side ace, you 'might' have |
| 6♡³ | 6♠⁴ | coughed up a splinter jump to |
| pass | | 4◇ after partner bid 2♠. |

### TALK ABOUT HAVING THE RIGHT HAND!

| Opener | Responder (you) | |
|--------|-----------------|---|
| ♠ A K 8 7 4 3 | ♠ J 9 6 5 2 | |
| ♡ K 8 5 2 | ♡ — | |
| ◇ A K | ◇ J 7 5 4 | |
| ♣ 2 | ♣ A 7 4 3 | |
| | | 1. 1430. |
| 1♠ | 4♠ | 2. '1' (♣A) with a heart void. |
| 4NT¹ | 6♡² | 3. Opener knows of ten, possibly |
| 7♠³ | pass | eleven, total trumps. |

# THE BOTTOM LINE

These are the responses to RKB when holding a void:

- With '0' or '2' Keycards, usually '2', bid 5NT.
- With '1' or '3' Keycards, jump to six of the void suit. If the void suit is higher-ranking than the agreed suit, jump to the six of the agreed suit.
- After a void-showing response to RKB, the next step by the asker, excluding the trump suit (sign-off) and 5NT (SKA), is the queen-ask and if there is still room, new suits are Specific Suit Asks.
- No void-showing in double-agreement sequences.

# CHAPTER 6

# GAME-FORCING DOUBLE-AGREEMENT SEQUENCES

Our definition of a game-forcing double-agreement sequence is simultaneous (usually) agreement in two suits ending at the three- or four-level. A Keycard ask is possible by an unlimited hand or even by a limited hand that is facing a slam try. All of these game-forcing double agreement sequences include at least one major suit and come in three packages:

## 1. *Major-major double agreement*

| a) **Opener** | **Responder** | | b) **Opener** | **Responder** |
|---|---|---|---|---|
| 1♠ | 2♡ | | 1♡ | 2♠ |
| 3♣ | 3♠ | | 3♠ | 4♡ |
| 4♡ | ? | | ? | |

In each case '?' is unlimited and can ask for Keycards.

**After heart-spade or spade-heart double agreement, 4NT is RKB.**

If responder (a) asks for Keycards it is a 3014 ask because opener has shown extras by reversing (assuming the partnership plays 3♣ as showing extras). If opener (b) asks, it is a 3014 ask, because responder has jump-shifted.

## 2. *Minor-major double agreement*

| c) **Opener** | **Responder** | | d) **Opener** | **Responder** |
|---|---|---|---|---|
| 1♠ | 2♣ | | 1♣ | 1♡ |
| 3♣ | 3♠ | | 2♢ | 3♣ |
| ? | | | 3♡ | ? |

| e) **Opener** | **Responder** |
|---|---|
| 1♡ | 2♢ |
| 4♢ | 4♡ |
| ? | |

In each sequence the last bid completes a game-forcing double-agreement sequence.

After these three-level minor-major double agreements, four of the agreed minor is RKB. Yes, something new has been added!

After four-level minor-major double agreement, 4NT is RKB.

If opener (c) asks via 4♣, it is a 1430 ask — opener is asking. If responder (d) asks via 4♣, it is a 3014 ask — opener has shown extras by reversing. If opener (e) asks for Keycards via 4NT, it is a 1430 ask — opener is asking.

## 3. *Major-minor double agreement*

| f) **Opener** | **Responder** | | g) **Opener** | **Responder** |
|---|---|---|---|---|
| 1♠ | 2◇ | | 1♡ | 2♣ |
| 2♡ | 3♡ | | 2♠ | 3♠ |
| 4◇ | ? | | 4♣ | ? |

Once again, opener's last bid completes a game-forcing double-agreement sequence. In this group it can be argued that the last bid could be a cuebid as opposed to genuine support. Nonetheless we will treat it as a double-agreement sequence.

After major-minor double agreement ending in 4♣, 4◇ is RKB.

After major-minor double agreement ending in 4◇, the non-agreed major is RKB.

In (f) 4♠, the non-agreed major, is RKB (1430) — opener has neither jumped nor reversed. In (g) 4◇ is RKB (3014) — opener has reversed.

## 4. *Minor-minor double agreement*

This is the fourth and rarest of the three double-agreement possibilities and will discussed briefly later in the book in the section on the minors.

# RESPONSES TO RKB IN DOUBLE-AGREEMENT SEQUENCES

When responding to a double-agreement Keycard ask (1430 or 3014), the kings and queens of both suits are included in the response. In effect there are 6 Keycards, four aces and two kings. Buckle up.

*Note:* There are no void-showing responses when responding to a double-agreement ask.

## *Showing the queen(s)*

In double-agreement sequences, the first two responses to a 1430 or 3014 RKB remain unchanged. It's the queen-ask response that has undergone major reconstructive surgery. In double-agreement sequences there are three queen-showing responses! Assuming the ask is 4NT, these are the queen-showing responses when holding two Keycards. In other words, there are three third-step responses.

| | | |
|---|---|---|
| 5♡ | = | '2' with neither queen |
| 5♠ | = | '2' with one queen |
| 5NT | = | '2' with both queens |

OFF TO A FLYING START

| Opener | Responder | |
|---|---|---|
| ♠ A Q 5 3 2 | ♠ K J 8 | |
| ♡ A 6 4 2 | ♡ K Q 9 7 5 3 | |
| ◇ 9 4 | ◇ A 7 | 1. Double agreement. |
| ♣ Q 6 | ♣ A 4 | 2. RKB (1430) — opener hasn't jumped or reversed. |
| 1♠ | 2♡ | 3. '2' with one queen. |
| 3♡ | 3♠[1] | 4. Knows it's the ♠Q (good thinking) |
| 4♡ | 4NT[2] | and can count thirteen tricks: six |
| 5♠[3] | 7NT[4] | hearts, five spades and two aces. |

GOING A LITTLE FURTHER

| Opener | Responder | |
|---|---|---|
| ♠ A Q 8 7 3 | ♠ K J 5 | |
| ♡ A 9 8 2 | ♡ K Q J 6 3 | |
| ◇ 3 2 | ◇ A 9 4 | 1. Double agreement. |
| ♣ K 7 | ♣ A 5 | 2. RKB (1430) — opener hasn't jumped or reversed. |
| | | 3. '2' with one queen. |
| 1♠ | 2♡ | 4. SKA. |
| 3♡ | 3♠[1] | 5. ♣K. |
| 4♡ | 4NT[2] | 6. Thirteen tricks: five spades, five |
| 5♠[3] | 5NT[4] | hearts, two clubs and one dia- |
| 6♣[5] | 7NT[6] | mond. |

## LADIES ABSENT

| Opener | Responder |
|---|---|
| ♠ A 8 7 3 2 | ♠ K J 5 |
| ♡ A 9 8 2 | ♡ K Q J 6 3 |
| ◇ K 2 | ◇ A 9 4 |
| ♣ Q 7 | ♣ A 5 |

| Opener | Responder | |
|---|---|---|
| 1♠ | 2♡ | 1. Double agreement. |
| 3♡ | 3♠[1] | 2. RKB (1430) — opener hasn't jumped or reversed. |
| 4♡ | 4NT[2] | 3. '2' with neither queen. |
| 5♡[3] | 6♡[4] | 4. The ♠Q is missing. |

### TWO-OVER-ONE PLUS DOUBLE AGREEMENT

This hand from the '99 Spingold illustrates how responders with strong hands tread water in game-forcing auctions to extract as much information as possible before using RKB.

| Opener | Responder |
|---|---|
| ♠ J 5 2 | ♠ A 10 7 |
| ♡ A K 10 8 6 3 | ♡ Q J |
| ◇ Q 7 4 | ◇ A 10 5 3 2 |
| ♣ Q | ♣ A K 8 |

| Opener | Responder | |
|---|---|---|
| 1♡ | 2◇[1] | 1. Game force. |
| 2♡ | 2NT[2] | 2. Looking for more info before 'busting out'. |
| 3◇ | 3♡[3] | 3. Double agreement. |
| 4♡[4] | 4NT[5] | 4. Nothing more to say. |
| 5♠[6] | 6♡[7] | 5. RKB (1430) — opener hasn't jumped or reversed. |
| pass | | 6. '2' with one of the agreed queens. |
| | | 7. 1 Keycard missing. |

## Showing the queen(s) when the RKB ask is lower than 4NT

When the RKB is lower than 4NT, there is more room so you get a queen-showing bonus, an extra step, when holding 2 Keycards. (The first two steps remain the same.) The following chart means there are four 'third-step' responses.

| | | |
|---|---|---|
| 1st step | = | '2' with nary a queen |
| 2nd step | = | '2' with the lower-ranking queen only |
| 3rd step | = | '2' with the higher-ranking queen only |
| 4th step | = | '2' with both queens |

When contracting for a small slam in double-agreement sequences, you are looking to have at least five of the six missing Keycards plus the queen of the agreed suit. Of course it doesn't hurt to have both queens.

## THE OTHER SIDE OF THE COIN

| Opener | Responder |
|---|---|
| ♠ K J 10 7 2 | ♠ A 6 3 |
| ♡ K Q J 5 | ♡ A 2 |
| ◇ 9 | ◇ A 5 4 |
| ♣ K Q 6 | ♣ A J 7 3 2 |
| | |
| 1♠ | 2♣ |
| 2♡ | 3♠[1] |
| 4♣[2] | 4◇[3] |
| 5♣[4] | 5NT[5] |
| 7♣[6] | |

1. Game force.
2. Double agreement.
3. RKB (1430) — after double agreement when clubs is one of the agreed suits, 4◇ is RKB (4NT would be a diamond cuebid).
4. 4th step response = '2' with the lower-ranking queen only.
5. Grand slam try promising the four aces.
6. Can count thirteen tricks with clubs as trumps: five clubs, four hearts, two spades, the ◇A and a diamond ruff.

## PROTECTING ROYALTY

| Opener | Responder |
|---|---|
| ♠ K 5 | ♠ A 8 |
| ♡ A K 10 4 3 | ♡ Q J 6 |
| ◇ K 7 | ◇ 6 4 2 |
| ♣ A Q 10 5 | ♣ K J 7 3 2 |
| | |
| 1♡ | 2♣[1] |
| 4♣[2] | 4♡[3] |
| 4NT[4] | 5♠[5] |
| 6NT[6] | pass |

1. Not a game force.
2. Game-forcing, slam-invitational.
3. Natural, not forcing.
4. RKB (1430) — opener asking, double agreement.
5. '2' with one queen.
6. Protecting the ◇K.

## *The delayed queen-ask*

When partner makes a 1st or 2nd step response to a RKB ask (whether 4NT or not), unless the asker has both of the agreed-suit queens, the queen situation is unknown. To ask for the queens, the asker uses the next step, excluding the trump suit, but including 4NT. Again, four-step responses are in play (another bonus, are you thrilled?):

| | | |
|---|---|---|
| 1st step | = | no queen |
| 2nd step | = | lower-ranking queen only |
| 3rd step | = | higher-ranking queen only |
| 4th step | = | both queens |

## IT'S NICE TO KNOW WHICH QUEEN PARTNER HAS

| Opener | Responder | |
|---|---|---|
| ♠ K Q J | ♠ A 8 | |
| ♡ Q 7 6 5 | ♡ A K 8 3 2 | |
| ◇ A J 3 | ◇ 6 | 1. Double agreement. |
| ♣ 6 5 2 | ♣ A K 10 9 4 | 2. RKB (1430), double agreement. |
| | | 3. '1'. |
| 1♣ | 2♡ | 4. Queen-ask with a three-step |
| 3♡ | 4♣[1] | response. |
| 4♡ | 4NT[2] | 5. 3rd step response = higher-rank- |
| 5♣[3] | 5◇[4] | ing queen only |
| 5NT[5] | 6♡[6] | 6. Opting to play in the stronger |
| pass | | trump suit |

Those who play 'stronger minor' would open 1◇ on this hand. Those who play the weak notrump would open 1NT.

## FINDING FEMININE ROYALTY

| Opener | Responder | |
|---|---|---|
| ♠ A 6 | ♠ 4 | |
| ♡ A Q 7 6 5 | ♡ K J 3 | |
| ◇ 8 2 | ◇ A Q 5 4 | 1. Game-forcing, double agreement. |
| ♣ K 7 6 3 | ♣ A J 10 5 2 | 2. Cuebid. |
| | | 3. RKB (1430) — opener hasn't |
| 1♡ | 2♣ | jumped or reversed. |
| 3♣ | 3♡[1] | 4. '3'. |
| 3♠[2] | 4♣[3] | 5. Queen-ask. |
| 4♡[4] | 4♠[5] | 6. 3rd step response = higher-rank- |
| 5◇[6] | 6♣[7] | ing queen only. |
| pass | | 7. Playing in the likely nine-card fit |
| | | and protecting the ◇Q from |
| | | immediate attack. |

## PLAYING IN THE RIGHT SUIT — ENDING ON A SWEET NOTE

4NT can be used as the queen-ask if it is the first legitimate step after an RKB response. In a double-agreement sequence, an agreed suit cannot be used as a queen-ask suit.

| Opener | Responder | |
|---|---|---|
| ♠ A Q 5 | ♠ K J 10 6 2 | 1. Game-forcing agreement. |
| ♡ A J 10 7 | ♡ 4 3 | 2. Double agreement. |
| ◇ A J 10 6 2 | ◇ K Q 5 | 3. RKB (3014)— opener has |
| ♣ 3 | ♣ A 8 4 | reversed. After three-level |
| | | diamond-spade agreement, 4◇, |
| 1◇ | 1♠ | the non-agreed minor, is RKB. |
| 2♡ | 3◇¹ | 4. '3'. |
| 3♠² | 4◇³ | 5. Cheapest queen-ask available — |
| 4♡⁴ | 4NT⁵ | 4♠ is to play. |
| 5♡⁶ | 7♠⁷ | 6. 3rd step response = the higher-|
| pass | | ranking queen. |
| | | 7. Can count thirteen tricks on the |
| | | presumption that partner has a |
| | | 3-4-5-1 hand pattern: five |
| | | spades, five diamonds, the ♡A, |
| | | the ♣A and a club ruff in |
| | | dummy. |

It's over!

- In double-agreement sequences there are six Keycards in play: the four aces plus the kings of both agreed suits. The double-agreement Keycard ask depends upon which two suits are agreed and the level of agreement:

  *After major-major agreement, 4NT is RKB.*
  *After minor-major agreement ending in 4♡ or 4♠, 4NT is RKB.*
  *After club-major or diamond-major agreement ending in 3♡ or 3♠, four of the agreed minor is RKB.*
  *After major-club agreement ending in 4♣, 4♢ is RKB.*
  *After major-diamond agreement ending in 4♢, the non-agreed major is RKB.*

- In double-agreement sequences the queens of both suits are considered equally important.

  *If the RKB ask is 4NT* there are three queen-showing responses when holding 2 Keycards:
      5♡ = '2' without either queen
      5♠ = '2' with one queen
      5NT = '2' with both queens

  *If the RKB ask is lower than 4NT,* there are four queen-showing responses when holding 2 Keycards. In other words, there are four 'third-step' responses:
      3rd step = '2' with neither queen
      4th step = '2' with the lower-ranking queen
      5th step = '2' with the higher-ranking queen
      6th step = '2' with both queens

  *After a 1st or 2nd step response to a RKB ask,* the queen situation is unresolved. To ask for the missing queen(s), use the next step after the response, excluding an agreed suit, but including 4NT. There are four steps:

      1st step = nary a queen
      2nd step = lower-ranking queen only
      3rd step = higher-ranking queen only
      4th step = both queens

- There are no void-showing responses in double-agreement sequences.

# CHAPTER 7

# THE SPECIFIC SUIT ASK (SSA)

After an RKB response, 5NT asks for specific kings. However the RKB bidder may not be interested in specific kings, he may be interested in a third-round control (a doubleton or the queen, or possibly even a singleton) for a grand. If the asker's only losers are in a side suit that looks like AKxx(x), he needs the queen or shortness for a grand slam.

Say the asker has Kxxx(x) in a side suit and knows partner has the ace. It's not enough. To ensure a no-loser suit, he must find A, Ax, or AQ(x) as opposed to Axx(x). Also, if the asker has Axxx(x) in a side suit, he needs to find partner with the Kx, the KQ(x) or a singleton to bid a grand slam with security; Kxx(x) is not enough.

In order to extract such exact (specific) information, the RKB bidder uses the Specific Suit Ask (SSA). A SSA is used in two scenarios:

1.  *Directly after a RKB response.*
2.  *Directly after the response to a queen-ask.*

| Opener | Responder | |
|---|---|---|
| 1♠ | 3♠[1] | 1. Limit. |
| 4NT[2] | 5♣[3] | 2. RKB (1430) — opener asking. |
| 5♡ or 6♣ or 6♢ | ? | 3. '1'. |

Here, 5♡, 6♣, or 6♢ by opener would be Specific Suit Asks (What do you have in this suit, partner?); note that 5♢ is still the queen-ask. Notice that a queen-ask (5♢ in this case), takes precedence over a SSA. If you wish to make a SSA in the queen-ask suit, you must do it at the next level, here by bidding 6♢.

A SSA above five of the agreed suit is a grand slam try. To justify a SSA at this level your only losers should be in the ask-suit. Partner's holding in that suit should be the key to the grand. Unfortunately, a SSA doesn't come up all that often, but when it does...

**Pep talk:** You are now entering the arena with two RKB asks (1430 and 3014), a queen-ask, a Specific King Ask (SKA) and now a Specific Suit Ask (SSA). Are you ready for these guys, or what?

# RESPONSES TO A SSA

Responses to a SSA are by steps. Most important to remember is that the return to the trump suit is the death response. It denies second- or third-round control in the ask-suit. It shows xxx(x) and does not count as a step. Also, if you have the ace of the ask-suit, partner knows you have it, so don't count it. Think of the ace as a small card: Ax= xx and Axx(x)= xxx(x), etc.

The step responses to a SSA are:

| | | |
|---|---|---|
| 1st step | = third-round control | xx, Qx(x), Ax, AQx |
| 2nd step | = second-round control | Kxx(x) |
| 3rd step | = Kx | |
| raise of the ask-suit | = KQ(x) | |
| jump in the trump suit | = singleton (but see next section) | |

## Responding to a SSA with a singleton:

1.  If you are the supporting hand, and the SSA ask is in a previously-bid suit, jump in the trump suit with four or more trumps, but make a first-step response showing a doubleton (or the queen) with fewer than four trumps. If the first step is the trump suit, sign off in the trump suit. There is such a thing as a trump lead, you know.
2.  If you are the supporting hand and the SSA is an unbid suit, jump in the trump suit with a singleton holding three or more trumps.
3.  If you are the long trump hand, jump in the trump suit with a singleton. Period.
4.  If your singleton is the ace, treat it as a singleton and bid accordingly.

LOOKING FOR GOLD, FINDING DUST

| Opener | Responder |
|---|---|
| ♠ A Q 7 6 4 2 | ♠ K J 8 3 |
| ♡ A | ♡ 9 6 |
| ◇ A K 6 5 2 | ◇ 7 4 3 |
| ♣ 8 | ♣ A K J 6 |

| Opener | Oppt. | Responder | Oppt. |
|---|---|---|---|
| 1♠ | 3♡ | 4♡[1] | pass |
| 4NT[2] | pass | 5♡[3] | pass |
| 6◇[4] | pass | 6♠[5] | all pass |

1. Strong spade raise.
2. RKB (1430) — opener asking.
3. '2 without'.
4. SSA in diamonds.

5. Denies second- or third-round control — the death response. Exchange responder's hearts and diamonds and a grand is bid. The response to 6$\diamond$ with xx is a first-step response of 6$\heartsuit$ and opener bids 7$\spadesuit$

## WHEN SECOND-ROUND CONTROL IS NOT QUITE ENOUGH

| Opener | Responder |
|---|---|
| $\spadesuit$ A 8 3 | $\spadesuit$ K Q J 10 6 2 |
| $\heartsuit$ 9 7 | $\heartsuit$ A K |
| $\diamond$ A J 6 4 2 | $\diamond$ 5 |
| $\clubsuit$ K 5 4 | $\clubsuit$ A 6 3 2 |
| 1$\diamond$ | 2$\spadesuit$ |
| 3$\spadesuit$ | 4NT[1] |
| 5$\heartsuit$[2] | 6$\clubsuit$[3] |
| 6$\heartsuit$[4] | 6$\spadesuit$[5] |
| pass | |

1. RKB (1430) Jump shifter asking.
2. '2' without.
3. SSA in clubs.
4. 2nd step response= Kxx(x).
5. Not enough. He needs Kx, KQ(x) or a singleton with three trumps to bid a grand. (Clubs is an unbid suit — had clubs been bid, he would need four trumps. A trump lead is expected.)

## NEEDING SO LITTLE, FINDING EVEN LESS

| Opener | Responder |
|---|---|
| $\spadesuit$ A Q | $\spadesuit$ 6 |
| $\heartsuit$ K J 5 2 | $\heartsuit$ A Q 8 6 4 3 |
| $\diamond$ A Q 7 5 | $\diamond$ 2 |
| $\clubsuit$ J 5 4 | $\clubsuit$ A K 6 3 2 |
| 1NT | 2$\diamond$[1] |
| 3$\heartsuit$[2] | 4NT[3] |
| 5$\clubsuit$[4] | 6$\clubsuit$[5] |
| 6$\heartsuit$[6] | pass[7] |

1. Transfer.
2. Four-card support — presumably with a side-suit doubleton.
3. RKB (3014) — a strong notrump opener is considered the strong hand when responder does the asking.
4. '3'.
5. SSA in clubs.
6. Negative — xxx(x).
7. An almost certain club loser staring responder in the face.

## DO THE RIGHT THING!

| Opener | Responder |
|---|---|
| $\spadesuit$ A | $\spadesuit$ 8 6 4 3 2 |
| $\heartsuit$ A K 7 6 5 3 | $\heartsuit$ Q J 2 |
| $\diamond$ A Q 5 4 2 | $\diamond$ 7 |
| $\clubsuit$ 8 | $\clubsuit$ A K 6 4 |
| 1$\heartsuit$ | 1$\spadesuit$ |
| 3$\diamond$ | 4$\heartsuit$[1] |
| 4NT[2] | 5$\clubsuit$[3] |
| 5$\diamond$[4] | 6$\clubsuit$[5] |
| 6$\diamond$[6] | 6$\heartsuit$[7] |
| pass | |

1. Good trumps, some slam interest.
2. RKB (1430) — opener asking.
3. '1'.
4. Queen-ask.
5. Yes, with the $\clubsuit$K.
6. SSA in diamonds.
7. With a singleton in response to a SSA in a previously-bid suit, jump in the trump suit with four-card support — do not go past the trump suit with only three trumps.

## A repeat SSA!

*For duplimaniacs only:* When responder makes a 1st step response to a SSA showing the queen or a doubleton, it seldom matters which it is. However, if the asker really wants to know, he can make a repeat ask in the same suit at the seven-level! This repeat ask requests partner to bid 7NT with the queen, but to return to the trump suit with a small doubleton. This may come up once in your lifetime, and you and partner both have to remember that you are playing it. Good luck.

TESTING THE OLD MEMORY

| Opener | Responder | |
|---|---|---|
| ♠ A 8 | ♠ 5 | 1. RKB 1430 — opener hasn't jumped, etc. |
| ♡ Q 7 5 3 | ♡ A K J 8 6 2 | |
| ◇ Q 4 | ◇ A K J 3 2 | 2. '2 with'. |
| ♣ A J 5 4 2 | ♣ 7 | 3. SSA in diamonds (looking for third-round control). |
| 1♣ | 1♡ | 4. 1st step response showing xx or the queen. The denial response of 6♡ does not count as a step. |
| 2♡ | 4NT[1] | |
| 5♠[2] | 6◇[3] | |
| 6♠[4] | 7◇[5] | 5. Repeat SSA for matchpoint players who want to get to 7NT on hands like this if partner has the ◇Q. Others will cheerfully bid 7♡ and make it even when diamonds are 5-1! |
| 7NT[6] | pass[7] | |
| | | 6. I have the queen. Don't come home lame on me. |
| | | 7. Not to worry; diamonds will not be 5-1 in this book. |

Strangely, this exact problem came up at the 2003 Long Beach Nationals and not one pair reached 7NT. No one had the tools — but you do!

CAREFUL!

| Opener | Responder | |
|---|---|---|
| ♠ A J 5 | ♠ K 7 | 1. Transfer. |
| ♡ K 6 3 | ♡ A Q J 10 7 4 | 2. RKB (3014) weak asking strong. A strong 1NT opener is considered the strong hand. |
| ◇ A Q 8 | ◇ 5 | |
| ♣ Q 6 5 4 | ♣ A 7 3 2 | 3. '3'. |
| 1NT | 4◇[1] | 4. SSA in clubs. |
| 4♡ | 4NT[2] | 5. 1st step response showing the queen or a doubleton. A return to 6♡ would have denied third-round control. |
| 5♣[3] | 6♣[4] | |
| 6◇[5] | 6♡[6] | |
| pass | | 6. No grand today. |

There is a risk involved in bidding 6♣ with this holding: a second-step response of 6♠ showing Kxx(x) puts you in a tight spot. You almost have to bid 6NT rather than gamble bidding 7♡. Consider the responses before making a six-level SSA unless you already have the ace and king of the suit between the two hands. (You may have the king and partner may have shown the ace in response to a RKB ask.)

A FIND — FINALLY

| Opener | Responder | |
|--------|-----------|---|
| ♠ A Q J 10 7 | ♠ K 9 5 2 | |
| ♡ A | ♡ J 8 6 3 | |
| ◇ A K Q | ◇ J 9 7 | |
| ♣ K 7 3 2 | ♣ A 5 | |
| | | 1. RKB (1430) — opener asking. |
| 2♣ | 2◇ | 2. '2 without'. |
| 2♠ | 3♠ | 3. SSA in clubs. |
| 4NT[1] | 5♡[2] | 4. First-step response showing third-round control. |
| 6♣[3] | 6◇[4] | |
| 7♠[5] | | 5. Just what the doctor ordered. |

By making a six-level SSA, a grand slam try, the asker promises joint possession of the four aces as well as the king and queen of the agreed suit.

**Reminder:** When responding to a SSA with the ace of the ask-suit, do not get carried away. Partner knows you have that card. That is not what he is looking for.

## An SSA in a previously-bid suit

When an SSA is made in a previously-bid suit, shortness responses are no longer an issue.

*Responses to a SSA in a previously-bid suit:*

| 1st step | = | the queen (could have the ace) |
|----------|---|---------------------------------|
| 2nd step | = | the king (could have the ace) |
| raise of the ask suit | = | king and queen |

As ever, a return to trump suit is the weakest possible response. It denies second- or third-round control and does not count as a step.

## LOOK WHAT I FOUND!

| Opener | Responder |
|---|---|
| ♠ Q 6 5 4 | ♠ A 8 |
| ♡ A 9 7 3 | ♡ K Q 6 5 2 |
| ◇ A | ◇ 9 8 6 |
| ♣ A Q 3 2 | ♣ K J 5 |
| | |
| 1♣ | 1♡ |
| 3◇[1] | 4NT[2] |
| 5♣[3] | 6♣[4] |
| 6◇[5] | 7♡[6] |
| pass | |

1. Nobody likes to splinter with a singleton ace, but that's what they dealt you. If you prefer to treat this as a balanced hand, jump to 4♡.
2. RKB (3014) — opener has jumped.
3. '3'.
4. SSA. After jump agreement in a first-bid major, the major is considered the agreed suit. Period.
5. The queen.
6. Knows he can dump a spade on a club as opener must have at least four clubs with a known singleton diamond.


## I NEED A NEW PARTNER– WHAT ELSE IS NEW?

| Opener | Responder |
|---|---|
| ♠ 6 | ♠ A 5 |
| ♡ A Q 9 6 5 | ♡ K 8 3 2 |
| ◇ A 7 | ◇ K Q J |
| ♣ A K 6 3 2 | ♣ 8 7 5 4 |
| | |
| 1♡ | 2NT[1] |
| 4NT[2] | 5♡[3] |
| 6♣[4] | 6♡[5] |
| pass[6] | |

1. Jacoby 2NT (four-card support plus opening bid values).
2. RKB (1430) — opener asking .
3. '2 without'.
4. SSA in clubs.
5. Zilch in clubs.
6. A club loser looms.


## TAKING IT SLOWLY

| Opener | Responder |
|---|---|
| ♠ A Q 10 8 7 5 | ♠ K J 6 2 |
| ♡ A K 7 2 | ♡ 4 3 |
| ◇ 8 | ◇ A 6 3 2 |
| ♣ K 5 | ♣ A 4 3 |
| | |
| 1♠ | 2NT[1] |
| 3◇[2] | 4♣[3] |
| 4NT[4] | 5◇[5] |
| 6♡[6] | 6NT[7] |
| 7♠[8] | pass |

1. Jacoby 2NT.
2. Singleton — could also bid 4NT.
3. Cuebid.
4. RKB (1430) — opener asking.
5. '3' (can't be '0', 2NT is a strong response).
6. SSA in hearts — looking for third-round control.
7. First-step response showing xx or the queen.
8. Looking good!

A nice grand to bid but an even nicer one to stay out of if responder has
$\heartsuit$xxx(x).

## THE BOTTOM LINE

The frequency of a SSA is low, but it serves a wonderful purpose. It can, among other things, uncover third-round control in the ask-suit. It also can distinguish Kx from Kxx(x), or Ax from Axx(x).

- A SSA can only follow a Keycard response or a king-showing response to a queen-ask. After a king-showing response to a queen-ask, 5NT asks for another king; bidding a non-agreed suit is a SSA.
- The SSA bidder must be prepared for any negative response, particularly if the ask is at the six-level. After a response to RKB, the asker has to decide what further information is needed — the trump queen, a specific king, a specific third-round control — what? Once that question is answered, it's a piece of cake.

# CHAPTER 8

# MORE MAJOR-SUIT AGREEMENT SEQUENCES AND ASKS

There are some sequences following a Stayman response that allow responder to make a direct Keycard ask below 4NT. Lower-level RKB asks lead to other lower-level asks including our old buddies the queen-ask, the SKA and the SSA.

## OPENER SHOWS A MAJOR IN RESPONSE TO STAYMAN

| Opener | Responder | |
|---|---|---|
| 1NT | 2♣[1] | 1. Stayman. |
| 2♡ or 2♠ | 4♣[2] | 2. Can profitably be used as RKB (3014) for opener's major. If this agreement is in place, the bid of 4NT by responder over 2♡ or 2♠ can be played as natural. |

### A LOW-LEVEL RKB ASK, A LOW-LEVEL SKA ASK

| Opener | Responder | |
|---|---|---|
| ♠ K J 5 | ♠ A Q 10 7 4 3 | 1. RKB for hearts (3014) — weak asking strong. |
| ♡ 10 6 5 2 | ♡ A K Q J | |
| ◇ A Q 7 3 | ◇ 6 | 2. '2 without'. |
| ♣ A J | ♣ 8 4 | 3. Specific king ask. When an RKB response is lower than 4NT (here it is 4♠), then 4NT, if not needed as a queen-ask (the queen has been shown or denied), can be used as a lower-level SKA. In all other RKB sequences starting with 4NT, the SKA is 5NT. |
| 1NT | 2♣ | |
| 2♡ | 4♣[1] | |
| 4♠[2] | 4NT[3] | |
| 5♠[4] | 7♡[5] | |
| pass | | |
| | | 4. The ♠K (denies any other king). |
| | | 5. The right one! |

## COUNT YOUR TRICKS!

| Opener | Responder |
|---|---|
| ♠ K Q J 7 2 | ♠ A 6 |
| ♡ A J 10 4 | ♡ K Q 7 3 |
| ◇ 4 3 2 | ◇ A 8 7 5 |
| ♣ 3 | ♣ A J 7 |
| | |
| 1♠ | 2NT[1] |
| 3♡ | 4♣[2] |
| 4♡[3] | 4NT[4] |
| 5♡[5] | 5NT[6] |
| 7♡[7] | pass |

1. Natural and forcing — intends to rebid 4NT to show 18-19 balanced.
2. Change of direction — cuebid for hearts (would bid 3♠ to set spades as trumps).
3. Minimum, no slam interest.
4. RKB for hearts (1430)— opener hasn't jumped or reversed.
5. '2 without' including the ♠K.
6. Specific kings.
7. Opener can count thirteen tricks if responder has at least three clubs: five spades, four hearts, two minor-suit aces and two club ruffs.

### Two points:
1. Responder's 5NT bid guarantees joint possession of the four aces as well as the king and queen of the agreed suit, hearts.
2. When a two-suited hand (opener) responds to a 4NT RKB ask made by a known balanced hand (responder), the kings of both suits are included in the response.

## COUNT 'EM BOTH!

| Opener | Responder |
|---|---|
| ♠ K Q 7 | ♠ — |
| ♡ A 6 4 | ♡ K J 9 3 2 |
| ◇ A 10 4 3 | ◇ K J 5 |
| ♣ K 7 6 | ♣ A Q J 10 4 |
| | |
| 1NT | 2◇[1] |
| 2♡ | 3♣[2] |
| 3♡[3] | 4♠[4] |
| 5♡[5] | 5♠[6] |
| 6♡[7] | pass |

1. Transfer.
2. Natural, game-forcing.
3. Minimum with three hearts.
4. Exclusion Keycard Blackwood (jump over game — remember?).
5. '3' — including the ♣K. When a two-suited hand asks for Keycards facing a balanced hand (or vice versa), the kings of both suits are included in the response.
6. Queen-ask, the next step, a grand slam try.
7. Negative (return to the agreed suit).

**Reminder:** When responding to an Exclusion ask, responses are by steps starting with '0' and the queen is not included. If there is room after an EKB response, the next step, excluding the agreed suit (to play) and excluding 5NT (the SKA) is the queen-ask. A bid in a new suit that is not the queen-ask is a Specific Suit Ask. Is this fun, or what?

FINDING EVERYTHING

| Opener | Responder | |
|---|---|---|
| ♠ K J 6 3 2 | ♠ A Q 7 4 | 1. Primary spades, unknown single- |
| ♡ A Q 6 2 | ♡ 9 | ton, strong hand. Playing this |
| ◇ A Q 5 | ◇ K 8 6 3 | method, a direct jump to 4♡ |
| ♣ 4 | ♣ A K 10 5 | shows a heart void. |
| | | 2. Next step asks for the singleton. |
| 1♠ | 3♡[1] | 3. Hearts. |
| 3♠[2] | 4♡[3] | 4. RKB 1430 — opener asking. |
| 4NT[4] | 5♠[5] | 5. '2 with'. |
| 5NT[6] | 6♣[7] | 6. Specific kings up the line. |
| 6◇[8] | 6♡[9] | 7. ♣K. |
| 7♠ | | 8. What about the ◇K? |
| | | 9. 1st step response showing |
| | | Kxx(x). A 2nd step response |
| | | shows Kx. A raise of the ask suit |
| | | shows KQx(x) and a return to the |
| | | trump suit denies the ◇K and |
| | | does not count as a step. |

**Reminder:** When the RKB bidder makes a grand slam try of 5NT, the SKA, a follow-up bid in a new suit is a further king-ask.

THINK AHEAD!

| Opener | Responder (you) |
|---|---|
| ♠ A Q 9 3 | ♠ 7 |
| ♡ K Q 5 2 | ♡ A J 10 9 6 4 3 |
| ◇ 9 5 | ◇ K Q J |
| ♣ Q 6 2 | ♣ K J |
| 1♣ | 1♡ |
| 2♡ | ? |

If you carelessly whip out 4NT now, a '2 with' response of 5♠ puts you in la-la land. When hearts are agreed, you have to be careful about using 4NT holding '1 without' facing a minimum opener. Instead, you might try making a slam-try splinter jump of 3♠ to see what develops. Yes, yes, playing Kickback, where a leap to 4♠ is RKB for hearts, works great here.

## RKB FACING A '4' RESPONSE

| Opener | Responder |
|--------|-----------|
| ♠ 5 | ♠ A J 10 3 2 |
| ♡ A K Q 10 4 3 | ♡ J 7 5 |
| ◇ A K 10 6 | ◇ Q |
| ♣ A 8 | ♣ K Q J 10 |
| | |
| 2♣[1] | 2♠[2] |
| 3♡ | 4NT[3] |
| 5◇[4] | 5♡[5] |
| 6◇[6] | 7NT[7] |

1. Strong and artificial.
2. Natural.
3. RKB for hearts (3014). Had responder wanted to agree spades, he would bid 3♠ Also, if a raise to 4♡ is played as forcing, responder should do that to let the big hand take charge.
4. '4'.
5. Queen-ask. After a '4' response, hearts agreed, 5♡ is the queen-ask, it is not to play!
6. Yes, with the ◇K.
7. Can count thirteen tricks.

## A KEYCARD ASK WITH NO KEYCARDS!

In the following example the RKB bidder doesn't have *any* Keycards — really far out. (Don't make a habit of this!)

| Opener | Responder |
|--------|-----------|
| ♠ A 4 | ♠ Q J 10 9 6 3 2 |
| ♡ A 6 | ♡ K Q J |
| ◇ Q J 10 5 | ◇ K 4 |
| ♣ A K Q 7 2 | ♣ 3 |
| | |
| 1♣ | 1♠ |
| 2◇ | 3♠ |
| 4♡[1] | 4NT[2] |
| 5♣[3] | 5♠[4] |
| pass | |

1. Cuebid for spades.
2. RKB (3014) — weak asking strong.
3. '3'.
4. Not enough. Forget slam when missing two Keycards. It might be a side-suit ace and the king of trumps (the good news?) or it might be two aces (awful news).

## THINKING MATCHPOINTS

| Opener | Responder |
|--------|-----------|
| ♠ A K J 7 | ♠ Q 10 6 4 2 |
| ♡ K 5 4 | ♡ A |
| ◇ A 3 | ◇ K Q 7 |
| ♣ J 8 6 3 | ♣ A Q 5 2 |
| | |
| 1NT | 2♡[1] |
| 3♠[2] | 4NT[3] |
| 5♣[4] | 5NT[5] |
| 6♡[6] | 6NT[7] |

1. Transfer.
2. Four spades with a likely doubleton.
3. RKB (3014)— weak asking strong. A 1NT opener is considered the strong hand.
4. '3'.
5. Asking for specific kings up the line.
6. ♡K, denying the ♣K.
7. At matchpoints, looking for the extra 10 points. At any other form of scoring settle for 6♠ in case partner has a small doubleton in clubs allowing for a club ruff in dummy.

## RESPONDING TO A SECOND KING-ASK

| Opener | Responder | |
|---|---|---|
| ♠ A K J 7 3 | ♠ Q 10 8 4 | 1. Waiting |
| ♡ A 6 2 | ♡ K 4 3 | 2. RKB 1430. If 3NT over 3♠ is |
| ◇ A K Q | ◇ 9 7 2 | played as forcing (a good idea), |
| ♣ A 2 | ♣ K 5 4 | opener can bid 3NT asking |
| | | responder to cuebid kings and |
| 2♣ | 2◇[1] | aces up the line. |
| 2♠ | 3♠ | 3. '0'. |
| 4NT[2] | 5◇[3] | 4. Queen-ask. |
| 5♡[4] | 6♣[5] | 5. Yes, with the ♣K. |
| 6♡[6] | 6NT[7] | 6. Do you have the ♡K? |
| pass[8] | | 7. A 1st step response, excluding |
| | | the agreed suit, shows Kxx(x)(x). |
| | | 8. Can only count twelve tricks. |

### IS THAT '1' OR '4', PARTNER?

Sometimes you can't be sure whether partner's 5♣ response shows '1' or '4'. Don't laugh, it can happen!

```
            North                      South
            ♠ 7 6                       ♠ A K Q J
            ♡ A K 7 6 5 3 2             ♡ J 4
            ◇ A 4                       ◇ 9
            ♣ A 7                       ♣ K Q J 10 3 2
```

| West | North | East | South |
|---|---|---|---|
| 4◇ | 4♡ | pass | 4NT[1] |
| pass | 5♣[2] | pass | 5♡[3] |
| pass | 6♡[4] | pass | 7NT[5] |
| all pass | | | |

1. RKB for hearts (1430). The player who overcalls is the weak hand in RKB sequences.
2. '1' or '4'.
3. To play facing '1', queen-ask facing '4'.
4. Denies the ♡Q.
5. Can count thirteen tricks.

This is one of the few times the asker can't be absolutely sure whether partner has 1 or 4 Keycards. The solution is to sign off in the agreed suit; partner passes with '1', but can't pass with '4'! Once responder here knows that opener has '4' (since he bid on over 5♡), he can count thirteen tricks: six clubs, four spades, two hearts and a diamond.

| Opener | | Responder | |
|---|---|---|---|
| ♠ A K 7 6 3 | | ♠ Q J 5 2 | |
| ♡ A 3 | | ♡ 9 8 6 | |
| ◇ A | | ◇ J 7 2 | |
| ♣ K J 6 5 2 | | ♣ A Q 4 | |

| Opener | Oppt. | Responder | Oppt. |
|---|---|---|---|
| 1♣[1] | 2♡[2] | dbl[3] | pass |
| 4NT[4] | pass | 5♣[5] | pass |
| 5◇[6] | pass | 5NT[7] | pass |
| 7♠[8] | all pass | | |

1. Holding a 5-5 monster, and trying to make it easier for partner to scrape up a bid.
2. Weak.
3. Negative — promising at least four spades.
4. RKB (1430) — opener unlimited, spades agreed by inference (as if partner responded 1♠).
5. '1'.
6. Queen-ask.
7. Yes, with no side-suit king, but with an important extra, the ♣Q.
8. Knowing the extra is the queen of the asker's first suit, South gambles that he can pitch dummy's losing hearts on good clubs, eventually ruffing a heart in dummy. Note: if responder has four clubs and three hearts, one sad post-mortem is coming up.

# CHAPTER 9

## RKB AFTER A SPLINTER

After a game-forcing major-suit agreement via a splinter, 4NT is RKB. In some of these splinter sequences the opener can ask for Keycards via 4NT or show them via step responses! (Back in the fast lane again.)

Consider this sequence:

| Opener (you) | Responder |
|---|---|
| 1NT | 2♡ |
| 2♠ | 4♣ or 4◇ or 4♡ |
| ? | |

Here responder's first bid is a transfer to spades. His second bid shows a singleton in the jump suit, and is a slam try with at least six spades. What do your rebids mean? Here's the latest from the ward in the psychiatric wing:

1) With no slam interest, sign off in the agreed suit — here, bid 4♠.
2) If you wish to take charge, bid 4NT, RKB (1430).
3) And here's the kicker. With certain hands it might be better to answer the splinter jump in steps treating it as if it were a RKB ask! *However, the agreed suit and 4NT are not counted as steps.*

Also, to pull one of these 'role reversals' you must have at least '2 with', since that's what the first step shows. There are actually three steps:

| 1st step | = | '2 with' |
|---|---|---|
| 2nd step | = | '3 without' |
| 3rd step | = | '3 with' |

Why do this? Because some hands (the ones with aces and spaces) are better suited to showing Keycards rather than asking for them. Others, the ones with fillers in the side suits, and suits headed by the KQ or KQJ, are better suited to asking for Keycards because it is easier to count tricks. Can we really have our cake and eat it too? Why not?

## A 'FILLER' ASK

| Opener | Responder |
|---|---|
| ♠ A Q | ♠ K J 10 6 3 2 |
| ♡ J 10 7 | ♡ 4 |
| ◇ K Q 5 2 | ◇ A 4 3 |
| ♣ K Q 7 6 | ♣ A 4 3 |
| 1NT | 2♡[1] |
| 2♠ | 4♡[2] |
| 4NT[3] | 5◇[4] |
| 6♠[5] | pass |

1. Transfer.
2. Singleton slam try.
3. RKB (1430) — opener asking.
4. '3'.
5. Opener has a good hand for spades, nothing wasted in hearts, plus fillers in the minors, making it easy to count tricks.

## ACES AND SPACES

On this hand, opener, with aces and spaces, elects to show Keycards rather than ask for them.

| Opener | Responder |
|---|---|
| ♠ A 8 3 | ♠ K Q J 6 5 4 |
| ♡ K 8 6 2 | ♡ A 5 4 |
| ◇ A 5 2 | ◇ 8 |
| ♣ A J 6 | ♣ K 7 2 |
| 1NT | 2♡[1] |
| 2♠ | 4◇[2] |
| 5♣[3] | 6♠ |
| pass | |

1. Transfer.
2. Singleton slam try.
3. 2nd step response, showing '3 without'. A 1st step response of 4♡ shows '2 with'. Note that 4♠, to play, and 4NT, RKB, are not counted as steps.

## TALK ABOUT THE WRONG HAND

| Opener | Responder |
|---|---|
| ♠ K Q J 4 | ♠ 8 |
| ♡ J 5 | ♡ A Q 6 4 3 2 |
| ◇ A Q 7 5 | ◇ K 6 3 |
| ♣ Q J 3 | ♣ A 4 2 |
| 1NT | 2◇[1] |
| 2♡ | 3♠[2] |
| 3NT[3] | pass[4] |

1. Transfer.
2. Singleton slam try.
3. To play, knowing partner has a singleton spade and six hearts, etc.
4. Faith.

## ANOTHER 'WRONG' HAND

| Opener | Responder |
|--------|-----------|
| ♠ J 6 | ♠ A K 7 5 3 2 |
| ♡ K Q J 4 | ♡ 8 |
| ◇ A Q 6 3 | ◇ K 5 2 |
| ♣ Q J 7 | ♣ K 5 4 |

| Opener | Responder |
|--------|-----------|
| 1NT | 2♡[1] |
| 2♠ | 4♡[2] |
| 4♠[3] | pass |

1. Transfer.
2. Singleton slam try.
3. Would like to go in reverse back to 3NT, but the rules don't permit it and 4NT is RKB.

## TAKING CHARGE

| Opener | Responder |
|--------|-----------|
| ♠ K 8 2 | ♠ A 5 |
| ♡ K 4 | ♡ A Q J 7 6 3 |
| ◇ A K 6 4 3 | ◇ 2 |
| ♣ K 7 2 | ♣ Q 6 4 3 |

| Opener | Responder |
|--------|-----------|
| 1NT | 2◇[1] |
| 2♡ | 4◇[2] |
| 4NT[3] | 5♠[4] |
| 6♡ | pass |

1. Transfer.
2. Singleton slam try.
3. RKB (1430) — opener asking.
4. '2 with'.

A reasonable contract. In order to make a singleton slam try in this sequence, responder should have a six-card suit and a minimum of 13 'attractive' HCP. With a seven-card suit responder can fudge a point or two.

## SHOWING OFF YOUR NEW MOVES
Another sequence where an ask-show option is possible occurs when responder makes a four-level splinter response to an opening bid of 1♡ or 1♠.

| Opener | Responder |
|--------|-----------|
| ♠ A J 9 8 6 3 | ♠ K 7 4 2 |
| ♡ Q J 6 | ♡ K 7 4 3 |
| ◇ A 9 2 | ◇ 5 |
| ♣ 6 | ♣ K Q J 5 |

| Opener | Responder |
|--------|-----------|
| 1♠ | 4◇[1] |
| 4♡[2] | 4♠[3] |
| pass | |

1. Singleton diamond, opening bid values.
2. '2 with' (10 card fit assured).
3. Two aces missing.

# THE BOTTOM LINE

After a game-forcing major-suit agreement via a splinter, 4NT is RKB. In some of these splinter sequences the opener can ask for Keycards via 4NT or show them via step responses!

- With no slam interest, sign off in the agreed suit.
- If you wish to take charge, bid 4NT, RKB (1430).
- With the right kind of hand, you can answer the splinter jump in steps as if it were a RKB ask! The agreed suit and 4NT are not counted as steps. There are three steps:

  1st step = '2 with'
  2nd step = '3 without'
  3rd step = '3 with'

**Reminder:** These suggestions deal only with the sequences mentioned. Add others if you like — or junk it all. It's just an idea.

# MINOR -SUIT AUCTIONS

## PART THREE

# CHAPTER 10

# RKB AFTER TWO-LEVEL MINOR-SUIT AGREEMENT

Well gang, the fun and games are over. Your 4NT crutch to ask for Keycards is almost history with a capital 'H'. It's too elevated an ask once you've agreed to play in a minor suit. We can do better. If we arrange to make most of our RKB asks starting as low as 4♣ or 4◇, or just possibly 4♡, we will have room to make other asks without committing to slam if we discover we are missing two Keycards or one Keycard and the queen of trumps. Hold on, the ride is just beginning.

What follows are suggestions on what these lower asks are and when they apply. After all, one is playing with fire when bids such as 4♣, 4◇, and 4♡ (not to mention last-resort measures of 4♠ and 4NT) can all be used to ask for Keycards. Wait, don't leave!

Before embarking on this little adventure, it pays to start out by saying that with few exceptions (all noted in the chapter dealing with 2♣ opening bids) *the agreement is not the ask.* Even in a sequence where there is jump agreement, from 2♣ to 4♣, say, it is still the agreement, not the ask. *The ask follows the agreement.* Remember that.

It is easiest to attack lower-level RKB asks by using what I call the **level of agreement** method. When you know the level at which the agreement takes place, you will know what the ask is — assuming an ask is possible. Here are the suggested RKB asks after two-level agreement with the opponents keeping a respectful (and awed) silence.

## THE RKB ASK AFTER TWO-LEVEL SUIT AGREEMENT

If you are not playing inverted minors whereby a single raise shows a limit raise or better, this chapter may not be for you. In other words, don't hold your breath waiting for partner to ask you for Keycards after a weak single raise. And even if you play Crisscross by a non-passed hand (jumping from 1♣ to 2◇ or from 1◇ to 3♣ showing limit raises in opener's minor and playing the direct jump to the three-level as preemptive), there still don't figure to be many direct RKB asks in your future.

However, some opening hands are so freakish that that even after hearing a limit raise or an even weaker single raise, a Keycard ask is possible. RKB asks after jump limit raises to the three-level as opposed to Crisscross are discussed in Chapter 12, not in this one.

Okay, are you ready?

*The direct RKB ask after two-level agreement, whether or not the auction is game-forcing, is a jump to the four-level of the agreed suit.*

## FINDING GOLD IN THEM THAR HILLS

| Opener | Responder |
|---|---|
| ♠ A 8 7 4 | ♠ K 5 |
| ♡ A K | ♡ 10 8 3 |
| ◇ 4 | ◇ A Q 7 |
| ♣ A K 8 7 5 2 | ♣ Q J 6 4 3 |
| | |
| 1♣ | 2♣¹ |
| 4♣² | 4◇³ |
| 4♠⁴ | 5♡⁵ |
| 7♣ | pass |

1. Game force.
2. RKB (1430) — opener asking.
3. '1'.
4. Specific Suit Ask (SSA).
5. 3rd-step response (excluding the agreed suit) shows Kx. The 1st step, 4NT, shows third-round control, xx or the queen. The 2nd step, 5◇, shows Kxxx(x). Jump in the trump suit (6♣) with a singleton.

## Fit-showing Jump

Another two-level agreement sequence that might lead to an immediate Keycard ask is when a passed hand jump shifts by agreement, showing a two-suited hand including a fit with opener's suit (a Fit-showing Jump):

| Opener | Responder | | Opener | Responder |
|---|---|---|---|---|
| | pass | | | pass |
| 1♣ | 2◇ or 2♡ or 2♠ | | 1◇ | 2♡ or 2♠ |
| ? | | | ? | |

Assuming these two-suited jumps show near-opening bids with at least five cards in opener's minor, a Keycard ask might be forthcoming. In each case, the ask is a jump to the four-level of the agreed minor.

| Opener | Responder |
|---|---|
| ♠ 7 | ♠ K Q 6 5 2 |
| ♡ A J 6 | ♡ 3 2 |
| ◇ A Q J 5 | ◇ 8 |
| ♣ K Q 8 7 3 | ♣ A 10 6 5 2 |
| | pass |
| 1♣ | 2♠¹ |
| 4♣² | 4◇³ |
| 6♣⁴ | pass |

1. Fit-showing Jump by a passed hand.
2. RKB (1430) — opener asking.
3. '1'.
4. Going for it.

## Can responder get into the act?

What about responder? Can the responder, the one who has made the agreement, ask for Keycards? Yes, but not always. If the single raise is played as a game force, four of the agreed minor by either player *at any time* is RKB. However, if the bidding slips past four of the agreed suit without an RKB ask, the next RKB off-ramp is 4NT.

RESPONDER'S TURN TO SHINE

| Opener | Responder | |
|---|---|---|
| ♠ 5 4 2 | ♠ A J | 1. Inverted, played as a game |
| ♡ A K 3 2 | ♡ 8 | force. |
| ◇ 7 | ◇ A Q 6 4 | 2. Heart cards. |
| ♣ A J 10 8 3 | ♣ K Q 7 6 5 2 | 3. RKB (1430) — opener has not |
| | | jumped or reversed. |
| 1♣ | 2♣[1] | 4. '2 with'. Responder is presumed |
| 2♡[2] | 4♣[3] | to have at least five clubs. |
| 4NT[4] | 5◇[5] | 5. SSA (any suit that is not the |
| 7♣[6] | pass | queen-ask). |
| | | 6. Singleton. |

Although it is odds-on opener has a major-suit king, it would be nice to be sure before bidding a grand. But how? Your partner's response has preempted you out of your SKA. Here's a thought: why not use the splinter suit, if it is not the queen-ask suit, for something? In fact, why not use it to ask for kings by number as follows:

first-step response        =        1 king
second step-response        =        2 kings
returning to the agreed suit denies a king

In our example, after 4NT responder bids 5◇ to ask about the number of kings, opener bids 5♡ showing one king and responder bids a cozy 7♣.

Another two-level agreement sequence that can lead to a Keycard ask:

| Opener | Responder |
|---|---|
| ♠ J 5 | ♠ K Q 7 3 |
| ♡ Q 6 | ♡ A K 8 |
| ◇ 10 8 5 2 | ◇ A K 6 4 3 |
| ♣ A K Q 5 4 | ♣ 6 |
| | |
| 1♣ | 1◇ |
| 2◇¹ | 4◇² |
| 4♡³ | 4♠⁴ |
| 4NT⁵ | ?⁶ |

1. Presumed four-card support.
2. RKB (1430) — opener hasn't jumped or reversed.
3. '1'.
4. Queen-ask.
5. Negative (see note 6).
6. Pass — or 5◇! When a queen-ask can be made as cheaply as 4♡ or 4♠, the responder can deny the queen by bidding 4NT and can show the queen (without a king) by returning to the five-level of the agreed suit. Given this agreement (thank you, Danny Kleinman), it is possible to get out in 4NT when two Keycards or even an ace and the queen of the agreed suit are missing. Great for matchpoints.

## RKB AFTER TWO-LEVEL AGREEMENT IN A COMPETITIVE AUCTION

Let's talk about interference directly after the two-level agreement.

| Opener | Oppt. | Responder | Oppt. |
|---|---|---|---|
| 1◇ | pass | 2◇ | 2♡ or 3♡ |
| ? | | | |

Let's start with two-level interference, the 2♡ bid. Whether or not the 2◇ raise is game-forcing, a jump to 4◇ is RKB. In other words, two-level interference is disregarded when it comes to making a direct RKB ask.

After three-level interference, it does matter whether the suit agreement is game-forcing or not. If the agreement is game-forcing, four of the agreed suit remains RKB. If the agreement is not game-forcing, then bidding four of the agreed minor is simply a competitive non-forcing bid; responder is expected to pass. In order to ask for Keycards, opener must *jump* to the cheapest unbid suit at the four-level. If the overcall was 3♠ (those rats) jump to 4NT.

Practice time:

| Opener | Oppt. | Responder | Oppt. |
|---|---|---|---|
| 1♣ | pass | 2♣ | 3◇ or 3♡ or 3♠ |

Assuming 2♣ is not a game force, how would you ask for Keycards after the various three-level interference bids in this auction?

Here's how:

> After 3◇, leap to 4♡
> After 3♡, leap to 4♠
> After 3♠, leap to 4NT.

All these are 1430 asks.

## WHEN THEY GET IN YOUR FACE

| **Opener** | | **Responder** | |
|---|---|---|---|
| ♠ A K J 7 | | ♠ 5 | |
| ♡ 3 | | ♡ K J 6 | |
| ◇ K Q 4 | | ◇ J 6 3 2 | |
| ♣ K Q J 9 4 | | ♣ A 10 7 5 2 | |

| **Opener** | **Oppt.** | **Responder** | **Oppt.** |
|---|---|---|---|
| 1♣ | pass | 2◇[1] | 3♡ |
| 4♠[2] | pass | 4NT[3] | pass |
| 5♣[4] | all pass | | |

1. Crisscross. The equivalent of a 3♣ limit raise.
2. RKB (1430) — a jump to the cheapest unbid suit at the four-level. When a splinter and RKB conflict, the RKB ask takes precedence.
3. '1'.
4. All's well that ends well.

## THE BOTTOM LINE

- After either forcing or non-forcing two-level agreement, a leap to four of the agreed minor is RKB (1430).
- If the two-level agreement is game-forcing, either player can ask for Keycards via four of the agreed suit.
- If the agreement is not game-forcing (the more likely scenario) opener figures to be the one, if anyone, to do the asking.
- After game-forcing two-level agreement followed by two- or three-level interference, four of the agreed minor is RKB.
- After non-game-forcing two-level agreement followed by two-level interference, a jump to the four-level of the agreed suit is RKB.
- After non-game-forcing two-level agreement followed by three-level interference, a jump to the four-level of the cheapest unbid suit is RKB. If the interference is 3♠, the ask is 4NT.

# CHAPTER 11

# RKB AFTER THREE-LEVEL MINOR-SUIT AGREEMENT

Three-level agreement sequences come up more often than two- and four-level agreement sequences combined. After three-level agreement the unlimited hand does the asking. When both hands are unlimited, either hand can ask for Keycards. For a limited hand to ask for Keycards, partner must have made a slam try. If the suit agreement is game-forcing, four of the agreed minor is RKB. (After a Two-over-One game-forcing response, either hand can use four of the agreed minor to ask for Keycards).

Game-forcing sequences are easiest to deal with because the ask can be made at the lowest level possible, assuming, of course, that the unlimited hand is strong enough.

## *Three-level game-forcing agreement sequences*

LOOKING, LOOKING, LOOKING

| Opener | Responder |
|--------|-----------|
| ♠ A 5 | ♠ Q 8 6 3 2 |
| ♡ A K J 10 | ♡ 8 7 4 |
| ◇ K Q 10 7 5 2 | ◇ A J 6 |
| ♣ 3 | ♣ Q 8 |
| | |
| 1◇ | 1♠ |
| 2♡ | 3◇¹ |
| 4◇² | 4♡³ |
| 4NT⁴ | 5◇⁵ |
| pass⁶ | |

1. Game-forcing agreement.
2. RKB (1430) — opener asking.
3. '1'. After a '1' response, the next step is the queen-ask. If the next step happens to be partner's first-bid major suit, so be it, it is still the queen-ask. However, if the major has been rebid, it is to play.
4. SKA (4♠ would be the queen-ask). Note that a SKA of 4NT is not necessarily a grand slam try. This bid does not promise joint possession of all four aces and the king-queen of the agreed suit as the SKA of 5NT does.
5. No side-suit king.
6. No king, no slam. Opener is willing to play 6◇ if partner has the ♠K. At worst it will be on a heart finesse.

## JUMP SHIFT + AGREEMENT + BRAKES

| Opener | Responder | |
|---|---|---|
| ♠ A K J 6 | ♠ 3 2 | |
| ♡ K 5 | ♡ Q J 6 4 3 | |
| ◇ 9 | ◇ A 7 5 | |
| ♣ A Q J 7 4 3 | ♣ 10 8 2 | |

| Opener | Responder | |
|---|---|---|
| 1♣ | 1♡ | 1. Game-forcing three-level agreement |
| 2♠ | 3♣[1] | 2. RKB (1430) — opener asking. |
| 4♣[2] | 4◇[3] | 3. '1'. |
| 5♣[4] | pass | 4. Could be off two aces. |

## EYE CATCHING

| Opener | Responder |
|---|---|
| ♠ 8 5 2 | ♠ A K |
| ♡ J 10 8 | ♡ A |
| ◇ A 9 6 | ◇ K Q 10 7 4 3 2 |
| ♣ A K Q 3 | ♣ 6 5 4 |

| Opener | Responder | |
|---|---|---|
| 1♣ | 2◇[1] | 1. Strong jump shift. |
| 3◇[2] | 4◇[2] | 2. Game-forcing three-level agreement. |
| 4NT[3] | 5♣[4] | 3. RKB (1430) — responder is the strong hand. |
| 6♣[5] | 7NT[6] | 4. '2 without'. |
| pass | | 5. SSA in clubs. Most Specific Suit Asks contain the ace or king of the ask suit, usually both. This SSA with neither is only possible because the ask is low enough that any response can be handled. |
| | | 6. KQ(x) The raise of an ask suit shows the KQ with any length — the ace has already been accounted for. |
| | | 7. Can count thirteen tricks. |

## WHEN A HAND FITS

This 26-point slam comes rolling home mainly because responder has the perfect holding (no wasted secondary honors) in opener's short suit.

| Opener | Responder | |
|---|---|---|
| ♠ A K Q 7 4 | ♠ 3 | 1. Game-forcing splinter (by agreement). Some play 3◇ here as a splinter since 2◇ is forcing. Others use 3◇ to show a strong 5-5. Have an agreement. Murphy's Law: whichever way you decide to play 3◇, you will always get the 'other' hand. |
| ♡ 6 4 2 | ♡ A K 10 3 | |
| ◇ 10 | ◇ 4 3 2 | |
| ♣ A J 6 2 | ♣ K Q 10 7 5 | |

| Opener | Responder | |
|---|---|---|
| 1♠ | 2♣ | 2. RKB (3014) — opener has jumped. |
| 3◇[1] | 4♣[2] | 3. '2 without'. |
| 4♠[3] | 6♣ | |
| pass | | |

## BIZARRE, REALLY BIZARRE

| Opener | Responder |
|--------|-----------|
| ♠ 7 6 | ♠ K Q J 4 |
| ♡ K Q J 5 | ♡ 3 |
| ◇ K J | ◇ A Q 10 9 6 3 2 |
| ♣ A K Q 5 2 | ♣ 7 |
| | |
| 1♣ | 1◇ |
| 2♡ | 2♠ |
| 3◇[1] | 4◇[2] |
| 4NT[3] | ?[4] |

1. Game-forcing three-level agreement.
2. RKB (3014) — opener has jumped.
3. '2 without'.
4. At matchpoints, 'pass' is clear. Opener figures to have the missing kings and queens to justify a jump shift. If 'pass' is too unsettling, bid 5◇.

## A '3 OR 0' RESPONSE OF 4♠ TO A 1430 ASK USUALLY SHOWS ZILCH

| Opener | Responder |
|--------|-----------|
| ♠ 5 | ♠ K Q 7 4 3 |
| ♡ A K 7 | ♡ 6 2 |
| ◇ A K 9 8 6 3 | ◇ Q J 5 2 |
| ♣ K Q 4 | ♣ 8 6 |
| | |
| 1◇ | 1♠ |
| 2♡ | 3◇[1] |
| 4◇[2] | 4♠[3] |
| 5◇[4] | pass |

1. Game-forcing three-level agreement.
2. RKB (1430) opener asking.
3. 2nd step = '0' (can't be '3' — asker has '3').
4. Reminder: the asker has the option of signing off in 4NT after a zero response.

## PIECE OF CAKE

| Opener | Responder |
|--------|-----------|
| ♠ K 8 6 4 | ♠ A |
| ♡ 7 | ♡ K Q 5 4 3 |
| ◇ A Q 3 | ◇ 8 2 |
| ♣ A J 8 7 3 | ♣ K Q 6 5 2 |
| | |
| 1♣ | 2♡[1] |
| 2♠ | 3♣[2] |
| 4♣[3] | 4NT[4] |
| 6♣ | pass |

1. Strong.
2. Primary clubs.
3. RKB (3014) — when responder jump shifts, responder is the strong hand. At all other times the opener is the strong hand (1430) when opener asks.
4. '2 with'.

## COMPLEX AUCTION
(North America vs. Italy, Nations Cup)

| Opener | Responder |
|--------|-----------|
| ♠ K 4 | ♠ A J 6 3 |
| ♡ K 7 2 | ♡ A 5 |
| ◇ K 8 4 | ◇ A 2 |
| ♣ A 10 7 5 4 | ♣ K Q 6 3 2 |
| | |
| 1♣ | 1♠ |
| 1NT | 2♣[1] |
| 2◇[2] | 3♣[3] |
| 3NT | 4♣[4] |
| 4◇[5] | 4NT[6] |
| 6NT[7] | 7♣[8] |

1. Checkback to create a forcing auction — some use 2♣ as invitational and 2◇ as a game force.
2. Denies four hearts or three spades.
3. Game-forcing three-level agreement.
4. RKB (1430) — opener minimum.
5. '1'.
6. Specific King Ask.
7. Shows three kings.
8. Knows partner has Kx of spades having denied three spades with

## THE FROG AND THE PRINCE

After responder makes a three-level game-forcing splinter, a slam try, a limited opener can break ranks and ask for Keycards. The Keycard ask is four of the agreed minor (1430). This is one of the few times a minimum limited opener actually asks for Keycards. Think of a frog turning into a dashing prince.

| Opener | Responder |
|--------|-----------|
| ♠ 9 8 5 | ♠ 3 |
| ♡ K 4 | ♡ A 7 6 3 2 |
| ◇ K 8 | ◇ A J 5 |
| ♣ A K 9 6 4 3 | ♣ Q 8 7 5 |
| | |
| 1♣ | 1♡ |
| 2♣ | 3♠[1] |
| 4♣[2] | 4NT[3] |
| 6♣ | pass |

1. Game-forcing splinter.
2. RKB (1430) — opener asking. The prince in action. After a game-forcing splinter, the limited hand comes to life with the magic holding of xxx(x) in the splinter suit.
3. '2 with'.

A beautiful 24-point slam because responder has the right singleton. Give responder:

♠ 3   ♡ A 7 6 3 2   ◇ A 6 5   ♣ 8 7 5 2

and a 21-point slam comes rolling home!

## Three-level agreement after the fourth suit

Consider this sequence:

| Opener | Responder |
|--------|-----------|
| 1♣ | 1♡ |
| 1♠ | 2♢[1] |
| 2NT[2] | 3♣[3] |

1. Fourth suit forcing (could be artificial — always a 'good' hand).
2. Minimum with a diamond stopper.
3. Three-level agreement after the fourth suit.

The question is: is 3♣ a game force?

If responder wishes to invite game in clubs, he can bid 3♣ over 1♠. By interjecting the fourth suit, he promises a stronger hand. In other words, responder should have opening-bid values, minimum. In this book, right or wrong, it is assumed that the fourth suit followed by three-level agreement is a game force.

To make a Keycard ask after 3♣ (a game force) opener must be unlimited. If opener makes a non-jump rebid after the fourth suit, he is considered limited for RKB purposes. So no asks for this opener unless or until responder makes a slam try.

However, responder, who is unlimited, can ask for Keycards by bidding 4♣.

THE FOURTH SUIT IN ACTION

| Opener | Responder |
|--------|-----------|
| ♠ A J 6 3 | ♠ K 5 2 |
| ♡ 7 4 | ♡ A K 6 2 |
| ♢ K J 6 | ♢ 4 |
| ♣ K J 8 2 | ♣ A Q 7 6 3 |
| | |
| 1♣ | 1♡ |
| 1♠ | 2♢[1] |
| 2NT[2] | 3♣[3] |
| 3NT[4] | 4♣[5] |
| 4♠[6] | 6♣ |
| pass | |

1. 4th suit
2. Minimum, usually fewer than three hearts.
3. Game-forcing three-level agreement.
4. Not interested.
5. RKB (1430) — too much to be turned off.
6. '2 without'.

| Opener | Responder | |
|---|---|---|
| ♠ A K J 8 5 | ♠ 6 4 | 1. Fourth suit. |
| ♡ 9 3 | ♡ A 7 2 | 2. Minimum, likely with five 'nice' |
| ◇ K J 5 2 | ◇ A 10 6 3 | spades and no heart stopper. |
| ♣ 4 2 | ♣ A K J 7 | 3. Game-forcing three-level minor- |
| | | suit agreement. Intending to bid |
| 1♠ | 2♣ | 4◇, RKB, next. (Responder could |
| 2◇ | 2♡[1] | have jumped to 4♡ over 2◇ to |
| 2♠[2] | 3◇[3] | ask for Keycards as well.) |
| ?[4] | | 4. Opener, limited, has to come up |
| | | with a bid. 4◇ (not RKB by a |
| | | limited hand) is reasonable. It |
| | | will lead to either an aggressive |
| | | 6◇ or a conservative 5◇. |

## Double agreement in the minors

Double agreement in the minors is a rare bird. Here are a couple of possibilities:

| a) | Opener | Responder | b) | Opener | Responder |
|---|---|---|---|---|---|
| | 1◇ | 2♣ | | 1♣ | 1◇ |
| | 3♣ | 3◇ | | 3♡[1] | 4♣[2] |
| | ? | | | ? | |

1. Game-forcing splinter.
2. Diamonds (4◇ would be RKB).

The implications of Auction (a) depend upon whether 2♣ is played as a game force. If it is, there is double agreement in a game-forcing auction ending in 3◇. Given this scenario, 4♣ is RKB and responder counts the kings and queens of both suits. If 3♣ is not game-forcing, there is no Keycard ask coming from the opener at this point.

In Auction (b), 3♡ is clearly a game-forcing splinter agreeing diamonds and responder could have asked for Keycards via 4◇ (3014). The 4♣ bid could be a cuebid or it could be a support-showing bid. In any event this is considered a double agreement sequence. These might be the two hands:

| Opener | Responder | |
|---|---|---|
| ♠ A Q 6 | ♠ J 5 | 1. Game-forcing splinter agreeing |
| ♡ 8 | ♡ Q J | diamonds. |
| ◇ K J 7 3 | ◇ A Q 6 5 4 | 2. Ambiguous — probably length. |
| ♣ A Q J 6 2 | ♣ K 5 4 3 | 3. RKB (double agreement). |
| | | 4. Two with the higher-ranking |
| 1♣ | 1◇ | queen only (four-step responses |
| 3♡[1] | 4♣[2] | when RKB ask is below 4NT). |
| 4◇[3] | 5◇[4] | 5. Hoping to use the clubs to |
| 6◇[5] | pass | discard a spade from dummy if |
| | | dummy has a doubleton. |

In a contract of 6♣, also a 5-4 fit, you need to take a spade finesse, but in 6◊ you don't. Because partner has the doubleton spade, your clubs will be more useful as a side suit than as a trump suit. (You can only get rid of one spade on dummy's fifth diamond if clubs are trumps.)

| Opener | Responder | |
|---|---|---|
| ♠ Q J 6 | ♠ 8 3 | |
| ♡ A | ♡ K Q | |
| ◊ J 7 3 2 | ◊ A K Q 10 4 | |
| ♣ A J 9 5 4 | ♣ K Q 6 2 | 1. Strong jump shift. |
| | | 2. Club support — 4◊ would be |
| 1♣ | 2◊[1] | RKB. |
| 3◊ | 4♣[2] | 3. Cuebid probably denying a |
| 4♡[3] | 5◊[4] | spade control. |
| pass | | 4. No spade control. |

# THREE-LEVEL NON-FORCING AGREEMENT (NFA) SEQUENCES, ONE HAND UNLIMITED

What do the two following sequences have in common?

| Opener | Responder | | Opener | Responder |
|---|---|---|---|---|
| 1◊ | 1♡ | | 1◊ | 1♡ |
| 1♠ | 1NT | | 2♣ | 2NT |
| 2◊ | 3◊ | | 3♣ | 3◊ |
| ? | ? | | | |

In each sequence both players are limited and the final bid is not forcing. Nobody asks for Keycards in these sequences, so we bid them them a fond RKB adieu.

Now we can concentrate on non-forcing three-level agreement sequences where one hand is unlimited. (Both hands can't be unlimited because one has to have made a non-forcing bid.)

## *Two or more unbid suits*

After non-forcing three-level agreement, an unlimited hand can pass, invite game, bid game, invite slam, bid slam or ask for Keycards. A few applicable sequences:

| Opener | Responder | Opener | Responder | Opener | Responder |
|---|---|---|---|---|---|
| 1♣ | 3♣[1] | 1♣ | 1◊ | 1◊ | 1NT |
| ? | | 3◊[1] | ? | 2♠ | 3◊[1] |
| | | | | ? | |

1. Limit raise.          1. Non-forcing jump.          1. NFA after the 1NT response.

In each sequence the final bid is not forcing, but the facing hand is unlimited. There is yet another similarity: in each sequence there are two or three unbid suits. So what?

The reason this is important is this: after three-level non-forcing agreement, the Keycard ask depends upon the number of unbid suits there are! When there are two or three unbid suits, the raise to four of the agreed suit is RKB. This means that bidding an unbid suit in one of these sequences is a presumed game try (it could also be a slam try in disguise). After a game try, a return to four of the agreed suit by either player is to play. The rationale is this: since there are at least two suits available as game tries, it is safe to play the raise as RKB.

As a memory help, try this rhyme dealing with Keycard asks and unbid suits after three-level non-forcing agreement:

> When there are two or three (unbid suits)
> The raise is free for RKB

### EVERYTHING YOU NEED

This hand features the three necessary ingredients for the raise to be the Keycard ask:

1. Non-forcing three-level agreement.
2. The facing hand is unlimited.
3. Two unbid suits.

| Opener (you) | Responder | |
|---|---|---|
| ♠ A | ♠ J 9 6 | 1. One-round force. |
| ♡ A K Q 5 | ♡ 6 4 2 | 2. Three-level NFA — two unbid suits. |
| ◇ K J 9 8 7 3 2 | ◇ 10 6 5 | 3. RKB (1430) — opener asking. |
| ♣ 7 | ♣ A K 4 3 | 4. '1'. |
| 1◇ | 1NT | 5. Queen-ask. |
| 2♡¹ | 3◇² | 6. Denial. |
| 4◇³ | 4♡⁴ | 7. Bid 5◇. You are off an ace plus |
| 4♠⁵ | 4NT⁶ | the ◇Q. Also, if you are missing |
| ?⁷ | | the ◇A, partner may not have |
| | | the ◇10, which is bad news. |
| | | There is also that *&%* fourth |
| | | heart to deal with. Take the |
| | | money and run. |

## TAKING A STAND AND SAVING A STEP

| Opener | Responder |
|---|---|
| ♠ A | ♠ Q 8 3 |
| ♡ 6 | ♡ A J 4 |
| ◇ A Q J 9 7 4 | ◇ K 6 5 3 2 |
| ♣ A 7 6 4 2 | ♣ 5 3 |
| | |
| 1◇ | 3◇[1] |
| 4◇[2] | 4NT[3] |
| 5♣[4] | 5♡[5] |
| 6◇[6] | pass |

1. Limit raise. (Playing Crisscross the response would be 3♣.)
2. RKB (1430) — three unbid suits and an unlimited opener asking.
3. '2 without' — five-card support presumed.
4. SSA in clubs.
5. 2nd step response = third-round control, the queen or a doubleton.
6. A club loser.

## SPACE SAVER

A low-level Keycard ask allows for a SSA below game in the agreed suit, a big, big plus.

| Opener | Responder |
|---|---|
| ♠ Q 5 2 | ♠ A J 7 |
| ♡ A 9 8 5 2 | ♡ Q 4 |
| ◇ K Q 3 2 | ◇ A J 10 7 5 |
| ♣ 6 | ♣ A Q 5 |
| | |
| 1♡ | 2◇[1] |
| 3◇[2] | 4◇[3] |
| 5♣[4] | 5♡[5] |
| 6◇[6] | pass[7] |

1. Not a game force.
2. Considered limited when 2◇ is not a game force.
3. RKB (1430) — opener limited, two unbid suits. In this sequence it doesn't matter whether 2◇ is a game force or not, the ask is still 4◇.
4. '2 with'.
5. SSA in hearts.
6. The return to the agreed suit denies second- or third-round heart control.
7. Looking at a heart loser

## SPACE SAVER #2

| Opener | Responder |
|---|---|
| ♠ A 5 | ♠ 8 |
| ♡ K 7 5 3 2 | ♡ A 4 |
| ◇ K 6 | ◇ A Q 7 3 |
| ♣ K 10 8 3 | ♣ A Q 7 5 4 2 |
| | |
| 1♡ | 2♣[1] |
| 3♣ | 4♣[3] |
| 4♠[3] | 4NT[4] |
| 5◇[5] | 5♡[6] |
| 5♠[7] | 7♣[8] |
| pass[9] | |

1. Not a game force.
2. RKB (1430) — opener limited, two unbid suits.
3. '2 without'.
4. SKA.
5. ◇K, may have the ♡K.
6. Do you have the ♡K?
7. Yes — 1st step response showing the king.
8. He has so much fun making up these perfect fitting hands.
9. Don't you think everybody knows that?

*Reminder:* In response to a repeat king-ask in a previously bid suit, there are three responses.

1. A return to the agreed suit denies the king.
2. A first-step response shows the king
3. A raise of the ask-suit shows the KQ.

A low-level Keycard ask allows for a low-level second king-ask. If RKB is higher than 4♣, responder can't get in that 5♡ ask.

STOPPING ON A DIME

It is important to be able to get out at the four-level after non-forcing three-level agreement followed by an invite. The rule is that if either player returns to four of the agreed suit, the bidding can end right there.

| Opener | Responder |
|--------|-----------|
| ♠ K Q J 8 3 | ♠ 6 |
| ♡ J 6 | ♡ 7 4 2 |
| ◇ 5 3 | ◇ A Q J 4 |
| ♣ A J 10 7 | ♣ K Q 6 4 2 |
| | |
| 1♠ | 2♣¹ |
| 3♣² | 3◇³ |
| 3♠⁴ | 4♣⁵ |
| pass | |

1. Not a game force. Two-over-One bidders might respond 1NT (forcing) with this hand.
2. Considered limited for RKB purposes.
3. Game try — two unbid suits, so 4♣ is RKB (1430).
4. No heart stopper — strongish spade suit.
5. Not forcing. Opener doesn't figure to have a heart stopper and the hand has too many holes to bid game; besides, opener can still take another bid. And guess what? Even 4♣ may be too high!

CHEAP ASK AVAILABLE

| Opener | Responder |
|--------|-----------|
| ♠ K 8 3 | ♠ A Q 5 |
| ♡ 6 | ♡ K Q 10 4 |
| ◇ A 8 7 5 | ◇ K J 6 4 2 |
| ♣ A Q J 4 3 | ♣ 7 |
| | |
| 1♣ | 1◇ |
| 3◇¹ | 4◇² |
| 4NT³ | ?⁴ |

1. NFA.
2. RKB (3014) — opener has shown extras. When there are two or three, the raise is free.
3. '2 without'.
4. Pass or bid 6◇? The partnership is missing an ace plus the ◇Q. With a nine-card trump fit including the AKJ the odds favor bidding the slam (just). At matchpoints, if you aren't going to bid 6◇, pass 4NT.

## Only one unbid suit

Now for a second group of three-level non-forcing sequences:

| Opener | Responder | Opener | Responder | Opener | Responder |
|---|---|---|---|---|---|
| 1◇ | 1♡ | 1♣ | 1◇ | 1♣ | 1◇ |
| 1♠ or 2♣ | 3◇¹ | 1♡ or 1♠ | 3♣¹ | 1♡ | 1♠¹ |
| ? | | ? | | 3◇² | ? |

1. NFA.

1. NFA.

1. Natural — 2♠ would be the fourth suit
2. NFA.

| Opener | Responder | Opener | Responder |
|---|---|---|---|
| 1♡ | 1♠ | 1♡ | 1♠ |
| 2♣ | 3♣¹ | 2◇ | 3◇¹ |
| ? | | ? | |

1. NFA.

1. NFA.

Again, every sequence features three-level non-forcing agreement facing an unlimited hand. But this time there are *either zero or one unbid suits*.

When there are zero or one unbid suits, it may be awkward make an intelligent game try. To avoid this problem, the raise of the agreed suit to the four-level becomes invitational (as is bidding the unbid suit). To ask for Keycards, the unlimited hand must put on his jumping shoes.

*A leap from 3♣ to 4◇ and a leap from 3◇ to 4♡ is RKB (1430).* And, of course, there is another rhyme to get you through this madness.

> When there are zero or one (unbid suits)
> The jump (to RKB) is fun

HAVING FUN JUMPING WITH ONE

| Opener | Responder |
|---|---|
| ♠ A | ♠ 8 3 2 |
| ♡ K 5 | ♡ A Q 6 3 |
| ◇ A Q 9 8 5 2 | ◇ K J 6 4 |
| ♣ K J 5 3 | ♣ 7 4 |

| Opener | Responder | |
|---|---|---|
| 1◇ | 1♡ | 1. Not forcing. |
| 2♣ | 3◇¹ | 2. RKB (1430) — opener asking. The raise to 4◇ is invitational (one unbid suit). |
| 4♡² | 5♣³ | |
| 6◇ | pass | 3. '2 without'. |

Is this operation a success or did the patient die? Only time will tell.

## HOW MUCH FUN CAN 'ONE' PERSON HAVE?

| Opener | Responder |
|--------|-----------|
| ♠ 5 | ♠ A K 7 4 2 |
| ♡ A K 8 5 3 2 | ♡ 6 |
| ◇ 9 | ◇ Q 6 3 |
| ♣ A Q 8 6 3 | ♣ J 5 4 2 |
| 1♡ | 1♠ |
| 2♣ | 3♣[1] |
| 4◇[2] | 4♡[3] |
| 5♣[4] | pass |

1. Not forcing.
2. RKB (1430) — opener asking. The raise to 4♣ would be invitational.
3. '1'.
4. Too risky to gamble 6♣ — could be off two aces.

## MATCHPOINT MANIA

| Opener (you) | Responder |
|--------------|-----------|
| ♠ A K 10 6 | ♠ 4 |
| ♡ A Q 7 | ♡ J 5 2 |
| ◇ 6 | ◇ K Q J 4 3 |
| ♣ K J 6 4 2 | ♣ A 9 5 3 |
| 1♣ | 1◇ |
| 1♠ | 3♣[1] |
| 4◇[2] | 4♡[3] |
| 4♠[4] | 4NT[5] |
| ?[6] | |

1. Non-forcing agreement, one unbid suit.
2. RKB (1430).
3. '1'.
4. Queen-ask.
5. Denial. After minor suit agreement the queen-ask denial, if available, is 4NT. When 4NT is available, a return to the five-level of the trump suit confirms the queen but denies a side-suit king.
6. You are off an ace plus the queen of trumps, not to mention other possible problems; pass 4NT. At matchpoints if you don't pass, bid 6♣ rather than 5♣.

## A BONUS SEQUENCE (ARE YOU THRILLED?)

| Opener | Responder |
|--------|-----------|
| ♠ A K J 9 5 | ♠ 3 |
| ♡ J 4 | ♡ A K Q 6 |
| ◇ A 3 | ◇ K Q J 4 |
| ♣ 10 7 5 2 | ♣ Q J 6 3 |
| 1♠ | 2♣[1] |
| 3♣[2] | 4NT[3] |
| pass | |

1. Not a game force.
2. Presumed limited.
3. Natural — 4♣ is RKB.

Whether 3♣ is game-forcing, a one-round force, or not forcing at all, there is a way to ask for Keycards lower than 4NT in this sequence: 4♣. If the sequence is played as game-forcing, 4♣ is RKB. If the sequence is not played as game-forcing, 4♣ is still RKB because there are two unbid suits. This agreement liberates the jump to 4NT to be played as natural, to describe a hand too strong to bid 3NT, but not strong enough to bid 6NT. A 'tweener'.

## TEST YOURSELF - ✌

Let's see if any of this has made sense.

Say you wish to ask for Keycards in the following three-level agreement sequences. Determine what the ask is, assuming an ask is possible, and decide whether it is a 1430 or a 3014 ask.

| a) **Opener** | **Responder** | b) **Opener** | **Responder** |
|---|---|---|---|
| 1♣ | 1◇ | 1♡ | 1♠ |
| 1♠ | 3♣[1] | 2◇ | 3◇[1] |
| ? | | ? | |

1. Not forcing

1. Not forcing

In (a) you are unlimited, and there is one unbid suit. To ask for Keycards, jump to 4◇, 1430. (When there are zero or one, the jump is fun.)

In (b) you are unlimited and there is one unbid suit. To ask for Keycards jump to 4♡ (1430).

**Note 1:** After three-level non-forcing diamond agreement, one unbid suit, 4♡ by the unlimited hand is RKB, even if hearts is a first-bid suit, because 3♡ in these sequences is always forcing. (Important agreement.)

**Note 2:** In sequences where 4◇ can be used as RKB, jumps to 4♡ are natural.

| c) **Opener** | **Responder** | d) **Opener** | **Responder** |
|---|---|---|---|
| 1◇ | 1♠ | 1♣ | 1◇ |
| 2♣ | 3♣[1] | 1♡ | 1♠[1] |
| ? | | 3◇[2] | ? |

1. Not forcing.

1. Natural, not fourth suit;.
   2♠ would be fourth suit.
2. Not forcing.

In (c) after three-level non-forcing club agreement, one unbid suit, RKB is a leap to 4◇ (1430) and a raise to 4♣ is invitational.

In (d) after three-level non-forcing diamond agreement, one unbid suit, 4♡ is RKB (3014) — opener has jumped. When 4♡ is RKB after three-level diamond agreement, a raise to 4◇ is invitational.

## *Breathing life into a limited hand — more on splinters*

After three-level game-forcing minor-suit agreement, four of the agreed suit by the unlimited hand is RKB. Furthermore, after a splinter jump, a limited opener can come to life and ask for Keycards. But what about a limited responder, one who has shown weakness (has made a single or a limit raise) and suddenly hears partner make a slam try splinter? Is he an orphan for evermore, or what? It's a well-known fact that the value of a limited hand (any hand for that matter) can skyrocket after a splinter jump. Nonetheless, a weak limited hand is better advised to cuebid rather than become the general and ask for Keycards. As a weak limited responder, think cuebid after partner splinters.

If partner splinters after you, the responder, have made a single or a limit raise, new suits by you (including 4NT) are cuebids. Holding two important cards outside of the agreed suit, or an ace plus the ace or king of the agreed suit, start cuebidding. Just do it! With one important card that can be shown beneath the game-level, show it. 4NT shows strong trumps (two of the top three honors or an extra trump and the ace or king), but no cuebid available:

| Opener | Responder | |
|--------|-----------|--|
| 1♣ | 3♣[1] | 1. Limit raise. |
| 4◇[2] | ? | 2. Slam-invitational splinter. |

Now 4♡ and 4♠ by responder are cuebids, while 4NT shows strong trumps with no cuebid available.

ONCE A FROG, ALWAYS A FROG

| Opener | Responder | |
|--------|-----------|--|
| ♠ A 9 2 | ♠ 7 3 | |
| ♡ A K 6 3 | ♡ 7 2 | |
| ◇ 5 | ◇ A J 6 3 | |
| ♣ A Q J 7 2 | ♣ K 10 8 6 4 | 1. Limit raise. |
| | | 2. Slam-try splinter: 4♣ would be |
| 1♣ | 3♣[1] | RKB |
| 4◇[2] | 5◇[3] | 3. Cuebid (two important cards — |
| 6♣ | | ◇A, ♣K). |

UGH

| Opener | Responder | |
|--------|-----------|--|
| ♠ A 9 2 | ♠ 7 3 | 1. Limit raise. |
| ♡ A K 6 3 | ♡ J 2 | 2. Slam-invitational splinter. |
| ◇ 5 | ◇ K J 6 3 | 3. Wasted diamond strength with |
| ♣ A Q J 7 2 | ♣ K 10 8 6 4 | no ace or king to cuebid. |
| | | 4. A trusting opener should proba- |
| 1♣ | 3♣[1] | bly pass, but will die a thousand |
| 4◇[2] | 5♣[3] | deaths if responder tables Qx of |
| ?[4] | | hearts. |

## (This is worse than school)

Here are several more three-level agreement sequences. See if you can figure out what the RKB ask is, assuming an ask is possible, of course.

| Opener | Responder |
|--------|-----------|
| 1♡ | 2◇ |
| 2NT | 3♣ |
| 3◇ | ? |

If you are in a game-forcing sequence, 4◇ is RKB (1430) — opener has neither jumped nor reversed to show extras. If you are not in a game-forcing sequence, count the unbid suits! There is only one, so a jump to 4♡ is RKB (1430), opener not having jumped or reversed; a raise to 4◇ is invitational. It helps if the partnership knows when three-level minor suit agreement sequences are game-forcing or not. This is a recording.

| Opener | Responder | |
|--------|-----------|---|
| 1◇ | 2♣¹ | 1. Not a game force. |
| 2◇ | 3◇² | 2. Invitational. |
| ? | | |

Don't tell me you fell for this one! Both hands are limited, so no Keycard ask.

| Opener | Responder |
|--------|-----------|
| 1◇ | 1♠ |
| 2♡ | 3◇ |
| ? | |

Assuming 3◇ is a game force, 4◇ by either hand is RKB because both hands are unlimited. It's 1430 by the opener, 3014 by the responder. If you play 3◇ isn't a game force, 4♡ is RKB (1430) – one unbid suit.

| Opener | Responder | |
|--------|-----------|---|
| 1♠ | 2♣¹ | 1. Not a game force. |
| 2♡ | 2NT² | 2. 11-12 HCP. |
| 3♣³ | ? | 3. Forcing. |

Yes, 3♣ is forcing, but is it a game force? In any case responder is limited and opener hasn't splintered (or made a slam try) so a Keycard ask is off the wall bizarre at this point.

   **Reminder:** if 2♣ is played as a game force (Two-over-One), either player can use 4♣ as RKB after three-level agreement.

| Opener | Responder | |
|--------|-----------|---|
| 1♡ | 2♣[1] | 1. Not a game force. |
| 3♣[2] | 3♢[3] | 2. Forcing, but not to game |
| ? | | 3. Game try, supposedly; 4♣ is RKB. |

You are considered limited and partner has neither splintered nor made a clear-cut slam try (3♢ is a one-round force and is considered, at least temporarily, a game try). The bottom line is that you can't logically ask for Keycards at this point. If you had a great hand for clubs and wanted to ask for Keycards straight away, you could have leaped to 4♢. (Check out the chapter on two-level non-agreement sequences.)

If you play that the 2♣ response is not a game force, then as opener, with a strong hand for clubs, you do best to make a stronger agreement than 3♣. Consider splintering, jumping to 4♣, or bidding a new suit and then supporting clubs.

---

## THREE-LEVEL AGREEMENT FOLLOWED BY 3NT FOLLOWED BY A SLAM TRY

If you are the 3NT bidder, you are a limited hand. If partner makes a slam try, 4NT by you is to play and new suits are cuebids. In other words, there is no Keycard ask by the 3NT bidder; cuebid if you are interested in slam.

If the three-level agreement preceding the 3NT bid was game-forcing, four of the agreed minor by the *unlimited* hand is still RKB. If the three-level agreement preceding the 3NT bid was not game-forcing, bidding four of the agreed minor over 3NT is not RKB. Please.

| a) Opener | Responder | | b) Opener | Responder |
|-----------|-----------|---|-----------|-----------|
| 1♠ | 2♣ | | 1♠ | 2♣ |
| 3♣ | 3NT | | 2♢ | 3♢ |
| ? | | | 3NT | ? |

| c) Opener | Responder | | d) Opener | Responder |
|-----------|-----------|---|-----------|-----------|
| 1♣ | 1♡ | | 1♣ | 1♡ |
| 2♢ | 3♢ | | 2♠ | 3♣ |
| 3NT | ? | | 3NT | ? |

In (a) if 2♣ was a game force, 4♣ by the opener is RKB (1430). Playing Two-over-One, either player can ask for Keycards after three-level agreement because they are both considered unlimited. However after one bids 3NT, limiting his hand, that player can't ask for Keycards if a cuebid follows. If 2♣ was not a game force, there is no Keycard ask in the foreseeable future — both hands are limited. When a limited hand pulls 3NT to four of the agreed minor, a good case can be made for the bid to be non-forcing.

In (b) if 2♣ was a game force, 4◇ by the responder would be RKB (1430) — opener hasn't jumped or reversed. If 2♣ was not a game force and 3◇ isn't played as forcing, both hands are limited so there is no Keycard ask. The real issue is whether a pull to 4◇ should be considered forcing.

In (c) if 3◇ is a game force, 4◇ by responder, unlimited, is RKB (3014) — opener has reversed.

In (d) the auction is game-forcing and responder is unlimited, so 4♣ by the responder is RKB (3014).

*Review:* If the player facing the 3NT bidder makes a four-level slam try cuebid, the 3NT bidder can cuebid, bid 4NT (natural), or even leap to slam. What he can't do is pass or ask for Keycards.

### I WANT OUT!  I WANT IN!

| Opener | Responder | |
|---|---|---|
| ♠ K Q J 8 4 | ♠ 5 3 | |
| ♡ K Q 10 | ♡ 8 | |
| ◇ Q 6 3 2 | ◇ A J 7 4 | |
| ♣ 4 | ♣ A K Q 6 3 2 | 1. Game force. |
| | | 2. Game-forcing agreement. |
| 1♠ | 2♣¹ | 3. RKB (1430). |
| 2◇ | 3◇² | 4. '0'. |
| 3NT | 4◇³ | 5. Sign-off. |
| 4♠⁵ | 4NT⁶ | 6. After a '0' response to an RKB |
| pass | | ask, 4NT is to play! |

| Opener | Responder |
|---|---|
| ♠ A Q 8 6 4 | ♠ 5 3 |
| ♡ A J 5 | ♡ 8 |
| ◇ K 10 3 2 | ◇ A J 7 4 |
| ♣ 4 | ♣ A K Q 6 3 2 |
| | |
| 1♠ | 2♣¹ |
| 2◇ | 3◇² |
| 3NT | 4◇³ |
| 4NT⁴ | 6◇ |
| pass | |

1. Game force.
2. Game-forcing agreement.
3. RKB (1430).
4. '2 without'.

# INTERFERENCE PRECEDES A THREE-LEVEL NFA — ALL IS FORGIVEN

When there is interference *preceding, but not following,* three-level agreement, happy days are here again — even rhyme time (dealing with the number of unbid suits) is back. You bid as if the interference never happened. Also, any suit the opponents have bid is considered an unbid suit — providing it can be cuebid below four of the agreed suit.

| Opener | Oppt. | Responder | Oppt. |
|--------|-------|-----------|-------|
| 1♠ | 2♣ | 2◇ | pass |
| 3◇ | pass | ? | |

RHO has passed after the non-forcing agreement (3◇). Rhyme time. Two suits are available for game tries, 3♡ and 4♣. 'When there are two or three, the raise (to RKB) is free': 4◇ is RKB (1430).

| Opener | Oppt. | Responder | Oppt. |
|--------|-------|-----------|-------|
| 1♣ | 2♡[1] | 3♣ | pass |
| ? | | | |

1. Weak.

Disregard the interference when it is made by LHO, it's only your RHO who can you do in. But remember your rhymes! In this sequence you have three game tries available beneath 4♣: 3◇, 3♡, and 3♠, therefore 4♣ is RKB (1430).

BRUSHING THEM ASIDE AGAIN

| Opener | Responder |
|--------|-----------|
| ♠ K Q 5 3 | ♡ 7 2 |
| ♡ A K 4 | ♡ 8 5 3 |
| ◇ 7 | ◇ K J 6 |
| ♣ K Q 8 5 4 | ♣ A 7 6 3 2 |

| Opener | Oppt. | Responder | Oppt. |
|--------|-------|-----------|-------|
| 1♣ | 2♡[1] | 3♣ | pass |
| 4♣[2] | pass | 4◇[3] | pass |
| 5♣[4] | all pass | | |

1. Weak.
2. RKB 1430 (three unbid suits).
3. '1'.
4. Not enough.

# INTERFERENCE FOLLOWS THREE-LEVEL AGREEMENT — BAD NEWS, VERY BAD NEWS

| Opener | Oppt. | Responder | Oppt. |
|--------|-------|-----------|-------|
| 1♣ | 2♡¹ | 3♣ | 3♡ |
| ? | | | |

1. Weak.

Say RHO bids directly after non-forcing three-level agreement (the nerve!). When RHO intervenes after non-forcing three-level agreement, four of the agreed minor is not forcing, it is competitive (fighting for the contract). So goodbye four of the agreed minor as RKB, and goodbye 'rhyme time'.

To ask for Keycards after RHO interferes, it's 'jump time'. You have to jump to the cheaper (or only) unbid suit at the four-level. If none is available, jump to 4NT.

| Opener | Oppt. | Responder | Oppt. |
|--------|-------|-----------|-------|
| 1♡ | 1♠ | 2♣ | pass |
| 3♣ | 3♢ | ? | |

Your 2♣ bid is not a game force in competition, so 3♣ is not forcing. Looking at the bright side, you are unlimited so you can ask for Keycards — but what is the ask? There are no unbid suits to jump to (you can't use one of their suits to ask for Keycards — ever). You have to leap to 4NT (1430).

Let's look at some other sequences where RHO ruins your party. Say you are the opener. How would you compete, make a game try, or ask for Keycards in the following sequence?

| Opener | Oppt. | Responder | Oppt. |
|--------|-------|-----------|-------|
| 1♣ | pass | 3♣¹ | 3♢ or 3♡ or 3♠ |
| ? | | | |

1. Limit raise.

If the overcall is 3♢, 3♡ and 3♠ are game tries, possibly slam tries; 4♣ is to play, 4♡, a leap to the cheaper unbid suit, is RKB (1430) and 4♠ is a splinter. If the overcall is 3♡, 3♠ is a game try (or more), 4♣ is not forcing, 4♢ is a slam try, 4♡ is a cuebid, and 4♠, the one suit you can jump in, is RKB (1430). If the overcall is 3♠, forget about leaping to any suit at the four-level to ask for Keycards. Now 4♣ is not forcing, 4♢, 4♡ and 4♠ are all slam try cuebids and 4NT is RKB (1430).

Now try it with this sequence. Given the various intervening bids, how would you compete, make game tries or ask for Keycards?

| Opener | Oppt. | Responder | Oppt. |
|--------|-------|-----------|-------|
| 1♢ | pass | 3♢¹ | 3♡ or 3♠ or 4♣ |
| ? | | | |

1. Limit raise.

After 3♡, 3♠ and 4♣ are game tries, maybe more, 4◇ is to play, and 4♠, the only suit you can jump to, is RKB (1430). After 3♠, 4♣ is a game try, 4◇ is to play, 4♡ is a slam try, 4♠ is a cuebid and 4NT is RKB. Once they overcall 3♠, 4NT is the only RKB ask. If the interference is 4♣, 4◇ is to play, 4♡ and 4♠ are cuebids and 4NT is RKB (1430).

DEAL WITH IT!

| Opener | Responder |
|---|---|
| ♠ K Q 10 6 | ♠ J 5 2 |
| ♡ 9 | ♡ K Q J |
| ◇ A K 4 | ◇ 8 |
| ♣ A J 10 7 3 | ♣ Q 9 6 5 4 2 |

| Opener | Oppt. | Responder | Oppt. |
|---|---|---|---|
| 1♣ | pass | 3♣[1] | 3◇[2] |
| 4♡[3] | pass | 4NT[4] | pass |
| 5♣ | all pass | | |

1. Limit.
2. Three-level interference from RHO.
3. RKB (1430) — a jump to the cheaper unbid suit.
4. The big '0'.

## THE BOTTOM LINE

- A minimum limited hand cannot ask for Keycards unless partner makes a slam try. A splinter jump is considered a slam try.
- After game-forcing three-level agreement, four of the agreed minor by an unlimited hand is RKB. If both hands are unlimited or there has been a game-forcing two-over-one response, four of the agreed suit by either player is RKB. However, if one of the player bids 3NT, that player cannot ask for Keycards. Period.
- After non-game-forcing three-level agreement, it's rhyme time assuming an unlimited hand wishes to ask for Keycards.
- When there are zero or one (unbid suits), a jump to 4◇ over 3♣ or to 4♡ over 3◇ is RKB. Bidding the unbid suit is considered invitational.
- When there are two or three unbid suits, the raise of the agreed suit is RKB; other suits are considered game tries. After a game try, a return to four of the agreed minor by either hand is to play.
- When both hands have made non-forcing bids leading to three-level agreement, there is no Keycard ask.

If you can handle this chapter, you can handle anything.

# CHAPTER 12

# THE QUEEN-ASK AFTER MINOR-SUIT AGREEMENT

One of the advantages of a low-level RKB ask is a low-level queen-ask. Here are the responses to the low-level queen-asks of 4♡ or 4♠, the cheapest possible queen-asks.

## Responses to the 4♡ or 4♠ queen-ask

1. A response of 4NT denies the queen.
2. Bidding five of the agreed suit shows the queen but denies a side-suit king or an extra.
3. Bidding a side suit at the five-level confirms the queen and shows the king of the side suit bid.
4. Bidding six of the agreed suit shows the queen and denies a side-suit king or a side-suit extra. It is the weakest queen-showing response.
5. Bidding 5NT confirms the queen, denies a side-suit king, but shows an 'extra'.

## When 4NT is the queen-ask

1. A return to five of the agreed suit denies the queen.
2. Bidding a suit at the five-level confirms the queen and shows the king of the bid suit.
3. Bidding six of the agreed suit shows the queen but denies a side-suit king or a side-suit extra. It is the weakest queen-showing response.
4. Bidding 5NT confirms the queen, denies a side-suit king, but shows an 'extra'.

*In order of importance, 'extras' are:*
1. The queen of partner's first-bid suit.
2. The queen of partner's second-bid suit if his first-bid suit is the trump suit.
3. Extra trump length if the responder has the long trump hand.
4. If no side suits have been bid, any third-round control.

## Responses to a queen-ask at or above five of the agreed suit

When a queen-ask is made at or above five of the agreed suit, *it is a grand slam try*. After all, the asker is prepared to play at the six-level even if responder does not have the queen!

Responses are:

1. 5NT confirms the queen, denies a side-suit king, but shows an 'extra'; 7NT may be in the game.
2. Bidding six of the agreed suit denies the queen.
3. Bidding six of some other suit shows the queen plus the king of the bid suit; 7NT may be a possibility.
4. Bidding a grand in the agreed suit shows the queen but denies a side-suit king or a side-suit extra.

## The queen-ask when the trump suit is the next step after the RKB response

After a 1st or 2nd step response to RKB, the trump queen may be an unknown quantity and the next step is normally the queen-ask. But what if the next step is the trump suit? Surely, the trump suit is reserved for sign-offs. Not always. The trump suit can be used as the queen-ask suit in two scenarios.

1. After a 1430 (strong asking weak) RKB ask and a second step response of '0 or 3'.

   If the response shows '3', the next step is the queen-ask. Period. When 'strong asks weak' and gets a '3' response, 'strong' is not signing off! No way. If the asker wants to know about the queen facing '0', the next step after the trump suit is the queen-ask. This happens less than seldom.
2. After a 3014 (weak asking strong) ask followed by a 2nd step response of '1 or 4'. (Surely '4' — a strong hand doesn't have '1'. Please.)

   If the next step is the trump suit, it is the queen-ask facing '4'. How can the asker want to sign off after a '4' response? What was he looking for?

## The 4NT rebid after a Keycard response (three possible meanings)

1. After a '0' response to RKB, a follow-up bid of 4NT, if available, is to play.

Here are two sequences: each starts with a make-believe 1430 ask and a '0' response. In the first sequence, pretend clubs is the agreed suit.

| Opener | Responder | |
|--------|-----------|---|
| .... | .... | 1. RKB (1430). |
| 4♣[1] | 4♡[2] | 2. '0'. |
| 4♠[3] | | 3. Queen-ask (next step). A bid of 4NT would be for play. |

In the next sequence pretend diamonds is the agreed suit and opener is asking for Keycards via a 4◇ (1430) ask. Once again opener gets the dreaded '0' response.

| Opener | Responder | |
|--------|-----------|---|
| .... | .... | 1. RKB 1430. |
| 4◇[1] | 4♠[2] | 2. '0'. |
| 4NT[3] | | 3. To play. This time, 5♣ is the queen-ask. |

## 4NT IN ACTION AFTER A '0' RESPONSE

| Opener | Responder | |
|--------|-----------|---|
| ♠ A K 5 3 2 | ♠ Q 8 | 1. Waiting. |
| ♡ K Q 10 | ♡ 9 6 | 2. Natural. |
| ◇ K J | ◇ Q 8 6 5 4 3 2 | 3. RKB 1430. (A perk for a 2♣ opener — being able to make a |
| ♣ A K Q | ♣ J 9 | Keycard ask following a natural 3♣ or 3◇ bid with a raise. |
| 2♣ | 2◇[1] | Coming up — hang in there.) |
| 2♠ | 3◇[2] | 4. '0'. |
| 4◇[3] | 4♠[4] | 5. To play (after a '0' response). |
| 4NT[5] | pass | |

2 & 3.     After a '1' response to a Keycard ask, 4NT, if the next step, is the queen-ask. If it is not the next step, it is the SKA.

| Opener | Responder | |
|--------|-----------|---|
| 1♣ | 1♡ | 1. Game-forcing three-level agreement |
| 2♠ | 3♣[1] | 2. RKB (1430) |
| 4♣[2] | 4◇[3] | 3. '1' |
| 4♡[4] | | 4. Queen-ask (next step). Here 4NT would be the SKA, while 4♠ is a SSA. |

Keep the faith.

# CHAPTER 13

## RKB AFTER FOUR-LEVEL MINOR-SUIT AGREEMENT

### FOUR-LEVEL AGREEMENT, NO PREVIOUS 3NT BID

Depending upon the previous bidding, four-level agreement can be a slam try, an invitational raise, or a non-forcing preference. Whatever, barring a major exception (a mega-strong hand making the agreement), *the agreement is not the ask*. If both hands are limited the agreement isn't even forcing so there is no Keycard ask. However, after game-forcing four-level agreement, normally a slam try, with no previous 3NT bid, a lower-level Keycard ask is available to both a limited or an unlimited hand.

> When clubs is the agreed suit, 4◇ is the ask and 4NT is a diamond cuebid
> When diamonds is the agreed suit, 4♡ is the ask and 4NT is a heart cuebid

Simple, but each rule comes with one exception. Sorry.

### *Club agreement auctions*

First, let's deal with the exception to the rule when clubs is the agreed suit. If diamonds is a first-bid suit and clubs is a second bid suit, and clubs have neither been rebid nor jump-supported, 4◇ is best played as natural and 4♡ takes over as RKB for clubs. If hearts is also a first-bid suit (unlucky), 4♠ is RKB. The incidence is small, but there is a valid reason to keep 4◇ natural.

Sequences like these are the ones in question:

| a) **Opener** | **Responder** | | b) **Opener** | **Responder** |
|---|---|---|---|---|
| 1♡ | 2◇ | | 1◇ | 1♠ |
| 3♣ | 4♣ | | 3♣ | 4♣ |
| 4◇ | | | 4◇ | |

In both sequences diamonds is a first-bid suit, clubs a second-bid suit and clubs have not been rebid nor has the suit been jump-supported. Therefore 4◇ in each sequence is natural.

If opener (a) wants to ask for Keycards (clubs agreed) he must bid 4♠ (1430); 4♡ is natural and 4NT is a diamond cuebid. You knew that.

In Auction (b), both 4♢ and 4♠ are natural so the RKB winner is 4♡ (1430); 4NT is a heart cuebid.

To understand better the reason for the 'exception', say opener (a) has:

♠ 4   ♡ A K J 6 2   ♢ A Q 7   ♣ Q 6 3 2

Wouldn't he like to bid a natural 4♢ over 4♣? Diamonds could be a better trump suit than clubs. A strong 5-3 fit might offer more security than a shaky 4-4. A good bidder offers partner a choice of trump suits.

Opener (b) might be gazing at:

♠ K 5   ♡ 8   ♢ A Q J 6 5 3 2   ♣ A K 5

This hand is too strong to rebid a non-forcing 3♢, so 3♣ is certainly a possible rebid. After the raise to 4♣, wouldn't opener like to bid a natural 4♢?

## RULES, RULES, RULES

| Opener | | Responder (you) | |
|---|---|---|---|
| ♠ Q 5 2 | | ♠ 9 | |
| ♡ 3 | | ♡ A K Q J 7 6 | |
| ♢ A Q J 4 3 | | ♢ 5 | |
| ♣ K 6 4 2 | | ♣ A J 10 5 3 | |

| Opener | Oppt. | Responder | Oppt. |
|---|---|---|---|
| 1♢ | 1♠ | 2♡ | pass |
| 2NT | pass | 3♣ | pass |
| 4♣ | pass | ? | |

Given 'the exception' you can't use 4♢ or 4♡, both first-bid suits, to ask for Keycards. Those bids are natural. Using 4♠, a suit bid by the opponents, is also a super no-no. Guess what? You have to use 4NT (1430).

If you bid 4NT, partner responds 5♡, '2 without'. Now what? You can pass or gamble on the six-level knowing you are missing either one ace and the ♣Q or the ♣KQ. Either way, given that ♣J10, you are a favorite to make a slam in clubs or hearts.

## QUEEN-ASK DENIAL

| Opener | Responder |
|--------|-----------|
| ♠ 6 | ♠ A 10 5 3 |
| ♡ K 7 | ♡ Q J 3 2 |
| ◇ A Q J 6 | ◇ 5 4 |
| ♣ A K 9 6 5 3 | ♣ J 4 2 |
| | |
| 1♣ | 1♡ |
| 2◇ | 2NT[1] |
| 3♣ | 4♣[2] |
| 4◇[3] | 4♡[4] |
| 4♠[5] | 4NT[6] |
| 5♣[7] | pass |

1. Natural game-force.
2. The agreement, not the ask.
3. The ask (1430).
4. '1'.
5. Queen-ask.
6. The negative response to a queen-ask of 4♡ or 4♠ is 4NT. This response gives the asker the option of passing.
7. Opener knows the hand is off an ace, the ♣Q and perhaps the ◇K as well. There is just too much missing to bid on.

## DIAMONDS ARE USUALLY A GIRL'S BEST FRIEND WHEN CLUBS ARE AGREED

In the following sequence diamonds is not a first-bid suit so even though clubs is a second-bid suit that has not been rebid or jump-supported, 4◇ can be used as RKB.

| Opener | Responder |
|--------|-----------|
| ♠ A K 7 6 3 2 | ♠ 5 |
| ♡ 6 | ♡ K 8 7 5 3 2 |
| ◇ 10 | ◇ K Q |
| ♣ A J 10 6 5 | ♣ K Q 4 3 |
| | |
| 1♠ | 2♡ |
| 3♣ | 4♣[1] |
| 4◇[2] | 4♡[3] |
| 5♣[4] | pass |

1. The agreement, not the ask.
2. The ask. When opener asks, 1430.
3. '1'.
4. Two Keycards missing.

## CAN'T DO EVERYTHING

Once cuebidding is in motion after four-level agreement, 4NT is the next cheapest Keycard ask.

| Opener | Responder |
|--------|-----------|
| ♠ A Q | ♠ 9 8 4 |
| ♡ 6 | ♡ A J 10 3 |
| ◇ A K 6 5 2 | ◇ 4 3 |
| ♣ A J 9 5 4 | ♣ K Q 7 3 |
| | |
| 1◇ | 1♡ |
| 3♣ | 4♣ |
| ?[1] | |

1. It would be nice if 4◇ were RKB, but given 'the exception', it is natural. Here 4♠ is the Keycard ask (diamonds and hearts are both first-bid suits).

If you bid 4♠ (1430) here, partner responds 5♥, '2 with', and you can't bid a grand with any confidence given the diamond position (and a SSA in diamonds is already past 6♣!). After all, partner might have three small diamonds, not to mention that there is a possible spade loser even if partner has a doubleton diamond. Settle for 6♣ and make apologies later, if necessary.

## A REPLACEMENT CUEBID

After four-level club agreement when 4◇ is RKB, the usual case, 4NT is a diamond cuebid.

| Opener | Responder |
|---|---|
| ♠ 7 | ♠ A K Q 4 2 |
| ♡ 9 5 3 | ♡ 6 2 |
| ◇ A Q 8 | ◇ K J |
| ♣ A Q 10 9 6 5 | ♣ K J 4 3 |
| | |
| 1♣ | 1♠ |
| 2♣ | 4♣[1] |
| 4NT[2] | 5♣[3] |
| pass | |

1. Four-level jump raises and four-level jump preferences are game-forcing agreements, not RKB asks. No exceptions.
2. Diamond cuebid (4◇ is RKB), surely denying a heart control.
3. No heart control + no heart control = no slam.

## STRIKING GOLD, FINALLY

| Opener | Responder |
|---|---|
| ♠ 4 | ♠ A K 6 3 2 |
| ♡ Q J 9 5 4 | ♡ — |
| ◇ A K 6 | ◇ 10 7 3 |
| ♣ K 7 5 2 | ♣ A Q 6 4 3 |
| | |
| 1♡ | 1♠ |
| 2♣ | 4♣[1] |
| 4NT[2] | 6♣[3] |
| pass | |

1. The agreement, not the ask.
2. Diamond cuebid (4◇ is RKB).
3. Likes what he hears.

## GETTING YOUR MONEY'S WORTH

After a '1' response to RKB, a next-step rebid in either player's second suit is the queen-ask.

| Opener | Responder |
|---|---|
| ♠ A K Q 7 6 | ♠ 3 |
| ♡ 4 | ♡ J 10 9 5 3 |
| ◇ 4 | ◇ A K 10 6 2 |
| ♣ A K 9 5 3 2 | ♣ Q 6 |

| Opener | Responder |
|--------|-----------|
| 1♣ | 1♡ |
| 2♠ | 3◇ |
| 3♠ | 4♣¹ |
| 4◇² | 4♡³ |
| 4♠⁴ | 5◇⁵ |
| 6♣⁶ | pass |

1. Game-forcing four-level agreement.
2. RKB (1430) — opener asking.
3. '1'.
4. Queen-ask
5. Yes, with the ◇K.
6. One Keycard missing.

The previous hand brings to mind this hand: I'll present it to you as a problem, but you'll have to accept the opening bid. You hold:

♠ A K Q 7 4     ♡ K J     ◇ K     ♣ A 9 6 5 3

You are forced to open 1♣ (with 20 HCP there is something to be said for opening 1♣ in order to make it easier for partner to respond). In any case the bidding continues:

| Opener (you) | Responder |
|--------------|-----------|
| 1♣ | 1◇ |
| 2♠ | 3♡ |
| 3♠¹ | 4♣² |
| ? | |

1. Got that fifth spade in there
2. Strength not clear

Partner's 4♣ has the aura of a slam try. Lacking an agreement, one seldom uses the fourth suit with a weak hand after a jump shift. What now? Your options are: 1) 4◇ –- RKB; 2) 4♡ -- cuebid; 3) 5♣ signoff; 4) 6♣ — getting it over with.

Say you try 4◇, RKB (1430), and partner responds 4NT ('2 without'). Now what? You are probably thinking you never would have been in this mess had you opened 1♠. Okay, but what now?

It's not clear. You are missing the ♣Q plus another Keycard. In addition, your trump suit is shaky. Actually, the winning action was to pass 4NT or bid 5♣. Partner's hand:

♠ 5     ♡ A 9 6 3     ◇ A J 10 7 4     ♣ J 8 2

Slam would be playable if partner had the ♣10 instead of a smaller club. Tough hand. Tough game.

### THE RETURN TO PARTNER'S FIRST-BID MAJOR

After a response to RKB, if the RKB bidder returns to partner's first-bid major, a suit that has been rebid, close the books, it's all over but the shouting. If the suit has not been rebid and it's the next step, it's the queen-ask. If it is not the next step, it's a SSA.

| Opener | Responder | |
|---|---|---|
| ♠ K Q 7 6 4 3 | ♠ J 5 | |
| ♡ J 8 | ♡ A 4 | |
| ◇ J 6 | ◇ K Q 5 | 1. Game-forcing club agreement. |
| ♣ K J 3 | ♣ A Q 10 6 4 2 | 2. RKB (1430)— opener hasn't |
| | | jumped or reversed. |
| 1♠ | 2♣ | 3. '1'. |
| 2♠ | 3◇ | 4. To play. After a '1' response a |
| 4♣[1] | 4◇[2] | return to partner's first bid major, |
| 4♡[3] | 4♠[4] | a suit that has been rebid, is to |
| pass | | play with a capital 'P'. |

## FOUR-LEVEL JUMP-PREFERENCE AGREEMENT
*Reminder:* After four-level jump agreement in clubs, 4◇ is RKB. Period.

| Opener | Responder | |
|---|---|---|
| ♠ K Q J 6 | ♠ A 3 | |
| ♡ A | ♡ 9 6 2 | |
| ◇ A 4 2 | ◇ K Q 6 5 | 1. The agreement, a slam try. |
| ♣ A Q 7 6 4 | ♣ K J 3 2 | 2. RKB (1430) — jump shifter ask- |
| | | ing. |
| 1♣ | 1◇ | 3. '2 without'. |
| 2♠ | 4♣[1] | 4. Specific Suit Ask (clubs agreed). |
| 4◇[2] | 4NT[3] | 5. A raise of the ask suit shows the |
| 5◇[4] | 6◇[5] | KQ with any length. |
| 7NT[6] | pass | 6. Can count thirteen tricks. |

## ANOTHER JUMP AGREEMENT

| Opener | Responder | |
|---|---|---|
| ♠ A K | ♠ 9 | 1. Jump agreement. |
| ♡ 5 | ♡ A Q 7 6 3 | 2. Cuebid (4◇ is RKB and 4♡ is |
| ◇ Q 9 8 4 | ◇ A J 5 | natural). |
| ♣ A Q J 7 6 2 | ♣ K 5 4 3 | 3. RKB (3014) — opener has |
| | | reversed. |
| 1♣ | 1♡ | 4. '2 with'. |
| 2◇ | 4♣[1] | 5. Grand slam try looking for an |
| 4♠[2] | 4NT[3] | extra. Remember 5NT is not a |
| 5♠[4] | 5NT[5] | king-ask after minor-suit |
| 6♣[6] | pass | agreement. |
| | | 6. Fearing a diamond loser. |

If responder wishes to take charge in this auction, over 2◇ he bids 3♣ creating a game-forcing auction, and then 4♣, RKB (3014), on the next round.

## AND YET ANOTHER JUMP AGREEMENT (RENO NATIONALS, 2004)

| Opener | Responder | |
|--------|-----------|---|
| ♠ 5 2 | ♠ A 8 6 4 3 | 1. Game-forcing jump agreement. |
| ♡ A 8 6 4 | ♡ 3 | Partner is encouraged to cuebid. |
| ◇ 8 7 | ◇ A | 2. Cuebid. |
| ♣ A K J 10 6 | ♣ Q 8 7 5 3 2 | 3. RKB (1430) — opener hasn't |
| | | jumped or reversed. |
| 1♣ | 1♠ | 4. '3'. |
| 2♣ | 4♣[1] | 5. SSA in spades. |
| 4♡[2] | 4NT[3] | 6. A 1st step response shows sec- |
| 5◇[4] | 5♠[5] | ond-round control — the queen |
| 5NT[6] | 6♣[7] | or a doubleton. |
| pass | | 7. Knowing of a spade loser. |

Give opener a singleton spade with one more diamond and he jumps to 7♣ over 5♠. When responding to a SSA holding a singleton, jump in the trump suit. A SSA (or any ask for that matter) above five of the agreed suit is a grand slam try.

### THE JUMP CUEBID

| Opener | Responder (you) | |
|--------|-----------------|---|
| ♠ A Q J 7 6 | ♠ 5 | 1. Jump cuebid, agreeing clubs with |
| ♡ A | ♡ K J 5 3 2 | a diamond control — a serious |
| ◇ K 8 4 | ◇ A 6 3 | slam try. Some use the jump to |
| ♣ K Q 9 4 | ♣ A J 5 2 | show a singleton in the jump suit. |
| | | However, after opener has bid |
| | | two suits, the singleton is usually |
| 1♠ | 2♡ | in partner's first-bid suit render- |
| 3♣ | 4◇[1] | ing the jump quasi-obsolete. |
| 4NT[2] | 5♡[3] | 2. RKB (1430). |
| 5NT[4] | ?[5] | 3. '2 without'. |
| | | 4. Grand slam try looking for an |
| | | extra. |
| | | 5. Do you have a significant extra |
| | | given your previous slam try? |
| | | Close call. |

***Note:*** The jump to 4◇ is not RKB. In order to ask for Keycards after three-level non-agreement, the suit must have been rebid (see Chapter 20).

## A BETTER WAY?

A hand I kibitzed:

| Opener | Responder |
|---|---|
| ♠ Q 7 5 | ♠ A K 9 |
| ♡ 6 | ♡ K 10 5 4 3 |
| ◇ A K Q J 10 | ◇ 9 |
| ♣ K 6 5 2 | ♣ A Q 9 4 |

| | |
|---|---|
| 1◇ | 1♡ |
| 2♣ | 2♠ |
| 3NT | 6♣ |
| pass | |

Clubs were 3-2 and the contract came rolling home. All's well that ends well. However, I wondered how the bidding would go if responder jumps to 3♠ over 2♣, a fit-showing slam-try cuebid for clubs showing strong clubs (at least two of the top four club honors or any five clubs). If opener is sufficiently impressed, he can try 4♣, RKB (1430), and the same contract is reached. If opener chickens out and rebids 3NT, responder can still bid 4♣, RKB (1430), if he wishes.

### ROSENBLUM QUALIFYING

| Opener (Alan Sontag) | Responder (Me) |
|---|---|
| ♠ 7 4 | ♠ K 9 |
| ♡ 8 3 | ♡ A K Q |
| ◇ A K Q 6 4 | ◇ J 7 |
| ♣ K 8 3 2 | ♣ Q J 10 7 6 5 |

| Opener | Oppt. | Responder | Oppt. |
|---|---|---|---|
| 1◇ | 1♠ | 2♣ | 3♠[1] |
| 4♣[2] | pass | 4◇[3] | pass |
| 4NT[4] | pass | 5♣[5] | all pass |

1. Preemptive.
2. The agreement.
3. The ask (1430) — opener hasn't jumped or reversed.
4. '2 without.
5. You didn't think I was going to put anything in here where we got to slam off two aces, did you?

Notice that even though diamonds is a first-bid suit, the exception (can't use 4◇ as RKB) does not apply as clubs is also a first-bid suit. For the exception to apply, clubs must be a second-bid suit that has not been rebid or jump-supported.

What is the Keycard ask in each of these sequences?

| Opener | Responder |
|--------|-----------|
| 1♡ | 2◇ |
| 3♣ | 4♣ |
| ? | |

The exception. You can't use 4◇ (diamonds are a first-bid suit when clubs is a second-bid suit) and you can't use 4♡, your own first-bid suit, so 4♠ (1430) is the winner. And what would 4NT mean? It would be a spade cuebid, perhaps with a diamond void. Keep the faith.

| Opener | Responder | |
|--------|-----------|--|
| 1♠ | 2♣[1] | |
| 2♡ | 3♣[2] | 1. Not game-forcing. |
| 4♣[2] | ? | 2. Invitational. |

In this sequence 3♣ and 4♣ are both invitational, so we have two limited hands facing each other, so in a sane game there will be no Keycard ask forthcoming.

| Opener | Responder |
|--------|-----------|
| 1♣ | 1♡ |
| 2◇ | 4♣ |
| ? | |

RKB is 4◇ (1430). After four-level jump agreement, 4◇ is RKB. Period. Not only that, but clubs is a first-bid suit — another reason 4◇ can be used as RKB.

| Opener | Responder | |
|--------|-----------|--|
| 1◇ | 1♠ | |
| 3♣ | 4♣[1] | 1. Game-forcing agreement. |
| ? | | |

RKB is 4♡ (1430) — the exception. Diamonds is a first-bid suit, and clubs is a second-bid suit that has not been rebid or jump-supported. In this sequence both 4◇ and 4♣ are natural, 4♡ is RKB and 4NT is a replacement heart cuebid.

---

## Hearing from a new country: four-level diamond agreement

In this scenario 4♡ is RKB with the inevitable exception: after game-forcing four-level diamond agreement, 4♡ is RKB — unless hearts is the asker's first-bid suit. In that case 4♠ morphs into RKB because 4♡ is natural. If both hearts and spades are somebody's first-bid suit, 4NT is RKB.

And now for the kicker: if it makes no sense for 4♡ to show hearts, then even when hearts is partner's first-bid suit, 4♡ can and should be RKB for diamonds. But when does it make 'no sense'? It makes no sense if 4♡ is your fourth bid, partner having either opened 1♡ or responded 1♡, and never having rebid the suit. It is inconceivable to delay support that long for a first-bid major. Give me a break.

Say you are the opener in the following two sequences:

| a) Opener | Responder | | b) Opener | Responder |
|---|---|---|---|---|
| 1◇ | 1♡ | | 1♣ | 1♡ |
| 2♠ | 2NT | | 2◇ | 2NT |
| 3◇ | 4◇ | | 3◇ | 4◇ |
| 4♡? | | | 4♡? | |

In both sequences 4♡ is your fourth bid. Can you have heart support? Surely you would have coughed it up before this. Using 4♡ instead of 4♠ saves a step, but it must be your fourth bid and partner must not have rebid the suit.

How about this one?

| Opener (you) | Responder |
|---|---|
| 1♠ | 2♡ |
| 3◇ | 4◇ |
| 4♡? | |

Here 4♡ is natural, because it is your third, not your fourth, bid. If you want to ask for Keycards, bid 4NT (1430). The general rule is that first-bid majors cannot be used as the RKB suit.

| Opener | Responder (you) |
|---|---|
| 1♡ | 2◇ |
| 4◇ | 4♡? |

Again, 4♡ is natural. It is your second, not your fourth bid. In this sequence 4♠ is RKB (3014) and 4NT is a spade cuebid. From here on in, the 'fourth bid' exception is in place.

### TWO KINGS, PLEASE

When a two-suited hand faces a balanced hand, the kings of both suits are counted in the Keycard response no matter who asks.

| Opener | Responder |
|---|---|
| ♠ A 5 3 | ♠ K Q 7 4 2 |
| ♡ A 8 | ♡ 3 2 |
| ◇ A Q 7 6 4 | ◇ K 8 5 3 2 |
| ♣ A J 2 | ♣ 6 |

| Opener | Responder | |
|--------|-----------|---|
| 1◇ | 1♠ | 1. The agreement, not the ask. |
| 2NT | 4◇[1] | 2. RKB (1430). |
| 4♡[2] | 5♣[3] | 3. '2 without', including the ♠K. |
| 5NT[4] | 7◇[5] | 4. Grand slam try promising joint possession of the four aces plus the king-queen of the agreed suit. It is not the SKA in minor-suit auctions. |
| pass | | 5. Looks like the right hand to accept. |

EUROPEAN CHAMPIONSHIPS

| Opener | Responder |
|--------|-----------|
| ♠ K 7 | ♠ J 5 2 |
| ♡ A K 4 2 | ♡ Q 6 |
| ◇ A Q J 8 6 3 | ◇ K 5 |
| ♣ 4 | ♣ A K J 10 5 2 |

| Opener | Responder | |
|--------|-----------|---|
| 1◇ | 2♣ | 1. The agreement. |
| 2♡ | 3♣ | 2. The ask. RKB (1430) — opener asking. |
| 3◇ | 4◇[1] | 3. '2 without'. |
| 4♡[2] | 5♣[3] | |
| 6◇ | pass | |

Whether or not 2♣ is played as a game force, a reverse by opener facing a two-level responder is considered a game force. Opener might have rebid 3NT over 3♣, but what's the rush? In this sequence hearts is not a first-bid suit so 4♡ can be used as RKB after game-forcing four-level diamond agreement. When 4♡ is used as RKB, 4NT should be considered a heart cuebid.

AFTER A SINGLE RAISE

| Opener | Responder |
|--------|-----------|
| ♠ A J 6 4 3 | ♠ Q 5 |
| ♡ — | ♡ A K Q 4 2 |
| ◇ A 8 7 3 | ◇ K Q 6 5 2 |
| ♣ A 5 4 2 | ♣ 6 |

| Opener | Responder | |
|--------|-----------|---|
| 1♠ | 2♡ | 1. The agreement — not the ask. |
| 2♠ | 3◇ | 2. RKB (1430) — opener minimum. Hearts and spades are first-bid suits so 4NT is RKB. |
| 4◇[1] | 4NT[2] | 3. '3' (can't be '0'). Usually not a bright idea to show a void in partner's first-bid suit in response to a Keycard ask. |
| 5◇[3] | 5NT[4] | 4. Anything extra? I know you are short in hearts and have three aces. |
| 6◇[5] | pass | 5. As long as you know that, I've nothing else to report. |

| Opener | Responder (you) |
|---|---|
| ♠ A 8 | ♠ K 5 |
| ♡ A K J 6 3 | ♡ 8 |
| ◇ A K 6 5 | ◇ Q J 9 8 4 2 |
| ♣ 4 2 | ♣ K J 7 5 |
| | pass |
| 1♡ | 2◇ |
| 4◇ | ? |

It is very rare (off the wall) for a passed hand to use RKB, let alone to do it without a single Keycard! If you try this, be sure you know the ask, and be sure you can get out alive if two Keycards are missing.

Here 4♠ (3014) is the ask — opener has jumped and hearts is a first-bid suit. Consider the possible responses:

4NT  =  '3'. You can handle it: you will sign off in 5◇.

5♣  =  '4'. You can handle it: you will bid 6◇.

5◇  =  '2' (or '5') without. You can handle it. You will pass and go down! However if partner has five you will miss a cold grand!

Just kidding. If you have '5' and your partner does the asking, bid seven and expect to make nine, possibly ten. How can a grand not be cold if someone asks for Keycards and finds his partner with '5'? Give me a break. Besides, opener won't have '2 without' in this sequence.

In other words, it is safe to use RKB. If you do, you will get to six and you had better get the clubs right!

Now try this:

| Opener | Responder |
|---|---|
| 1♡ | 2◇ |
| 4◇ | 4NT |

What do you make of 4NT in this sequence? You know that 4♡ is natural so 4♠ is RKB (3014 —opener has jumped). Voila! 4NT is a spade cuebid, the cuebid partner has lost, probably denying a club control. Perhaps he has:

$$♠ A Q 6 \quad ♡ 7 2 \quad ◇ K Q 10 5 4 \quad ♣ 6 5 3$$

Tell me you're not having fun.

Played this one against two 'experienced' players (thousands of master points).

| Opener | Responder |
|---|---|
| ♠ J | ♠ K 10 6 4 2 |
| ♡ 10 5 3 | ♡ A K J |
| ◇ A Q 8 7 6 2 | ◇ J 10 |
| ♣ K J 5 | ♣ A 10 4 |
| 1◇ | 1♠ |
| 2◇ | 3♣ |
| 3◇ | 3♡ |
| 4♣ | 4◇ |
| pass! | |

Since it was a game-forcing four-level minor suit agreement sequence, it piqued my interest. In the face of the minimum diamond rebids, responder should sign off in 3NT. However, once he bids 4◇, a slam try, opener can't pass! He does best to bid 5◇... softly. Just kidding.

## RKB after the fourth suit

How would you ask for Keycards in this sequence?

| Opener (you) | Responder | |
|---|---|---|
| 1♡ | 2♣ | |
| 2◇ | 2♠ | |
| 3◇ | 4◇[1] | 1. The agreement, not the ask. |
| ? | | |

Yes, 4♠ (1430) is the winner. Hearts is your first-bid suit, so forget that. But If hearts were partner's first-bid suit, and it wasn't rebid, you could use 4♡ as RKB — if it was your fourth bid. Hang in there.

What's the RKB ask here?

| Opener (you) | Responder | |
|---|---|---|
| 1♠ | 2♣ | |
| 2◇ | 4◇[1] | 1. The agreement, not the ask. |
| ? | | |

An easy one: 4♡ (1430), and 4NT is a heart cuebid. Are you starting to get the hang of this? Humor me and nod.

How about this one?

| Opener (you) | Responder | |
|---|---|---|
| 1♡ | 2♣ | |
| 3◇[1] | 4◇ | 1. Natural (some play it as a splinter). |
| ? | | |

Again, 4♠ is RKB (1430). Hearts is your first-bid suit so that's out, but 4♠ is available and 4NT is a spade cuebid.

And this?

| Opener (you) | Responder | |
|---|---|---|
| 1◇ | 2♣ | |
| 2♡ | 2♠ | |
| 3◇ | 4◇[1] | 1. The agreement. |
| ? | | |

This time it is 4♡ (1430). After four-level diamond agreement, 4♡ is RKB if hearts is not a first-bid suit.

Another one:

| Opener (you) | Responder |
|---|---|
| 1◇ | 1♡ |
| 2♣ | 2♠ |
| 3◇ | 4◇ |
| ? | |

Again, 4♡ (1430). Here 4♡ is your fourth bid and partner has never rebid the suit, so it can be used as RKB after four-level game-forcing diamond agreement.

## THE BOTTOM LINE

- Four-level agreement is not the RKB ask. In almost all sequences the ask follows the agreement. There are a few (very few) times when the ask is the agreement.

   1. Opener reverses, responder rebids the same minor at the three-level, opener raises (the ask).
   2. Either opener or responder jump shifts, partner rebids the same minor at the three-level, the jump-shifter raises the minor (the ask).
   3. After a 2♣ opening, responder bids a natural 3♣ or 3◇, and opener raises (the ask). This one is coming up.

   It simplifies the auction when the strong hand is allowed to make a lower-level Keycard ask, when feasible.

- After four-level club agreement, 4◇ is RKB. After four-level diamond agreement, 4♡ is RKB (exceptions have been noted).

- When a bid lower than 4NT can be used to ask for Keycards, and 3NT has not reared its ugly head, 4NT is a replacement cuebid for the RKB ask suit.

# FOUR-LEVEL AGREEMENT (A SLAM TRY) FOLLOWS 3NT

When four-level minor-suit agreement follows 3NT, it is a slam try. The 3NT bidder, a limited hand, may or may not wish to accept. Since it is a slam try he can't pass; nor can he ask for Keycards — unless he has previously jumped in the agreed suit. In addition, a 4NT rebid is to play.

| Opener (you) | Responder |
|---|---|
| 1♣ | 1♡ |
| 3♣ | 3♢ |
| 3NT | 4♣ |
| ? | |

In this auction, you can ask for Keycards because you have jumped in the agreed suit. Here, 4♢ is RKB (1430).

Most of the time the 3NT bidder won't have jumped in the agreed suit and won't be able to ask for Keycards. However, with slam interest he can cuebid. He can also signoff in five of the agreed minor or even in 4NT with regressive hands that feature wasted strength in partner's short suit.

After a 3NT bidder cuebids, partner can ask for Keycards via 4NT, but 4NT by the 3NT bidder is to play.

| a) Opener | Responder (you) | | b) Opener | Responder (you) |
|---|---|---|---|---|
| 1♠ | 2♣ | | 1♠ | 2♢ |
| 2♢ | 3NT | | 3♠ | 3NT |
| 4♣ | ? | | 4♢ | ? |

In Auction (a), 4♣ is a slam try with short hearts. You can cuebid 4♢ or 4♡, bid a natural 4♠, or sign off in 4NT or 5♣. In Auction (b), 4♢ is a slam try. Even though diamonds is your first-bid suit, it is a not a suit you have jumped in, so you can't ask for Keycards, but you can cuebid 4♡ or 5♣. A bid of 4♠ is natural, and 4NT and 5♢ are both sign-offs.

Decide what your follow-up bids mean in these sequences after partner's four-level agreement slam try.

| c) Opener (you) | Responder | | d) Opener | Responder (you) |
|---|---|---|---|---|
| 1♢ | 2♣ | | 1♢ | 2♣ |
| 3NT | 4♢ | | 2♡ | 3NT |
| ? | | | 4♣ | ? |

In Auction (c), 4♡ and 4♠ are cuebids, 5♣ is natural, and 4NT and 5♢ are sign-offs. In Auction (d), 4♢ is ambiguous. It could be natural or it could be a cuebid, but it isn't RKB. For the rest, 4♡ and 4♠ are cuebids, while 4NT and 5♣ are sign-offs.

## FACING A SINGLETON

| Opener | Responder |
|--------|-----------|
| ♠ A Q 6 3 2 | ♠ 5 |
| ♡ A K 7 3 | ♡ Q J 5 |
| ◇ K 6 2 | ◇ A J 7 4 3 |
| ♣ 7 | ♣ K Q J 4 |

| | |
|--------|-----------|
| 1♠ | 2◇[1] |
| 2♡ | 3NT |
| 4◇ | 4NT[2] |
| pass | |

1. Not a game force.
2. Wasted secondary club strength facing partner's shortness.

| Opener | Responder |
|--------|-----------|
| ♠ A Q 6 3 2 | ♠ J 5 |
| ♡ A K 7 3 | ♡ Q 6 5 |
| ◇ K 6 2 | ◇ A Q J 7 4 |
| ♣ 7 | ♣ A J 4 |

| | |
|--------|-----------|
| 1♠ | 2◇[1] |
| 2♡ | 3NT |
| 4◇ | 5♣[2] |
| 6◇ | pass |

1. Not a game force.
2. Cuebid. A great hand, good trumps, along with an ace in partner's singleton suit. You want to get to at least 6◇ on this one.

### TWO MORE TRIAL SPINS

What do you think responder should bid in the following slam try sequences?

| Opener | Responder (you) |
|--------|-----------------|
| ♠ A K J 6 4 3 | ♠ 5 2 |
| ♡ 7 | ♡ K J 4 |
| ◇ Q 6 5 | ◇ A J 2 |
| ♣ A Q 6 | ♣ K J 5 3 2 |

| | |
|--------|-----------------|
| 1♠ | 2♣ |
| 3♠ | 3NT |
| 4♣[1] | ? |

1. Opener, unlimited, is making a slam try presumably with six spades and three clubs.

This is a mixed bag. You suspect a red-suit singleton, but don't know where. Nevertheless, the hand is worth a 4◇ cuebid. Incidentally, a follow-up cuebid by a 3NT bidder who has made a two-level response, promises two Keycards, minimum, in blood. After your diamond cuebid, opener will jump to 6♣.

| Opener | Responder (you) |
|---|---|
| ♠ A K J 6 4 3 | ♠ 5 |
| ♡ 7 | ♡ K Q 10 4 |
| ◇ Q 6 5 | ◇ K J 10 |
| ♣ A Q 6 | ♣ K 7 5 3 2 |

| Opener | Responder | |
|---|---|---|
| 1♠ | 2♣ | 1. Opener, unlimited, is making a |
| 3♠ | 3NT | slam try presumably with six |
| 4♣[1] | ? | spades and three clubs. |

Having secondary honors in both majors, you have an obvious 4NT signoff; opener passes.

### ACELESS WONDER

| Opener | Responder (you) |
|---|---|
| ♠ A K J 6 4 3 | ♠ 2 |
| ♡ 7 | ♡ K J 4 2 |
| ◇ Q 6 5 | ◇ K 8 2 |
| ♣ A Q 6 | ♣ K J 5 3 2 |

| Opener | Responder | |
|---|---|---|
| 1♠ | 2♣ | 1. Opener, unlimited, is making a |
| 3♠ | 3NT | slam try presumably with six |
| 4♣[1] | ? | spades and three clubs. |

Looking at an aceless wonder with a stiff spade, 5♣ looks best. Opener, not hearing a red-suit cuebid, passes.

## DIAMOND JUMP AGREEMENT AFTER A NATURAL, MINIMUM, 2NT REBID

| Opener | Responder |
|---|---|
| ♠ J 10 7 3 | ♠ — |
| ♡ 10 5 | ♡ K J 6 4 2 |
| ◇ K Q J 10 6 | ◇ A 8 5 3 2 |
| ♣ A K | ♣ Q 9 7 |

| Opener | Oppt. | Responder | Oppt. |
|---|---|---|---|
| 1◇ | 1♠ | 2♡ | pass |
| 2NT[1] | pass | 4◇[2] | pass |
| 5♣[3] | pass | 6◇ | all pass |

1. Minimum.
2. Game-forcing jump preference.
3. Cuebid.

This is a hand from a local team championship. At both tables 5◇ was the final contract, but it seems 6◇ might have been reached. After the 4◇ bid, 4NT is to play and 4♠ and 5♣ are cuebids. A 5♣ cuebid should be music to responder's ears and he should chance 6◇. Even if the ♡AQ are missing, the spade bidder is a favorite to have the ace.

*Note:* Jumps to 4♣ after a previous bid of 1NT or 2NT are often played as Gerber, not as agreement jumps. (Coming up.)

## A FINISHING TOUCH

| Opener | Responder | |
|---|---|---|
| ♠ A K 7 3 2 | ♠ 6 5 | |
| ♡ 4 | ♡ A Q J | |
| ◇ A K 6 3 | ◇ 7 5 2 | |
| ♣ K 6 2 | ♣ A Q 7 4 3 | 1. Not a game force. |
| | | 2. Slam try with short hearts. |
| 1♠ | 2♣[1] | 3. Cuebid — a 3NT bidder can't |
| 2◇ | 3NT | ask for Keycards unless he has |
| 4♣[2] | 4♡[3] | previously jumped in the agreed |
| ? | | suit. |

Opener can cuebid 4♠ or maybe leap to 6♣ as responder has promised two Keycards with the cuebid. If opener wants to, 4NT (1430) is the ask.

## THE BOTTOM LINE

- Four-level agreement after a 3NT bid is a slam try.
- Unless the 3NT bidder has jumped in the agreed suit, he cannot ask for Keycards: with slam interest he cuebids. Rebidding 4NT or raising to five of the agreed minor are both sign-offs. Passing is not an option.
- If the 3NT bidder cuebids, partner can ask for Keycards via 4NT.

Congratulations! You've just made it through another chapter.

# CHAPTER 14

## EXCEPTIONS AND 'PERKS'

We've hinted earlier at the existence of some 'perks' in strong sequences, and it's time to talk about them. They come up in auctions after a strong, artificial 2♣ opening, a jump shift or a reverse.

*Note:* If you play a strong club system you may have to make a few adjustments, but it shouldn't be a problem. Besides, you are better placed being one level lower.

After hammering you for the last few chapters with 'the agreement is not the ask', the truth will out: in a few (very few) sequences the agreement *is* the ask! When, exactly, is the agreement the ask?

## RESPONDER BIDS A NATURAL 3♣ OR 3♢ AFTER A STRONG, ARTIFICIAL 2♣ OPENING

| Opener | Responder | |
|---|---|---|
| 2♣ | 3♣[1] | 1. Natural. |
| 4♣[2] | | 2. RKB for clubs. |

| Opener | Responder | |
|---|---|---|
| 2♣ | 3♢[1] | 1. Natural. |
| 4♢[2] | | 2. RKB for diamonds. |

| Opener | Responder | |
|---|---|---|
| 2♣ | 2♢[1] | 1. Artificial. |
| 2♡ | 3♢[2] | 2. Natural. |
| 4♢[3] | | 3. RKB for diamonds. |

| Opener | Responder | |
|---|---|---|
| 2♣ | 2♡[1] | 1. Natural. |
| 2♠ | 3♣[1] | |
| 4♣[2] | | 2. RKB for clubs. |

In each sequence the agreement is the ask. Why? Because a truly strong hand should be able to ask for Keycards without agreeing the suit first. In the case of a 2♣ bidder, any minor suit bid naturally at the three-level will do.

## A 'PERK' IN ACTION

| Opener | Responder |
|---|---|
| ♠ A K Q J | ♠ 5 2 |
| ♡ A K 9 5 2 | ♡ 4 3 |
| ◇ A J 6 | ◇ K Q 10 7 5 4 |
| ♣ Q | ♣ K 6 2 |
| | |
| 2♣ | 3◇ |
| 4◇[1] | 4♡[2] |
| 4♠[3] | 5♣[4] |
| 6NT[5] | pass |

1. RKB (1430) after a natural 3◇ response.
2. '1'.
3. Queen-ask.
4. Yes, with the ♡K.
5. A home run (call 911 if partner has a singleton king of clubs!).

## MORE 'PERKS'

| Opener | Responder |
|---|---|
| ♠ A K J 7 6 | ♠ 4 |
| ♡ K 3 | ♡ A J 10 4 2 |
| ◇ A 8 | ◇ 7 6 5 |
| ♣ A K 5 2 | ♣ Q J 9 3 |
| | |
| 2♣ | 2♡[1] |
| 2♠ | 3♣[1] |
| 4♣[2] | 4◇[3] |
| 4♡[4] | 5♣[5] |
| 5NT[6] | 6♣[7] |
| pass | |

1. Natural; does not promise two of the top three honors.
2. RKB (1430) — the agreement is the ask.
3. '1'.
4. Queen-ask. After a '1' response, a return to the agreed suit or the asker's first-bid suit is to play. A return to the responder's first-bid suit is the queen-ask. However, if the suit has been rebid or supported, it is to play. An important distinction.
5. Shows the queen but denies a side-suit king or a side-suit extra; 4NT would deny the queen.
6. Grand slam try, not a king-ask. Opener knows that responder does not have the ♠Q, the ◇K or extra club length (no 5NT response to the queen-ask), but may have the ♡Q.
7. Sorry, boss, no got.

## A STUMBLING BLOCK?

| Opener (you) | Responder |
|---|---|
| ♠ A Q 6 4 3 | ♠ 7 |
| ♡ A | ♡ 9 6 2 |
| ◇ A K Q 5 | ◇ J 8 7 6 4 2 |
| ♣ K Q 6 | ♣ A J 3 |

| Opener | Responder | |
|--------|-----------|---|
| 2♣ | 2◇¹ | 1. Waiting. |
| 2♠ | 3◇² | 2. Natural. |
| 4◇³ | 4♡⁴ | 3. RKB (1430). |
| ? | | 4. '1'. |

What now? Assuming partner has six diamonds (looking at your diamonds it is a near-certainty) along with the ♣A, a grand is right around the corner. If partner has three or more hearts, thirteen tricks are there for the taking. if partner has a 2-2-6-3 pattern without the ♠K, then, and only then, will you be reduced to a spade finesse. Go for it.

Just for drill, check out what these other bids (4♠, 4NT, 5♣, 5◇, 5♡ and 5♠) would mean after the 4♡ response:

4♠ and 5◇ are to play.

4NT is the queen-ask, next cheapest step.

5♣ and 5♡ are Specific Suit Asks.

But what in the world is 5♠? It would be nice if it were a SSA, and perhaps it should be, but lacking a firm agreement, this is a scary rabbit to pull out of your hat! When it comes to scary bids, particularly scary bids that haven't been discussed, don't make them! Just don't! That's the best advice you will get in this entire book. After this pep talk, 7◇ still looks like a good bet.

## OPENER REVERSES, RESPONDER BIDS AND REBIDS A MINOR TO THE THREE-LEVEL

| Opener | Responder | |
|--------|-----------|---|
| 1◇ | 2♣ | |
| 2♡ | 3♣ | |
| 4♣¹ | | 1. RKB (1430). |

| Opener | Responder |
|--------|-----------|
| 1♠ | 2◇ |
| 3♣ | 3◇ |
| 4◇? | |

If this sequence (considered a reverse by many) promises reversing values, a raise to the four-level is RKB. If it does not promise extras, 4◇ is the agreement, and 4♡ is the ask. This sequence requires a meeting of the minds.

GO FOR IT!

| Opener | Responder | |
|---|---|---|
| ♠ A K 5 4 | ♠ 6 2 | |
| ♡ A | ♡ J 10 7 | |
| ◇ A J 10 6 3 | ◇ K 5 | |
| ♣ K 8 2 | ♣ A Q J 10 4 3 | 1. RKB (1430), The raise is the ask |
| | | by a reversing opener after |
| 1◇ | 2♣ | responder rebids a minor. |
| 2♠ | 3♣ | 2. '1'. |
| 4♣[1] | 4◇[2] | 3. Queen-ask, |
| 4♡[3] | 5◇[4] | 4. Yes, with the ◇K, |
| 7♣[5] | pass | 5. Just 6♣ would be wimpy. |

# OPENER JUMP-SHIFTS, RESPONDER BIDS AND REBIDS A MINOR TO THE THREE-LEVEL

| Opener | Responder | |
|---|---|---|
| 1♣ | 1◇ | 1. Game-forcing jump shift. |
| 2♡ or 2♠[1] | 3◇[2] | 2. Minor-suit rebid. |
| 4◇[3] | | 3. RKB 1430, diamonds agreed. |

A DOSE OF REALISM

| Opener | Responder | |
|---|---|---|
| ♠ A K J 7 | ♠ Q 3 2 | |
| ♡ 4 | ♡ J 10 6 | |
| ◇ A 6 3 | ◇ Q 10 7 5 4 2 | |
| ♣ A K 6 5 3 | ♣ J | |
| | | |
| 1♣ | 1◇ | |
| 2♠ | 3◇ | 1. RKB (1430) — the 'perk' . |
| 4◇[1] | 4♠[2] | 2. '0'. |
| 5◇[3] | pass | 3. That's all she wrote. |

Again the ask comes before the agreement. As always, it is a super-strong hand that breaks 'the agreement is not the ask' rule.

**Reminder:** After a '0' response to RKB, 4NT is to play. However this is definitely not the time to do that!

# OPENER JUMP-SHIFTS AFTER A 1NT RESPONSE, RESPONDER INTRODUCES A MINOR AT THE THREE-LEVEL

| Opener | Responder | |
|--------|-----------|---|
| 1♠ | 1NT | 1. Game-forcing jump shift. |
| 3♣[1] | 3◇[2] | 2. New minor at the three-level, |
| 4◇[3] | |    presumably a six-card suit. |
| | | 3. RKB (1430). |

## TALK ABOUT SEEING RED

| Opener | Responder |
|--------|-----------|
| ♠ K 10 6 5 3 | ♠ — |
| ♡ A | ♡ J 7 6 4 2 |
| ◇ A Q 5 | ◇ K J 10 6 4 3 2 |
| ♣ A Q 10 2 | ♣ 6 |

| Opener | Responder | |
|--------|-----------|---|
| 1♠ | 1NT | |
| 3♣ | 3◇ | 1. RKB (1430). |
| 4◇[1] | 4♡[2] | 2. '1'. Does not count a void in |
| 6◇ | pass |    partner's first-bid suit. |

Opener caught responder with a real freak and 6◇ is quite playable. The downside here is that opener cannot make a natural raise of 3◇ to 4◇.

# RESPONDER JUMP-SHIFTS, OPENER REBIDS HIS MINOR AT THE THREE-LEVEL

Really big hands usually want to ask for Keycards as cheaply as possible. Call it a 'big hand perk'. For such hands, after partner has shown minor-suit length, four-level agreement is the ask (*Noblesse Oblige*). Responder can get into the act as well. If responder makes a strong jump shift and opener rebids his original minor at the three-level, a raise of that minor is RKB (1430). *Noblesse Oblige* again.

| Opener | Responder | |
|--------|-----------|---|
| 1♣ | 2◇ or 2♡ or 2♠ | |
| 3♣ | 4♣[1] | 1. RKB (1430). |

| Opener | Responder | |
|--------|-----------|---|
| 1◇ | 2♡ or 2♠ or 3♣ | |
| 3◇ | 4◇[1] | 1. RKB (1430). |

| Opener | Responder | |
|--------|-----------|--|
| ♠ K Q 6 | ♠ 4 | |
| ♡ 3 | ♡ A K Q 5 4 | |
| ◇ A J | ◇ K Q 8 | |
| ♣ Q J 10 6 5 4 2 | ♣ K 8 7 3 | 1. Strong. |
| | | 2. RKB (1430) The agreement is the |
| 1♣ | 2♡¹ | ask by the 'jump shifter' after |
| 3♣ | 4♣² | partner rebids a minor. |
| 4◇³ | 5♣⁴ | 3. '1'. |
| pass | | 4. Two aces missing. |

# A CHEAP EKB ASK!

It's beneath the dignity of a 2♣ opener to waste time splintering. A mega-powerful hand wants to ask for, not dish out, information. Jumps by a 2♣ bidder after partner makes a natural suit response should therefore be reserved for something else; but what?

Some play that the jump shows a solid suit and asks partner to cuebid aces and kings. This book suggests that when a mega-strong hand (either opener or responder who has jump-shifted, an opener who has reversed, or a 2♣ opener) makes a single jump after partner has rebid a suit, the jump should be treated as an Exclusion Ask. In the case of the 2♣ opener, the responder need not have rebid the suit. Just bidding a suit naturally is enough to allow a 2♣ opener to make an EKB ask by jumping.

CHEAP EXCLUSION ASK

| Opener | Responder | |
|--------|-----------|--|
| ♠ J 6 4 3 | ♠ Q 7 6 5 2 | 1. Waiting. |
| ♡ A K Q J 7 | ♡ 6 2 | 2. EKB (a 'perk' given to a 2♣ |
| ◇ — | ◇ A 8 5 | opener). |
| ♣ A K Q J | ♣ 10 9 8 | 3. '0'. |
| | | |
| 2♣ | 2◇¹ | |
| 2♡ | 2♠ | |
| 4◇² | 4♡³ | |
| 4♠ | pass | |

Nice to stay out of trouble on a hand like this.

# THE FLIP SIDE OF THE COIN

After the strong 2♣ bidder shows his suit, a single jump by the responder is a splinter showing a fit plus a singleton. A double jump shows a fit plus a void in the jump suit. *It is not EKB.* The weak hand avoids asking the 2♣ bidder for anything. The weak hand tells.

This is beginning to remind me of what my partner of many years, Billy Eisenberg, once lamented: 'Eddie, our convention basket is leaking.' Onward.

### RESPONDER GETS INTO THE ACT

When four-level minor-suit splinter agreement bypasses the four-level of the agreed suit, the cheapest *unbid* suit is considered RKB. But after major-suit splinter agreement, 4NT is always the RKB ask.

| Opener | Responder | |
|---|---|---|
| ♠ A K Q | ♠ 7 4 | |
| ♡ K | ♡ A Q 6 5 4 3 | |
| ◇ A J 8 2 | ◇ 6 | |
| ♣ A K Q J 3 | ♣ 10 7 6 5 | 1. Natural. |
| | | 2. Splinter, stiff diamond, club support. |
| 2♣ | 2♡¹ | |
| 3♣¹ | 4◇² | 3. RKB (1430). |
| 4♠³ | 4NT⁴ | 4. '1'. |
| 7♣⁵ | pass | 5. My diamond losers are covered. |

# THE BOTTOM LINE

There are a few selected sequences where the raise to four of the last-bid minor is RKB, not the agreement. These RKB 1430 'raise asks' can only be made by a mega-strong hand.

### *Excluding these exceptions, the agreement is not the ask:*
- When a 2♣ opener faces a partner who makes a natural bid of 3♣ or 3◇, a raise to four of responder's minor is RKB (1430).
- After a 1♣ or 1◇ opening bid, responder jump-shifts, opener rebids the minor at the three-level and responder raises to the four-level. The raise is a 1430 RKB ask.
- After a 1♣ opening and 1◇ response, opener jump-shifts to 2♡ or 2♠, responder bids 3◇, opener raises to 4◇. The raise is a 1430 RKB ask.
- Opener reverses at the two-level after partner responds 2♣ or 2◇, responder rebids the minor at the three-level, opener raises the minor. The raise is a 1430 RKB ask.
- Opener jump-shifts or reverses after a 1NT response, responder introduces a minor at the three-level, and opener raises the minor. The raise is a 1430 ask.
- After a 2◇ response to an opening bid of 1♡ or 1♠, opener rebids 3♣, and responder rebids 3◇. If the 3♣ rebid is played as showing extras, the raise to 4◇ is RKB (1430). If it does not promise extras, 4◇ is a forcing raise and 4♡ is RKB (1430).

### *Remember too:*
- A player who opens 2♣ cannot splinter, but his partner can. A jump by the opener after a natural response is EKB.
- When a splinter jump bypasses four of the agreed minor, the cheapest unbid suit at the four-level can be used to ask for Keycards. If none is available, 4NT can be used.
- A player who makes a single raise or a limit raise of an opening bid is not the hand that asks for Keycards. In fact, he is barred. The mega-strong hand is the one that usually asks for Keycards. The weaker hand thinks 'cuebid' or 'splinter'. Amen.
- A jump by a 2♣ opener, a jump-shifter or a reversing opener after partner has rebid his minor is an Exclusion Ask. Keep the faith.

# CHAPTER 15

# RKB AFTER GF MINOR-SUIT SPLINTER AGREEMENT

A splinter jump by an unpassed hand is a game force and frequently attracts a Keycard ask. After game-forcing minor-suit splinter agreement, either player can use four of the agreed minor to ask for Keycards.

## *After a three-level splinter*

After a *three-level* splinter the partner of the splinter bidder has options:

| Opener | Responder | |
|--------|-----------|--|
| 1◇ | 3♠[1] | 1. Game-forcing splinter. |
| 4◇[2] | | 2. RKB (1430) — opener asking. |

Opener's other options here include 3NT (probably wasted values in the splinter suit), 5◇ (to play — strong trumps with nothing to cuebid), and cuebids of 4♣, 4♡, and 4♠.

Once a cuebid bypasses four of the agreed minor, the next RKB off-ramp is 4NT. If the splinter jump bypasses four of the agreed suit, the cheapest unbid suit at the four-level can be used as RKB. If no unbid suits are open, 4NT it is. When there are two unbid suits, a cuebid in one implies a lack of control in the other. Cuebidding the splinter suit denies a control in an unbid suit(s).

Finally, when both hands are limited there is no Keycard ask unless someone splinters. After a splinter, a limited partner can ask for Keycards.

MAGIC FACING A SPLINTER
When the player facing a splinter has xxx(x) in the splinter suit, the sky could be the the limit.

| Opener | Responder |
|---|---|
| ♠ 7 5 4 | ♠ A K |
| ♡ 3 | ♡ 10 9 4 |
| ◇ A 6 2 | ◇ K 10 8 7 5 4 3 |
| ♣ A K 10 6 5 4 | ♣ 2 |

| Opener | Responder | |
|---|---|---|
| 1♣ | 1◇ | 1. Limited — both hands now limited. |
| 2♣ | 3◇[1] | 2. Splinter. |
| 4♡[2] | 4♠[3] | 3. RKB (1430) — cheapest unbid. |
| 5♣[3] | 6◇ | 4. '2 without'. |
| pass | | |

## NOT MUCH WASTED

| Opener | Responder |
|---|---|
| ♠ A J 5 | ♠ K 6 3 |
| ♡ 7 | ♡ A 6 5 4 2 |
| ◇ A Q 10 8 6 3 | ◇ K 7 4 2 |
| ♣ J 5 2 | ♣ 9 |

| Opener | Responder | |
|---|---|---|
| 1◇ | 1♡ | 1. Game-forcing splinter, |
| 2◇ | 4♣[1] | 2. RKB (1430) — opener asking. Not much wasted in the splinter suit. |
| 4◇[2] | 5♣[3] | 3. '2 with'. Ten-card fit — opener presumed to have six diamonds in this sequence. |
| 6◇ | pass | |

## THAT'S ALL SHE WROTE

| Opener | Responder |
|---|---|
| ♠ 7 | ♠ Q 6 2 |
| ♡ A K J 5 | ♡ Q 3 |
| ◇ K Q 10 7 | ◇ J |
| ♣ Q 6 4 3 | ♣ A K J 10 7 5 2 |

| Opener | Responder | |
|---|---|---|
| 1◇ | 2♣ | 1. Game-forcing splinter. |
| 3♠[1] | 5♣[4] | 2. Clubs man, just clubs. Nothing to cuebid. |
| pass | | |

## POINTS SCHMOINTS

| Opener | Responder |
|---|---|
| ♠ A 7 4 | ♠ K J 3 |
| ♡ K Q 10 5 | ♡ A 6 2 |
| ◇ J 9 7 | ◇ 3 |
| ♣ A 8 2 | ♣ K Q 7 6 4 3 |

| Opener | Responder | |
|--------|-----------|---|
| 1♣ | 3♢[1] | 1. Game-forcing splinter. |
| 3♡[2] | 4♣[3] | 2. Heart strength. |
| 4♠[4] | 6♣ | 3. RKB (1430) — opener hasn't |
| pass | | jumped or reversed. |
| | | 4. '2 without'. |

**Reminder:** When opener uses RKB, 1430. When responder uses RKB, 1430 unless opener has shown extras by reversing, jumping, opening a strong 1NT or 2NT or a strong 2♣. In those cases, responder's ask is a 3014 ask.

## Splintering after a Weak Two

The partner of a preemptor is considered the strong hand (see Chapter 24). Translation: if the partner of the preemptor uses RKB, it is 1430. If the preemptor uses RKB, it is a 3014 ask, and the responder should get a new partner.

| Opener | Responder | |
|--------|-----------|---|
| ♠ 7 | ♠ A 8 5 | |
| ♡ A J 10 7 4 3 | ♡ K 5 | |
| ♢ Q 6 2 | ♢ K 8 | 1. Forcing, natural. |
| ♣ Q 8 3 | ♣ A K J 6 5 4 | 2. Splinter,-agreeing clubs. |
| | | 3. RKB (1430) — opener has |
| 2♡ | 3♣[1] | preempted. |
| 4♠[2] | 4NT[3] | 4. '1'. |
| 5♣[4] | 6♣[5] | 5. Opener figures to have the ♣Q |
| pass | | or four clubs. |

**Note:** A four-level splinter jump in spades, clubs agreed, forces partner to use 4NT as RKB. To preserve partnership harmony, that jump therefore promises at least one Keycard — in blood.

## Opener splinters after a two-level response

Not everyone plays these three-level jumps as splinters — it's a matter of partnership agreement.

| Opener | Responder | |
|--------|-----------|---|
| ♠ A K Q J 6 | ♠ 5 4 | |
| ♡ Q 7 5 | ♡ A 6 3 | |
| ♢ 7 | ♢ A 8 4 | 1. Game-forcing splinter (some play |
| ♣ A Q 7 4 | ♣ K J 6 5 2 | it natural). |
| | | 2. Cuebid. |
| 1♠ | 2♣ | 3. RKB (1430) — opener asking. |
| 3♢[1] | 3♡[2] | 4. '3'. |
| 4♣[3] | 4♡[4] | 5. Can count thirteen tricks includ- |
| 7♣[5] | | ing a diamond ruff in dummy. |

Here it works well to play 3◇ as a splinter since 2◇ is forcing. However, you do give up the jump shift to show a strong 5-5. Choices, choices, choices.

## When either hand can ask

When both hands are strong, there may be a question as to who should ask and who should tell (cuebid). In general, after a splinter jump, a balanced hand with aces and spaces cuebids and the hand with the strong side suit asks. It is easier to count tricks when the hand with the strong side suit asks.

| Opener | Responder | |
|---|---|---|
| ♠ A J 10 5 | ♠ K Q 4 | 1. Game-forcing splinter (5+ clubs). |
| ♡ A 10 7 | ♡ 6 | 2. RKB (1430) — opener asking. |
| ◇ 5 | ◇ A Q 2 | 3. '1'. |
| ♣ A K 7 6 2 | ♣ J 10 8 5 4 3 | 4. SSA in spades. |
| | | 5. KQ(x) — a raise of a SSA shows KQ(x). |
| 1♣ | 3♡[1] | 6. Here we go again. Another commercial where you have just the right cards. He's shameless. |
| 4♣[2] | 4◇[3] | |
| 4♠[4] | 5♠[5] | |
| 7♣[6] | pass[7] | 7. You'd do the same thing. |

SPLINTER WITH A FLOURISH

| Opener | Responder | |
|---|---|---|
| ♠ A 6 4 3 | ♠ 7 | |
| ♡ J 5 | ♡ A K 7 | |
| ◇ K 7 5 4 2 | ◇ J 8 6 3 | |
| ♣ A 4 | ♣ K Q J 6 3 | |
| | | 1. Game-forcing splinter — three- or four-card support after a suit has been rebid. |
| 1◇ | 2♣ | |
| 2◇ | 3♠[1] | |
| 4♣[2] | ? | 2. Cuebid (aces and spaces). |

At this point you can try 4◇, RKB, or cuebid 4♡. Which is better and why? There are several compelling reasons to bid 4◇, RKB.

1) You have a trick-taking side suit
2) It will be a lower ask than 4NT, partner's only available ask after you cuebid.
3) A lower ask allows for a queen-ask below five of the agreed suit.

If you bid 4◇, RKB (1430), the response is 4♠ showing '3', and now you have room for a 4NT queen-ask. When opener denies the queen, settle for 5◇. If you cuebid 4♡ and opener bids 4NT, RKB (1430), your '1' response is 5♣ and a 'safe' queen-ask is lost.

Conclusion: With a choice between cuebidding or making a lower-level ask, lean toward the ask, particularly if your cuebid would force partner to use 4NT to ask for Keycards.

## Cuebidding beyond four of the agreed suit

Once a cuebid following a splinter jump bypasses four of the agreed suit, the next possible RKB ask is 4NT, and other suits are cuebids.

A BYPASS

| Opener | Responder |
|---|---|
| ♠ 7 5 | ♠ A K 3 |
| ♡ 9 8 7 | ♡ 6 |
| ◇ A Q J | ◇ K 7 6 3 |
| ♣ K Q 8 6 2 | ♣ A J 5 4 3 |
| 1♣ | 3♡¹ |
| 4◇² | 4NT³ |
| 5♠⁴ | 6♣ |
| pass | |

1. Game-forcing splinter.
2. The bypass cuebid suggesting zilch in spades. Opener's hearts make slam a live possibility.
3. RKB (1430) — opener hasn't jumped or reversed.
4. '2 with'.

## THE BOTTOM LINE

- After a game-forcing splinter jump, four of the agreed minor by either hand, if available, is RKB, other suits are cuebids and 3NT is to play.
- After a cuebid that follows a splinter jump bypasses four of the agreed suit, 4NT is the next possible RKB ask.
- If a four-level splinter bypasses four of the agreed minor, four of the cheapest unbid suit is RKB. If there are no unbid suits, 4NT is RKB. No suit bid by an opponent, or the splinter suit itself, can be used to ask for Keycards.
- A splinter jump to 4♠ agreeing clubs promises at least one Keycard... in blood.
- It usually works out better if the player with aces and spaces cuebids allowing the player with a possible strong side suit to use RKB. However, in close cases, the player who can make the cheaper ask should take charge.

# CHAPTER 16

# HANDLING VOIDS AFTER MINOR-SUIT AGREEMENT

In the majors, Exclusion Asks are leaps in the void suit *above* game in your major. These jumps come after major-suit agreement — or sometimes without agreement when the last bid is a major. Partner is obliged to answer Keycards in steps, starting with '0'. There are four Keycards: the three aces outside the void suit, plus the king of the agreed suit or last-bid major. The queen is not included in the response. Most major-suit Exclusion Asks are at the five-level, which allows the asker to bow out gracefully at that level facing a disappointing response.

After minor-suit agreement, an Exclusion Ask is one level higher than a splinter jump. After two-level agreement, when a three-level jump is a splinter, a four-level jump is EKB. So far, so good. However, after three- (or four-)level agreement, an Exclusion jump must come a the five-level. Five-level jumps are Exclusion Asks. The problem is that if you get a discouraging response you are doomed to play at the six-level. The bottom line is this:

1) Five-level Exclusion Asks are rare (or should be);

2) Six-level Exclusion Asks are, for practical purposes, non-existent;

3) You can live beautifully without this chapter.

If you are still there: after an Exclusion response, the next step (including the void suit, 4NT or 5NT) is the queen-ask. A return to the agreed suit is always to play. New suits that are not the queen-ask are Specific Suit Asks.

You are now ready for some EKB action!

## EKB AFTER TWO-LEVEL AGREEMENT (YOUR LUCKY DAY)

After two-level agreement, a jump to four of the agreed suit is RKB. When the agreed suit is the RKB ask suit, a jump one level higher than a splinter jump is EKB.

| Opener | Responder | |
|--------|-----------|---|
| 1♣ | 2♣ | 1. EKB — a jump one level higher |
| 4◇¹ | | than a splinter jump. |

## JUMPING FOR JOY

| Opener | Responder |
|---|---|
| ♠ A Q J 7 | ♠ 4 3 |
| ♡ — | ♡ K J 6 |
| ◇ K J 9 8 6 3 | ◇ A 7 5 4 2 |
| ♣ K Q 5 | ♣ A 6 2 |
| | |
| 1◇ | 2◇[1] |
| 4♡[2] | 5♣[3] |
| 5♠[4] | 5NT[5] |
| 6◇[6] | pass |

1. Inverted
2. EKB — one level higher than a splinter jump; 4◇ would be RKB.
3. '2'.
4. SSA. A new suit that is not the queen-ask.
5. 1st step response shows third-round spade control. It must be xx as the asker has the queen.
6. Bidding a grand on a finesse is against the odds. However, bidding a small slam on a finesse offers acceptable odds.


## LIFE-SAVING SECOND ASK

| Opener | Responder |
|---|---|
| ♠ K Q | ♠ A 5 |
| ♡ — | ♡ A J 8 |
| ◇ A Q J 6 5 4 | ◇ K 8 7 3 2 |
| ♣ A K 7 6 3 | ♣ 8 4 2 |
| | |
| 1◇ | 2◇[1] |
| 4♡[2] | 5♣[3] |
| 6♣[4] | 6◇[5] |
| pass | |

1. Inverted.
2. EKB — a jump one level higher than a splinter; 4◇ would be RKB.
3. '2'.
4. SSA in clubs (prepared to bid a grand facing a 1st step response of 6♡ showing third-round control).
5. A return to the trump suit denies third-round control and does not count as a step.


## LOOKING FOR '2', FINDING ONLY '1'

| Opener (you) | Responder |
|---|---|
| ♠ K Q J 5 | ♠ 7 3 |
| ♡ A Q 6 2 | ♡ 5 4 |
| ◇ — | ◇ A K 8 |
| ♣ A Q 9 6 4 | ♣ K J 8 7 3 2 |
| | |
| 1♣ | 2♣[1] |
| 4◇[2] | 4♠[3] |
| 6♣[4] | pass |

1. Inverted — setting the trump suit.
2. EKB — one level higher than a splinter; 4♣ is RKB.
3. '1' — 2nd step response. Doesn't count the ◇A.
4. Partner has the wrong ace. He needs the ♠A for you to be interested in a grand.

| Opener (you) | Responder |
|---|---|
| ♠ — | ♠ A K 6 |
| ♡ K Q J 5 | ♡ 4 3 |
| ◇ A K J | ◇ Q 8 7 |
| ♣ K Q 7 6 4 2 | ♣ J 10 9 5 3 |
| 1♣ | 2◇[1] |
| 4♠[2] | 4NT[3] |
| ?[4] | |

1. A Crisscross limit raise. Think 3♣ if you play limit raises.
2. After two-level agreement, jumps one level higher than a splinter are EKB asks. If you play 3♣ as a limit raise, a leap to 4♠ over that is a splinter so you have to keep 5♠ to make an Exclusion ask. A bit high!
3. '0'.
4. You are off two aces and partner has about 9-10 HCP. Partner has at most 3 HCP in the minors and no ♡A. Guess where partner's points are? At matchpoints consider passing, particularly with the lead coming up to partner's spade strength! Yes, you've read that last sentence correctly, and no, you can't have your money back for the book.

## THE BOTTOM LINE

- After two-level agreement, four-level jumps are EKB asks. But after 1◇-2◇, 4♣ is a splinter so 5♣ is EKB.

## EKB AFTER TWO-LEVEL NON-AGREEMENT

Exclusions Asks are so rare in non-agreement sequences that we will only consider EKB after a minor suit has been rebid

After two-level club non-agreement, 4◇ is RKB. *Translation:* If your void is in diamonds, EKB is 5◇. If your void is in another suit, the EKB ask must be one level higher than a splinter jump. After two-level diamond non-agreement, the RKB ask can be 4♡ or 4♠. *Translation:* If your void is in the RKB ask suit, jump one level higher to use EKB. If your void is not in the RKB ask suit, jump one level higher than a splinter jump to use EKB.

In non-agreement sequences you are dealing with dangerous five-level EKB asks. Keep in mind that there is no law that says you have to use EKB just because you have a void, particularly at the five-level. You need a whale of a hand to use EKB at the five-level. After all, if you wind up missing two Keycards, it's not going to be pretty. Maybe you should have been cuebidding instead. Forewarned is forearmed.

| Opener | Responder |
|--------|-----------|
| 1♡ | 2♣ |
| ? | |

Here 4♢ is RKB. If you have a diamond void, 5♢ is EKB. If you have a spade void, 3♠ is a splinter so 4♠ is EKB.

| Opener | Responder |
|--------|-----------|
| 1♠ | 2♢ |
| ? | |

Now 4♡ is RKB. If you have a heart void, 5♡ is EKB. If you have a club void, 4♣ is a splinter so 5♣ is EKB.

Now suppose you hold:

♠ A Q 6 5 3 2    ♡ K 4    ♢ —    ♣ A J 7 4 2

| Opener | Responder (you) |
|--------|-----------------|
| 1♡ | 1♠ |
| 2♣ | ? |

You are thinking 'Exclusion in diamonds', but how high to jump? Plenty high: 4♢ is RKB, so 5♢ is EKB. If partner shows '2' (5NT), you still have to deal with the spade position for a grand. You are too high to find out partner's exact spade holding. A gambler would bid 7♣ hoping partner has a void, a singleton, the king, or that the finesse works if partner has a doubleton.

TWO VOIDS

EKB (and RKB) asks are easier to deal with after a suit has been rebid.

| Opener | Responder (you) | |
|--------|-----------------|--|
| ♠ A 10 7 2 | ♠ — | |
| ♡ A 6 3 | ♡ K 8 5 | |
| ♢ K J 7 5 4 2 | ♢ A 8 6 3 | 1. 3♠ would be a splinter, so 4♠ is EKB. |
| ♣ — | ♣ A K J 5 4 2 | |
| | | 2. '2' excluding the ♠A. |
| 1♢ | 2♣ | 3. Queen-ask, the next step. |
| 2♢ | 4♠[1] | 4. On the assumption that partner |
| 5♢[2] | 5♡[3] | has four diamonds. If he doesn't, |
| 7♢[4] | pass | it's on my head. |

*Don't read this:* you might like to consider playing that after a queen-ask, a response in the void suit denies the queen, but shows maximum trump length and the inability to know whether the two hands have a ten-card trump fit. *I warned you.*

## ANOTHER STRIKE!

| Opener | Responder | |
|---|---|---|
| ♠ 3 | ♠ A K 8 5 4 | 1. Some rebid 1NT. |
| ♡ Q J 9 4 | ♡ — | 2. 3♡ is natural, 4♡ is a splinter, |
| ◊ A 7 6 | ◊ K J 8 3 | so 5♡ is EKB. Scary, isn't it? |
| ♣ A J 10 9 6 | ♣ K Q 8 7 | Some bridge players have yet to |
| | | make their first Exclusion Ask. |
| 1♣ | 1♠ | 3. '2'. |
| 2♣[1] | 5♡[2] | 4. If partner has six clubs, this |
| 6♣[3] | 7♣[4] | should be cold. If partner has |
| pass | | five clubs he should have a great |

play for it. Let's hope partner knows how to set up a long suit after a trump lead. Without a trump lead, there's a high cross-ruff for thirteen tricks.

## PUBLISHER'S CONTRIBUTION

Ray (Lee) was telling me about his own experiences with EKB. Some years ago, on the way to a Regional, he managed to persuade his wife, Linda, to add EKB to their system. She finally consented, confident that it would never come up anyway. Believe it or not, this was the second hand out of the box:

| Opener (Ray) | Responder (Linda) | |
|---|---|---|
| ♠ A K 10 7 6 4 | ♠ 3 | |
| ♡ 3 | ♡ Q J 5 | |
| ◊ A Q 8 7 5 2 | ◊ K J 9 6 3 | |
| ♣ — | ♣ A Q 4 2 | |
| | | 1. See, it does come up! |
| 1♠ | 2◊ | 2. '1'. |
| 5♣[1] | 5♡[2] | 3. And it works! |
| 6◊[3] | pass | |

This hand turned Linda into a believer!

# EKB AFTER THREE- (OR FOUR)-LEVEL AGREEMENT

After three- or four-level agreement, jumps to the five-level in unbid suits are EKB asks. Since there is no such animal as a five-level splinter, the good news is that there won't be any confusion. The bad news is that the ask is so high that you can seldom use it.

### UP, UP AND AWAY WE GO!

| Opener (you) | Responder | |
|---|---|---|
| ♠ A Q 7 6 4 3 | ♠ — | |
| ♡ — | ♡ 8 7 3 2 | |
| ◇ A Q 5 4 3 | ◇ K J 7 6 | |
| ♣ K 2 | ♣ A Q J 5 4 | |
| 1♠ | 2♣ | 1. EKB after three-level agreement. |
| 2◇ | 3◇ | 2. '2'. |
| 5♡[1] | 6♣[2] | 3. At the fork — either you go for it |
| ?[3] | | or you don't. |

After three-level agreement, jumps to the five-level (5♡ here) are EKB asks. However, five-level EKB asks commit you to a small slam. Are you willing to risk it? In this case it seems safe. Even if partner has an unlikely '0', you will still have a play for 6◇. However, you strike gold. Partner responds 6♣ showing '2', the ♣A and the ◇K. Notice that partner does not count the spade void. Once again greed enters the picture. If partner has likely spade shortness (or the king) there should be a great play for the grand — and there's always a finesse facing two small spades. Are you a gambler or not?

### SEVEN-FIVE COME ALIVE!

| Opener (you) | Responder | |
|---|---|---|
| ♠ — | ♠ K 5 2 | 1. Game-forcing agreement, not an |
| ♡ A K J 7 6 3 2 | ♡ — | ask. Jump raises show strong |
| ◇ Q J 6 5 4 | ◇ A K 10 2 | trumps and are slam tries. |
| ♣ J | ♣ K Q 7 5 4 3 | 2. EKB. Looks dangerous with only |
| 1♡ | 2♣ | one Keycard, but partner's |
| 2◇ | 4◇[1] | bidding suggests at least two, |
| 5♠[2] | 6◇[3] | possibly three Keycards. |
| pass [4] | | 3. '2' — does not count the heart |
| | | void. |
| | | 4. Has survived a five-level |
| | | Exclusion ask holding only one |
| | | Keycard. |

After opener or responder jump-shifts, a follow up jump by the jump-shifter after three- or four-level agreement is EKB. It is beneath the dignity of a jump-shifter to splinter. By our agreements, a jump-shifter asks for information, he doesn't dish it out via a splinter.

## WHEN TWO ARE MISSING, IT'S TIME TO CLOSE SHOP

| Opener | | Responder | |
|---|---|---|---|
| ♠ — | | ♠ J 8 6 5 | |
| ♡ A 3 | | ♡ K Q 5 2 | |
| ◇ A Q J 6 5 4 | | ◇ 8 7 2 | |
| ♣ K Q J 5 2 | | ♣ 6 3 | |

| Opener | Oppt. | Responder | Oppt. |
|---|---|---|---|
| 1◇ | pass | 1♡ | 1♠ |
| 3♣ | pass | 3◇[1] | pass |
| 4♠[2] | pass | 4NT[3] | pass |
| 5◇[4] | all pass | | |

1. Game-forcing three-level agreement — 4◇ would be RKB.
2. EKB.
3. A big fat '0'.
4. Two Keycards missing .

## AFTER OPENER JUMP-SHIFTS

| Opener | Responder |
|---|---|
| ♠ A K J 6 | ♠ 4 3 2 |
| ♡ K 6 2 | ♡ Q J 10 5 |
| ◇ — | ◇ J 10 4 |
| ♣ A K J 7 4 3 | ♣ Q 6 5 |
| 1♣ | 1♡ |
| 2♠ | 3♣[1] |
| 4◇[2] | 4♡[3] |
| 4♠[4] | 6♣[5] |
| pass[6] | |

1. Three-level game-forcing agreement.
2. EKB (4♣ would be RKB). A follow-up jump by a jump-shifter is Exclusion.
3. '0'.
4. Queen-ask.
5. Yes, with no side-suit king but I can't believe I'm actually jumping to slam with this hand.
6. Not to worry, I know for a fact that clubs are 2-2 and the ♠Q is onside. He can't stand to see any of his example hands go down.

This is an awkward sequence because the opener can't be sure responder is so weak. It helps if responder has an artificial bid to show a terrible hand facing a game-forcing jump shift.

| Opener | Responder |
|---|---|
| ♠ A Q J 5 | ♠ 7 |
| ♡ — | ♡ J 6 4 3 |
| ◇ A K 3 | ◇ Q J 10 7 5 2 |
| ♣ K Q 6 5 4 3 | ♣ A 2 |
| | |
| 1♣ | 1◇ |
| 2♠ | 3◇ |
| 4♡[1] | 4NT[2] |
| 5♣[3] | 6◇[4] |
| 7◇[5] | pass |

1. EKB (4◇ is RKB). No splinters by a jump-shifter, only EKB jumps.
2. '1' (♣A).
3. Queen-ask. Diamonds is the agreed suit. After an Exclusion jump and response, follow-up 'next step' bids at the five-level, even in the asker's first-bid suit, are queen-asks. A jump to 6♣ would be to play.
4. The queen.
5. Looks good. Partner has the ♣A, the ◇Q and diamond length.

## Don't read this, please don't!

The eternal problem. You can't make an Exclusion ask in any suit partner has bid. Jumps in partner's suits are natural. Maybe, just maybe, an agreement can be made that a jump to game in partner's first-bid major by a known strong hand after game-forcing three-level minor-suit agreement is EKB. After all, a three-level bid in that major is forcing. A truly frightening agreement.

SCARY, SCARY, SCARY

| Opener | Responder |
|---|---|
| ♠ K Q 7 6 | ♠ A 4 |
| ♡ — | ♡ J 8 5 3 2 |
| ◇ K Q 3 | ◇ A 5 4 |
| ♣ A K Q 7 3 2 | ♣ 6 5 4 |
| | |
| 1♣ | 1♡ |
| 2♠ | 3♣[1] |
| 4♡[2] | 5♣[2] |
| 7♣[4] | |

1. Game-forcing three-level agreement.
2. EKB. The scary agreement in action. If you buy into this (remember 3♡ would be forcing), you and partner should have it in writing, signed by both players — in blood.
3. '2'.
4. It may seem like a good idea on paper, but if partner ever passes one of these EKB asks, it's the end of the world — not to mention the partnership — not to mention what will become of this book.

# EKB JUMPS AFTER OPENER REVERSES

After opener reverses and responder rebids any suit, a jump by the reverser is EKB, not a splinter jump. It is beneath the dignity of a reverser, a strong hand, to splinter after partner rebids a suit.

| Opener | Responder | |
|---|---|---|
| ♠ K 6 | ♠ Q J 5 3 | 1. Game-forcing agreement. |
| ♡ — | ♡ A 9 2 | 2. EKB (4♣ would be RKB). A |
| ◇ A K 6 4 3 | ◇ 7 5 2 | follow-up jump by a reversing |
| ♣ A K 8 6 5 2 | ♣ Q 4 3 | opener after three-level |
| | | agreement is an EKB ask. |
| 1♣ | 1♠ | 3. '0'. |
| 2◇ | 3♣¹ | 4. Queen-ask (next step). If 4NT |
| 4♡² | 4♠³ | were not the next step, it would |
| 4NT⁴ | 6♣⁵ | be the SKA. |
| pass | | 5. Got it! |

At first glance this contract doesn't look so hot. But you have a chance. If you get a heart lead, ruff, and lead a low spade. If LHO has the ♠A, you're almost home free. If LHO ducks, win in dummy and pitch your ♠K on the ♡A. If LHO rises with ace, you have three diamond pitches coming — two on spades and one on the ♡A — a Morton's Fork.

# EKB AFTER RESPONDER JUMP SHIFTS

You can guess what's coming next. If opener rebids any suit, a second jump by the responder is EKB.

| Opener | Responder | |
|---|---|---|
| ♠ A Q 8 | ♠ — | |
| ♡ 6 2 | ♡ K J 7 | |
| ◇ Q 5 3 | ◇ A K J 10 7 6 2 | |
| ♣ A 7 6 4 2 | ♣ K 5 3 | 1. Strong jump-shift. |
| | | 2. The agreement. |
| 1♣ | 2◇¹ | 3. EKB (4◇ would be RKB). A |
| 3◇² | 4♠³ | follow-up jump by the jump-shifter |
| 5♣⁴ | 6◇ | after agreement. |
| pass | | 4. '1' — doesn't count the ♠A. |

# EKB IN A SUIT THEY HAVE BID

No problem: just buckle up and jump one level higher than a splinter jump.

| Opener | Oppt. | Responder | Oppt. |
|---|---|---|---|
| 1♣ | 1♡ | ? | |

Say you are gazing fondly at:

$$\spadesuit\, K\,Q\,5 \qquad \heartsuit\, — \qquad \diamondsuit\, K\,J\,6\,3 \qquad \clubsuit\, A\,Q\,J\,7\,6\,2$$

If you wish to 'exclude' in hearts, jump to 4♡, one level higher than a splinter.

## THE BOTTOM LINE

Before using EKB, leaping madly into outer space with a void, make sure you can handle the awkward '0' or '1' responses.

- EKB asks are leaps one level higher than a splinter jump.
  - After two-level agreement, three-level jumps are splinters and four-level jumps are EKB asks.
  - After three-level agreement, four-level jumps are splinters and five-level jumps are EKB asks.
- When responding to EKB, do not count a void, do not count the ace of the jump suit and do not include the queen of the agreed suit in your response. There are four Keycards, the three 'working' aces plus the king of the agreed or last-bid suit.
- An opener who has reversed or jump-shifted, a responder who has jump-shifted and a strong 2♣ opener are all 'exempted' from splintering. Follow-up jumps from these people after three-level or four-level agreement are EKB asks.
- After a response to EKB, the next step, including 4NT but excluding the agreed suit (which is to play), is a queen-ask.
- If 4NT is not needed as a queen-ask, it is the SKA. A bid of 5NT in EKB sequences is always a SKA.
- After an EKB response, a follow-up bid in any suit that is not a queen-ask is a SSA. A follow-up bid in the void suit is a SSA in the queen-ask suit.
- Solidify your splinter agreements if you intend to use EKB.
- After an EKB response, a return to five of the asker's first-bid suit (not the agreed suit) is not to play. It is either the queen-ask (next step) or a SSA (not the next step). However, a return to the asker's first-bid suit at the six-level is to play.

In case you haven't realized it, EKB jumps are accidents waiting to happen. Some would say this whole book is. If you can't remember the ask, or you don't think partner can, or if the level of the ask is so high that you can't handle an 'unfortunate' response, forget the whole thing. You can survive without EKB; millions have. However, it does come in handy when you have the right hand.

# RESPONDING TO RKB WITH A VOID

Voids, voids, voids. Love them or hate them, you have to deal with them. In the first part of this chapter the void was in the asker's hand. In the rest of it, the void will be in the hand of the responder to a RKB ask. From here on in, think of yourself as the one responding to RKB with a void.

## Clubs is the agreed suit

When *clubs* is the agreed suit, the Keycard ask will be 4♣ or 4◇ more than 90% of the time. Here are the void-showing responses to both asks. (Note that if your void is in partner's first-bid suit, you normally disregard it.)

Void-showing responses to RKB asks start with the raise of the ask-suit, the 5th step, and it is irrelevant whether the ask is 1430 or 3014. It helps if you remember that the 'raise of the ask-suit' is the first step in void-showing responses.

When 4♣ is the ask, clubs agreed, void-showing responses start with 5♣, and they are:

> 5♣ = '0 or 2' Keycards with an unknown void.
> 5◇, 5♡, 5♠ = '1 or 3' Keycards with a void in the jump suit.

Do not worry about '4' Keycards: '3' is a minor miracle unless it is a 3014 ask. Furthermore, in some sequences your 'unknown' void will be a 'known' void. You may have splintered, you may have bid two other suits, etc. In such sequences, partner will know, and you will know that partner knows; the opponents will know and you will know that they know. The whole world will know.

A 5♣ response is apt to show '2' rather than '0'. If the ask is 3014 — weak asking strong — it surely shows '2'. Only if your previous bidding has shown a pathetic hand should a 1430 asker ever assume '0'. As for partner deciding between '1' or '3' when you leap in your void suit, partner should be able to tell from your previous, beautiful, descriptive bidding which it is.

LIKE A CHARM

| Opener | Responder | |
|---|---|---|
| ♠ — | ♠ Q 6 5 3 | |
| ♡ K J 7 6 3 | ♡ 2 | |
| ◇ A 6 4 3 | ◇ K Q | |
| ♣ A J 5 2 | ♣ K Q 8 7 6 4 | |
| 1♡ | 2♣ | 1. Splinter. |
| 3♠[1] | 4♣[2] | 2. RKB 3014 — opener has |
| 5♣[3] | 6♣ | jumped. |
| pass | | 3. '2' with an obvious spade void. |

TOUGH CALL

| Opener | Responder |
|---|---|
| ♠ A K 7 | ♠ 4 3 2 |
| ♡ 6 | ♡ A J 10 5 3 |
| ◇ A 10 7 4 | ◇ — |
| ♣ A K 6 5 2 | ♣ Q J 8 7 3 |

| Opener | Responder | |
|---|---|---|
| 1♣ | 1♡ | 1. The agreement, not the ask. |
| 2◇ | 4♣[1] | 2. RKB (1430) — opener asking. |
| 4◇[2] | 6♣[3] | 3. '1' (can't be '3' when the asker has '3') with a diamond void. |
| ?[4] | | 4. Tempted to go for the moon. |

A jump to six of the agreed suit in respond to a RKB ask shows '1 or 3' Keycards with a void in a higher-ranking suit than the trump suit. Here it must be in diamonds. If the void were in spades, the response to RKB would be 5♠.

WHEN THE WHOLE WORLD KNOWS

| Opener | Responder |
|---|---|
| ♠ 5 | ♠ A 6 4 |
| ♡ K Q 7 3 | ♡ — |
| ◇ A K | ◇ Q 8 5 2 |
| ♣ A Q 8 7 6 3 | ♣ K J 9 5 4 2 |

| Opener | Oppt. | Responder | Oppt. |
|---|---|---|---|
| 1♣ | 1♡ | 3♡[1] | dbl |
| 4♣[2] | pass | 5♣[3] | pass |
| 7♣[4] | all pass | | |

1. Splinter, game force (4♡ would be EKB).
2. RKB (1430) — opener asking.
3. '0 or 2' (surely '2') with a heart void.
4. Can't see any losers.

## When 4◇ is the ask, clubs agreed

When 4◇ is the RKB ask, clubs agreed, void-showing responses still start with the raise of the ask suit, but this time it is 5◇.

| 5◇ | = '0 or 2' with an unknown void |
|---|---|
| 5♡, 5♠ | = '1 or 3' with a void in the jump suit |
| 6♣ | = '1 or 3' with a diamond void |

If the jump in your void suit would land you beyond 6♣, jump to 6♣. Partner will know that your void suit is in a higher-ranking suit than the trump suit.

## When diamonds is the agreed suit

When *diamonds* is the agreed suit, the RKB ask will be 4◇ or 4♡ more than 90% of the time. As ever, void-showing responses begin with the raise of the ask suit.

*When 4◇ is RKB, diamonds agreed*

| | |
|---|---|
| 5◇ | = '0 or 2' with an unknown void |
| 5♡, 5♠, 6♣ | = '1 or 3' with a void in the jump suit |

*When 4♡ is RKB, diamonds agreed*

| | |
|---|---|
| 5♡ | = '0 or 2' with an unknown void |
| 5♠, 6♣ | = '1 or 3' with a void in the jump suit |
| 6◇ | = '1 or 3' with a heart void |

## The queen-ask after a void-showing response

Whether the void is known or not, the next step after a void-showing response is the queen-ask and other suits are Specific Suit Asks.

IT WORKS, IT WORKS!

| Opener | | Responder (you) | |
|---|---|---|---|
| ♠ K Q 6 | | ♠ A 7 3 | |
| ♡ K Q | | ♡ A 9 5 | |
| ◇ A K J 6 | | ◇ 9 8 7 5 4 3 2 | |
| ♣ 8 7 6 5 | | ♣ — | |

| Opener | Oppt. | Responder | Oppt. |
|---|---|---|---|
| 1◇ | 3♣ | 4♣[1] | pass |
| 4◇[2] | pass | 5◇[3] | pass |
| 5♡[4] | pass | 7◇[5] | all pass |

1. Agrees diamonds, game force.
2. RKB (1430) — opener asking.
3. '0 or 2'. You hope partner will know your void is in clubs. Since 4♣ is a strong bid, you are presumed to have '2'.
4. Queen-ask.
5. Seven-card support equals a queen!

HOME GAME GRAND

| Opener (you) | Responder |
|---|---|
| ♠ A K | ♠ J 7 5 4 2 |
| ♡ K J 6 3 | ♡ — |
| ◇ A J 10 7 6 | ◇ K Q 5 4 2 |
| ♣ A 3 | ♣ Q J 8 |
| 1◇ | 1♠ |
| 2♡ | 4◇¹ |
| 4♡² | 6◇³ |
| ?⁴ | |

1. Jump preferences and jump raises to the four-level are agreements, not asks.
2. The ask (1430) — opener asking.
3. '1' or '3' (must be '1', opener has '3') with a heart void. A jump in the trump suit indicates a void in a suit that is higher-ranking than the trump suit and it can't be spades!
4. To bid on or not to bid on? Like death and taxes, if you make the losing decision, you will never hear the end of it. Never.

## After a jump response to RKB

| Opener | Responder (you) |
|---|---|
| ♠ 10 | ♠ A K Q |
| ♡ K Q 5 4 | ♡ — |
| ◇ A K 6 5 | ◇ J 8 4 3 2 |
| ♣ A K Q 7 | ♣ J 6 5 4 2 |
| 1◇¹ | 3♡² |
| 4◇³ | 5♡⁴ |
| 5♠⁵ | 6◇⁶ |
| pass | |

1. Some would open 1♣.
2. Game-forcing splinter showing at least five-card support — a possible stretch.
3. RKB (1430) — opener asking.
4. '1' or '3' (must be '1' opener has '3') with a heart void.
5. Queen-ask, next-ranking suit.
6. Negative. Given that you are known to have five diamonds, your response denies the queen. With six diamonds, jump to a grand.

## THE BOTTOM LINE

- Void-showing responses in response to RKB asks start with the 5th step, a raise of the ask-suit.
- After a void-showing response, the asker has the option of additional asks. The next step, including the void suit, is the queen-ask; other suits are specific suit asks.
- When responding to RKB, do not show a void in partner's first-bid suit.

Congratulations. You have survived another chapter.

# CHAPTER 17

## REVIEWING THE ASKS

It might be a good idea to step back and take a look at some iffy minor-suit slam hands and review the various asks.

### Review of the SKA

A new suit after a 4NT (or 5NT) SKA is a further king-ask. If the player being asked does not have the king, he signs off in the agreed suit. If the responder to a second king-ask has the desired king, he has two options:

1) A 1st step response, excluding the trump suit, shows Kxx(x).
2) A jump in the trump suit shows Kx or a singleton.
3) If a second king-ask is made in a suit in which the king has already been denied, it morphs into a third-round control ask.

Responses are:

1) Return to the trump suit = no third-round control
2) Nearest notrump = the queen
3) Jump in the trump suit = x or xx

### Review of responses to a five-level SSA in an unbid suit

1) Return to the trump suit denies second- or third-round control: (xxx(x))
2) 1st step response, excluding the trump suit = third-round control (xx or the queen)
3) 2nd step response = Kxx(x)
4) 3rd step response = Kx
5) Raise of ask suit = KQ(x)
6) Jump in trump suit = singleton

A HAPPY AND A SAD RESPONSE

After a king is shown in response to a queen-ask, a follow-up bid in a new suit is a Specific Suit Ask, while a follow-up bid of 5NT asks for any other king that has not been denied by the first king-showing response.

| Opener | Responder |
|---|---|
| ♠ A | ♠ K J 7 4 |
| ♡ A J 5 | ♡ 4 3 2 |
| ♢ A Q 6 2 | ♢ K 7 |
| ♣ A 10 7 5 3 | ♣ K Q 8 4 |
| | |
| 1♣ | 1♠ |
| 2♢ | 4♣[1] |
| 4♢[2] | 4♡[3] |
| 4♠[4] | 5♢[5] |
| 5♡[6] | 6♣[7] |
| pass[8] | |

1. The agreement, not the ask.
2. The ask (1430) — opener asking.
3. '1'.
4. Queen-ask (next ranking suit).
5. Yes, with the ♢K.
6. SSA in hearts.
7. Return to the trump suit = no second- or third-round heart control.
8. Risky bidding a grand facing xxx in hearts.

## A SECOND KING-ASK

**Reminder:** After a strong, artificial 2♣ opening and a natural first- or second-round response of 3♣ or 3♢, a raise of that minor is RKB. A 'perk' for a mega-strong hand. Keep in mind that the responder to any grand slam ask can bid a grand slam outright if he can count thirteen tricks.

| Opener | Responder |
|---|---|
| ♠ A J 7 | ♠ 5 3 2 |
| ♡ A K J 6 5 | ♡ 4 |
| ♢ A Q 8 4 | ♢ K J 6 3 2 |
| ♣ A | ♣ K 8 4 3 |
| | |
| 2♣ | 2♢[1] |
| 2♡ | 3♢[2] |
| 4♢[3] | 4♡[4] |
| 4NT[5] | 5♣[6] |
| 5♠[7] | 6♢[8] |
| ?[9] | |

1. Waiting.
2. Natural.
3. RKB (1430).
4. '1'.
5. SKA (4♠, the next ranking suit, would be the queen-ask).
6. ♣K (could still have a major-suit king).
7. SSA in spades; 5NT would ask for the ♠K. The SSA also picks off doubletons, queens and singletons.
8. Denies second- or third-round control; 5NT would show third-round control, 6♣ would show the king.
9. Touch and go. There is a chance of setting up hearts for spade discards.

| Opener | Responder |
|--------|-----------|
| ♠ A K Q 6 3 | ♠ 7 |
| ♡ J 9 | ♡ Q |
| ◊ J 7 6 | ◊ A K 4 |
| ♣ Q 7 3 | ♣ K J 10 9 6 5 4 2 |

| Opener | Responder | |
|--------|-----------|--|
| 1♠ | 2♣ | |
| 2♠ | 3◊ | 1. The agreement, not the ask. |
| 4♣[1] | 4◊[2] | 2. RKB (1430) — opener limited. |
| 4♡[3] | 5♣[4] | 3. '1'. |
| pass | | 4. 2 aces missing. |

This hand illustrates one advantage of using a lower-level ask when clubs is the agreed suit. It also illustrates why the agreement should normally *not* be the ask, particularly when the agreement is made by the weaker hand. The one who makes the agreement may not want to be the one who wants to make the ask. However, as we have seen, in sequences where the agreement is made by a super-strong hand, the raise to the four-level is best played as the ask.

### WHEN RESPONDER HAS THE GOODS — AND THEN SOME!

After an inverted minor raise, a *jump* to four of the agreed suit is RKB.

After a king is shown in response to a queen-ask, a follow-up bid in another suit, is a SSA, *not* another king-ask. A SSA is more flexible than a king-ask. If you want to know if partner has another king, bid 5NT. However, after a king is shown in response to a Specific King Ask, a follow-up bid in a new suit is another king-ask — assuming partner can have a king in that suit (i.e. it wasn't denied by the first king response).

| Opener | Responder |
|--------|-----------|
| ♠ K Q J | ♠ A 9 7 |
| ♡ K J 6 2 | ♡ A |
| ◊ 10 9 5 | ◊ A K J 3 |
| ♣ Q J 7 | ♣ A K 10 5 2 |

| Opener | Responder | |
|--------|-----------|--|
| 1♣ | 2♣[1] | 1. Inverted – unlimited. |
| 2NT[2] | 4♣[3] | 2. Presumed balanced minimum. |
| 4♡[4] | 4♠[5] | 3. RKB (1430) — opener hasn't jumped, etc. |
| 5♡[6] | 5♠[7] | 4. '3' or '0', this time '0'. |
| 6♠[8] | 7♣[9] | 5. Queen-ask. |
| pass | | 6. Yes, with the ♡K, possibly the ♠K, but no ◊K. |
| | | 7. SSA in spades. |
| | | 8. The KQ(x). A raise of the ask suit shows the KQ with any length. |

Thirteen tricks – as long as opener has four spades, either red queen or a doubleton diamond. Lacking all of this, the *worst* it can be is on a diamond finesse, plus a chance of ruffing out the ♡Q if partner has KJxx. You only live once.

*Reminder:* Responses to that SSA of 5♠, clubs agreed, are:

5NT: 1st step = third-round control, Qx(x) or xx
6♣: The agreed suit, denies second- or third-round control and doesn't count as a step.
6♢: 2nd step = Kxx(x)
6♡: 3rd step = Kx
6♠: Raise of the ask suit = KQ(x)
7♣: Jump in the trump suit = a singleton

MULTIPLE ASKS — THE BIG TIME

| Opener | Responder | |
|--------|-----------|---|
| ♠ A K 7 6 | ♠ 5 | 1. Presumed natural after a jump shift. |
| ♡ A | ♡ K 8 6 5 3 | |
| ♢ 4 3 2 | ♢ A K 7 5 | 2. The agreement, not the ask. Apparently a slam try with a diamond control. |
| ♣ A K J 10 6 | ♣ Q 8 2 | |
| 1♣ | 1♡ | 3. RKB after four-level club agreement (1430). |
| 2♠ | 3♢[1] | |
| 3NT | 4♣[2] | 4. '1'. |
| 4♢[3] | 4♡[4] | 5. Queen-ask. |
| 4♠[5] | 5♢[6] | 6. Yes, with the ♢K. |
| 5♡[7] | 5NT[8] | 7. SSA in hearts, a bid suit. After a queen-ask, the next ask is a SSA). |
| 7♣[9] | pass | 8. 2nd step response = the king. |
| | | 9. Voila! A resting place for my third diamond. |

*Reminder:* An SSA in a previously-bid suit (5♡ here), means shortness is not an issue. These are the responses:

return to the trump suit (6♣) denies the queen or king
1st step (5♠)                =        the queen
2nd step (5NT)            =        the king
raise of the ask suit (6♡)  =        the KQ

Keep in mind that the ace is already accounted for when responding to a SSA.

| Opener | Responder | |
|---|---|---|
| ♠ Q | ♠ A 8 7 3 | |
| ♡ A J 10 7 4 | ♡ 5 2 | 1. Game-forcing splinter. |
| ◇ A K 7 6 2 | ◇ Q J 10 8 5 4 | 2. RKB after game-forcing three-level |
| ♣ Q 6 | ♣ A | agreement; (3014) — opener |
| | | has jumped. |
| 1♡ | 2◇ | 3. '3'. |
| 3♠[1] | 4◇[2] | 4. Specific kings? (4♠ is the queen- |
| 4♡[3] | 4NT[4] | ask.) |
| 5◇[5] | 6◇[6] | 5. Zilch, sorry. |
| pass | | 6. You're sorry? |

After having splintered, opener is 'the strong hand' so it is 3014 responses if responder asks. Once responder knows of the singleton spade and later of the ♡A and the ◇AK, he need only find the ♣K or the ♡K to shoot the moon. No luck today.

## 30-POINT DECK = 24-POINT SLAM

Your hand has improved when you have xxx facing a known singleton. Ten of their high-card points are going to take one trick. In the other three suits, you are playing with a thirty-point deck and you don't need all thirty of those points to bid a slam.

| Opener | Responder (you) | |
|---|---|---|
| ♠ 6 | ♠ 8 7 3 | 1. Limit raise |
| ♡ A K 5 2 | ♡ 4 3 | 2. Splinter (4◇ would be RKB — |
| ◇ A Q 8 5 | ◇ K J 7 4 2 | see Chapter 13). |
| ♣ K Q 6 4 | ♣ A 5 2 | 3. Cuebid. When you are known |
| | | to be weak and have 2 Keycards |
| 1◇ | 3◇[1] | facing a slam try, put on your |
| 4♠[2] | 5♣[3] | cuebidding shoes. Slam must be |
| 6◇ | pass | close if not at your very door. |

After a game-forcing splinter, four of the agreed suit, by a limited or unlimited hand, is RKB. If the splinter jump bypasses the agreed suit, four of the cheapest unbid suit is RKB. If all else fails, there is always 4NT.

| Opener | Responder | |
|---|---|---|
| ♠ 9 8 5 | ♠ 2 | |
| ♡ 3 | ♡ A 10 7 5 4 | |
| ◇ K Q 2 | ◇ A J 6 3 | |
| ♣ A K 10 8 7 3 | ♣ Q J 2 | |
| | | 1. Game-forcing splinter. |
| 1♣ | 1♡ | 2. RKB (1430) — opener asking. |
| 2♣ | 3♠¹ | Opener's hand has improved |
| 4♣² | 4NT³ | dramatically after the splinter. |
| 6♣ | pass | Notice the spade holding. |
| | | 3. '2 with'. |

## THE BOTTOM LINE

- After a Specific King Ask of 4NT or 5NT, a follow-up bid in a non-agreed suit is a second king-ask. However, if the king of the second suit has been denied, the 'second king-ask' becomes a third-round control ask.
- Any ask above game in the agreed suit is a grand slam try. Translation: the four aces and the KQ of the agreed suit are accounted for. Responder need not answer one of these asks if thirteen tricks can be counted — responder can bid a grand slam outright.
- After a king-showing response to a queen-ask, new suits by the asker are Specific Suit Asks; 5NT asks for any other undenied king. Following a RKB response if there has been no queen-ask and no Specific King Ask, a new suit by the asker is a Specific Suit Ask.
- After a game-forcing three-level splinter agreement, either hand can ask for Keycards via four of the agreed minor. If the splinter jump bypasses four of the agreed suit, the cheapest unbid suit can be used to ask for Keycards.

# CHAPTER 18

# REMEMBERING THE RKB ASKS AFTER MINOR-SUIT AGREEMENT

Now that you have the hang of the responses, I hate to say this, but the real problem is knowing whether an ask is possible and if it is, what is it? You just don't want to confuse a natural 4♣ or 4◇ bid with an RKB ask — though it does make for a good story.

When clubs is the agreed suit, there are five possible Keycard asks: 4♣, 4◇, 4♡, 4♠ and 4NT! Scary, isn't it? Not really. About 80-90 % of the those asks will be 4♣ or 4◇.

In order not to fear using RKB with lower asks, here are some suggestions, keeping in mind that it is an *unlimited* hand that is doing the asking:

## WHEN 4♣ IS THE ASK FOR CLUBS

### 1. *After two-level agreement*

This occurs most often after an inverted raise.

| Opener | Responder | |
|--------|-----------|---|
| 1♣ | 2♣[1] | 1. Inverted. |
| 4♣[2] | | 2. RKB. |

### 2. *After opener reverses*

In the following sequence both hands are unlimited so either can ask via 4♣

| Opener | Responder | |
|--------|-----------|---|
| 1♣ | 1♡ | 1. Unlimited and game-forcing. |
| 2◇ | 3♣[1] | 2. RKB 1430 — opener asking. |
| 4♣[2] | | |

| Opener | Responder | |
|--------|-----------|---|
| 1♣ | 1♡ | 1. Unlimited and game-forcing. |
| 2◇ | 3♣[1] | 2. RKB 3014 — opener has |
| 3NT | 4♣[2] | reversed. A planned sequence. |

But remember in most RKB sequences the agreement comes before the ask:

| Opener | Responder | |
|--------|-----------|---|
| 1♣ | 1♡ | 1. Jump preferences and jump agreements are slam tries, not RKB asks. |
| 2◊ | 4♣¹ | |

## 3. After three-level game-forcing agreement

After three-level agreement in a game-forcing auction, four of the agreed minor by the unlimited hand is RKB.

| Opener | Responder | |
|--------|-----------|---|
| 1♣ | 1♡ | 1. Game-forcing agreement. |
| 2♠ | 3♣¹ | 2. RKB 1430 — opener asking, not to mention jump-shifter asking. When a jump-shifter asks it is always 1430; if a jump-shifter is asked, it is always 3014. |
| 4♣² | | |

After a three-level forcing splinter agreement, four of the agreed suit is RKB by either hand.

| Opener | Responder | |
|--------|-----------|---|
| 1♣ | 3♡¹ | 1. Game-forcing splinter. |
| 4♣² | | 2. RKB 1430. |

| Opener | Responder | |
|--------|-----------|---|
| 1♣ | 1♡ | 1. Game-forcing agreement by an unlimited hand. |
| 1♠ | 2◊ | 2. RKB — first the agreement and then the ask (excluding a few exceptional sequences). |
| 2NT | 3♣¹ | |
| 3◊ | 4♣² | |

It is assumed that the fourth suit followed by three-level agreement is a game force. If you are not of that persuasion, then 4◊, not 4♣, would be RKB; 4♣ would be invitational. (Know your three-level agreement structure!)

## 4. Clubs, the fourth suit, is raised naturally

| Opener | Responder | |
|--------|-----------|---|
| 1◊ | 1♡ | 1. Raising the fourth suit is a game force. |
| 1♠ | 2♣ | 2. RKB 1430 — opener has not jumped or reversed. |
| 3♣¹ | 4♣² | |

## 5. After a natural 2NT response to a 1♣ opening

| Opener | Responder | |
|---|---|---|
| 1♣ | 2NT | |
| 4♣[1] | | 1. RKB 1430 — opener asking. |

This is a form of Gerber, but more precise because it is Keycard Gerber, clubs agreed, allowing one to ferret out club royalty.

Similarly here:

| Opener | Responder |
|---|---|
| 1◇ | 2NT |
| ? | |

In this sequence it makes sense to play 4◇ as RKB for diamonds. If you agree, a leap to 4♣ is free to be used for something else, perhaps a strong diamond-club two-suiter.

And now for a sequence that doesn't fit the mold: using 4♣ as RKB clubs *before* agreement.

## 6. After a strong, artificial, 2♣ opening and a natural 3♣ bid by responder

| Opener | Responder | |
|---|---|---|
| 2♣ | 3♣[1] | 1. Natural. |
| 4♣[2] | | 2. RKB 1430. |

| Opener | Responder | |
|---|---|---|
| 2♣ | 2♠ | |
| 2NT | 3♣[1] | 1. Natural. |
| 4♣[2] | | 2. RKB 1430. |

## 7. After NF three-level agreement when there are two or three unbid suits

| Opener | Responder | |
|---|---|---|
| 1♣ | 3♣[1] | 1. Limit raise. |
| 4♣[2] | | 2. RKB 1430. |

After non-forcing three-level agreement, four of the agreed minor can be used as RKB — *if there are two or three unbid suits.* The unbid suits can be used as game tries. After a game try, if either player returns to four of the agreed suit, that can be passed

| Opener | Responder | |
|--------|-----------|---|
| 1♡ | 2♣ | |
| 3♣ | 4♣¹ | 1. RKB 1430. |

Whether this is played as a game-forcing sequence or not, there are two unbid suits, so 4♣ can be used to ask for Keycards. If the sequence is not played as game-forcing, bidding an unbid suit is a game try.

# WHEN 4♣ IS NOT THE CLUB ASK

There are three possibilities:

## 1. After NF three-level agreement, zero or one unbid suits

Excluding the exceptions noted above, the ask is 4◇.

| Opener | Responder | |
|--------|-----------|---|
| 1◇ | 1♠ | 1. Non-forcing three-level agreement. |
| 2♣ | 3♣¹ | 2. RKB 1430. One unbid suit, 4♣ |
| 4◇² | | is invitational. |

| Opener | Responder | |
|--------|-----------|---|
| 1♣ | 1♡ | 1. Non-forcing three-level agreement. |
| 1♠ | 3♣¹ | 2. RKB 1430. One unbid suit, 4♣ |
| 4◇² | | is invitational. |

## 2. When the agreement is 4♣

When the agreement is 4♣, 4◇ is RKB with one exception. If diamonds is a first-bid suit, clubs a second-bid suit, and clubs have not been rebid or jump-supported, 4◇ is natural. To make a RKB ask, use the unbid major. If both majors have been bid, use the major that was bid secondarily.

| Opener | Responder | |
|--------|-----------|---|
| 1◇ | 1♡ | 1. Four-level agreement. |
| 2♣ | 4♣¹ | 2. RKB 1430. Even though diamonds is a first-bid suit, clubs |
| 4♠² | | have been jump-supported. |

| Opener | Responder | |
|--------|-----------|---|
| 1♠ | 2♣ | 1. Four-level agreement (not the ask). |
| 2◇ | 3NT | 2. RKB 1430. Clubs is a first-bid |
| 4♣¹ | 4◇² | suit and diamonds isn't — not that it would matter. |

| Opener | Responder | |
|--------|-----------|---|
| 1◇ | 1♠ | 1. RKB 1430. Diamonds is a first-bid suit, clubs a second-bid suit, and clubs have not been rebid or jump-supported. In that case 4◇ is natural and the unbid major can be used as RKB. |
| 3♣ | 4♣ | |
| 4♡¹ | | |

### 3. After a cuebid above four of the agreed suit in a splinter sequence

| Opener | Responder | |
|--------|-----------|---|
| 1♣ | 2♣¹ | 1. Natural or inverted. |
| 3◇² | 4◇³ | 2. GF splinter. |
| 4NT⁴ | | 3. Cuebid. |
| | | 4. RKB 1430. |

## ALL ABOUT DIAMONDS

The rules and sequences for club agreement sequences are identical for diamond agreement sequences. However, when diamonds is the agreed suit, the majority of the RKB asks are either 4◇ or 4♡. A bid of 4♣ is *never* used as RKB for diamonds. In addition, if hearts is a first-bid suit, 4♠ must be used instead of 4♡. If both hearts and spades are first-bid suits, 4NT is RKB for diamonds. Here are some of the applicable sequences.

### 1. After opener jumps to 2NT and receives GF three-level diamond preference

| Opener | Responder | |
|--------|-----------|---|
| 1◇ | 1♠ | 1. 4◇ would be a jump preference — a slam try, but not RKB. |
| 2NT | 3◇¹ | 2. RKB 3014 — opener has jumped. |
| 3♡ | 4◇² | |

Responder is unlimited in a game-forcing three-level agreement sequence. Given these two necessary requirements, 4◇ is RKB.

| Opener | Responder | |
|--------|-----------|---|
| 1◇ | 1♠ | |
| 2NT | 3◇ | |
| 3♡¹ | 4♣¹ | 1. Cuebid. |
| 4◇² | | 2. RKB 1430. |

This time opener is limited but responder has made a cuebid indicating slam interest. A limited hand can ask for Keycards in a game-forcing sequence after partner either splinters or makes a slam try.

The actual hands were:

| Opener | Responder | |
|---|---|---|
| ♠ K 5 | ♠ A Q 6 3 2 | |
| ♡ A K Q | ♡ 8 7 4 | |
| ◊ A K 10 7 3 | ◊ Q 8 5 4 | |
| ♣ 6 4 2 | ♣ 9 | |
| | | |
| 1◊ | 1♠ | |
| 2NT | 3◊ | 1. RKB 1430. |
| 3♡ | 4♣ | 2. '1'. |
| 4◊¹ | 4♡² | 3. Queen-ask (see below). |
| 4♠³ | 5◊⁴ | 4. ◊Q with no side-suit king (see |
| 6◊ | pass | below). |

After a '1' response to RKB, a return to responder's first-bid major (if it hasn't been rebid) is the queen-ask. If it has been rebid, it is to play. In addition, when responding to a queen-ask of 4♡ or 4♠, 4NT is the denial response. A return to five of the agreed minor shows the queen but denies a side-suit king.

## 2. When responder has both minors in response to a 1NT or 2NT opening bid

| Opener | Responder | |
|---|---|---|
| ♠ A K 7 | ♠ 4 | |
| ♡ Q 6 2 | ♡ 4 | |
| ◊ K J 7 5 | ◊ A Q 10 4 3 2 | |
| ♣ A K 8 | ♣ Q J 6 5 4 | |
| | | 1. Both minors. |
| 2NT | 3♠¹ | 2. The agreement |
| 4◊² | 4♡³ | 3. RKB 3014 — facing a 2NT |
| 4NT⁴ | 6◊ | opening bid. |
| pass | | 4. '4' including the ♣K. |

When a balanced hand faces a two-suiter and a Keycard ask ensues, the kings of both suits are included in the response. After four-level diamond agreement, 4♡ is RKB unless hearts is a first-bid suit; if it is, 4♠ is RKB. If both are first-bid suits, 4NT is RKB. Where there's a will, there's a way.

### 3. Opener wants to ask for Keycards after a natural 2NT response

| Opener | Responder | |
|--------|-----------|---|
| 1♢ | 2NT | |
| 4♢[1] | ? | 1. RKB 1430, diamonds agreed. |

If this agreement is in place (a jump rebid of four of opener's minor over the 2NT response is RKB), a jump to 4♣ can be reserved for something else — perhaps a strong two-suiter.

These are only ideas. If you don't agree, make up your own agreements. Just have *some* agreement!

### 4. After a 1♢ opening and a non-jump rebid of 2NT, responder wants to Keycard for diamonds

| Opener | Responder | |
|--------|-----------|---|
| ♠ K Q 4 | ♠ 5 | |
| ♡ Q J 4 2 | ♡ A 8 6 | |
| ♢ A J 9 5 | ♢ K Q 8 4 | |
| ♣ 10 3 | ♣ A K J 8 5 | 1. GF three-level diamond agreement. |
| 1♢ | 2♣ | 2. RKB 1430 by an unlimited hand. |
| 2NT | 3♢[1] | A direct jump to 4♢ over 2NT |
| 3NT | 4♢[2] | would not have been RKB. |
| 4♡[3] | 6♢ | 3. '1'. |

Once responder creates a three-level game-forcing agreement, he can later use four of the agreed minor to ask for Keycards. Opener, limited, cannot ask for Keycards after 3♢.

This is not a slam to write home about, but not easy to stay out of with that whale responder has. As for opener having short diamonds, the likelihood of that is less than 5%.

### 5. After a 1♡ or 1♠ opening, a 2♢ response and a non-jump rebid of 2NT, responder wants to Keycard for diamonds

After a 2NT rebid, a jump to 4♣ (Gerber) agrees responder's suit and demands a Keycard response.

| Opener | Responder |
|--------|-----------|
| ♠ Q 10 4 | ♠ A 6 2 |
| ♡ A Q 6 4 3 | ♡ 2 |
| ♢ 8 2 | ♢ A K Q J 7 5 4 3 |
| ♣ K Q 2 | ♣ 3 |

| Opener | Responder | |
|---|---|---|
| 1♡ | 2♢ | 1. Balanced minimum. |
| 2NT[1] | 4♣[2] | 2. RKB 1430 for diamonds. |
| 4♢[3] | 6♢[4] | 3. '1'. |
| | | 4. Going for it with nine solid tricks. There's something to be said for bidding 6NT so that the lead comes up to partner's hand. Another marginal slam. |

## 6. After opener jump shifts and responder rebids diamonds

| Opener | Responder | |
|---|---|---|
| 1♣ | 1♢ | |
| 2♠ | 3♢ | |
| 4♢[1] | | 1. RKB 1430. A 'perk'. |

After opener or responder jump shifts, and partner rebids a minor at the three-level, the jump-shifter can ask for Keycards via four of the last-bid minor without having to agree the suit first (see Chapter 14).

## 7. After opener reverses and responder agrees diamonds at the three-level in a GF auction

| a) Opener | Responder | b) Opener | Responder |
|---|---|---|---|
| 1♣ | 1♡ | 1♣ | 1♡ |
| 2♢ | 3♢[1] | 2♢ | 3♢[1] |
| 4♢[2] | | 3♣ | 4♢[2] |

1. Game-forcing three-level diamond agreement.
2. RKB: 1430 in (a), opener asking — 3014 in (b) after the reverse.

After three-level game-forcing diamond agreement, 4♢ by the unlimited hand is RKB. In these sequences, both hands are unlimited, so either can use 4♢ to ask for Keycards.

## 8. After a strong 2♣ opening and a natural 3♢ bid by responder

| Opener | Responder | |
|---|---|---|
| | | 1. Natural, |
| 2♣ | 3♢[1] | 2. RKB 1430. Bypassing the agreement stage after a 2♣ opening. |
| 4♢[2] | | |

| Opener | Responder | |
|--------|-----------|---|
| 2♣ | 2♠ | |
| 3♣ | 3◇[1] | 1. Natural, |
| 4◇[2] | | 2. RKB 1430. Another bypass. |

## 9. When 4♡ can't be used as RKB after four-level diamond agreement

| Opener | Responder | |
|--------|-----------|---|
| 1♡ | 2◇ | 1. RKB 3014 — opener has |
| 4◇ | 4♠[1] | jumped. |

After four-level diamond agreement when hearts is a first-bid suit, 4♡ is natural and 4♠ has to be used to ask for Keycards. When 4♠ is RKB, 4NT morphs into a spade cuebid. When an unbid or secondary suit is used to ask for Keycards, a bid of 4NT instead is a cuebid in that suit.

## 10. The death diamond agreement sequence

| Opener | Responder | |
|--------|-----------|---|
| 1♡ | 1♠ | |
| 2◇ | 4◇[1] | 1. The agreement, not the ask. |
| 4NT[2] | | 2. RKB 1430 — opener asking. |

When both hearts and spades are first-bid suits, 4NT is the last RKB off-ramp after four-level diamond agreement.

# CHAPTER 19

# TWO-LEVEL MINOR-SUIT NON-AGREEMENT

Two-level non-agreement sequences (opener's second bid is 2♣ or 2♦ or responder's first bid is 2♣ or 2♦) that lead to direct Keycard asks are few and far between. It's *far* from clear that there should even be a Keycard ask after two-level non-agreement — at least until the suit has been rebid. Yes, you *can* leave home without it.

Let's take a look at some sequences where opener rebids his original minor at the two-level. There aren't many.

## OPENER REBIDS HIS MINOR AT THE TWO-LEVEL

| a) **Opener** | **Responder** | b) **Opener** | **Responder** |
|---|---|---|---|
| 1♣ | 1♦ or 1♡ or 1♠ | 1♦ | 1♡ or 1♠ |
| 2♣ | ? | 2♦ | ? |

When clubs is the suit, Auction (a), a leap to 4♦ is RKB (1430). What do you lose? Not much. If the response is 1♦ you lose a natural jump to 4♦. When is the last time you jumped to 4♦ in this sequence? If the response is 1♡ or 1♠, you lose a 4♦ splinter. What do you gain? A lower-level Keycard ask.

When diamonds have been rebid, Auction (b), a leap to 4♡ is RKB unless hearts is your first-bid suit. When that happens, you have to use a leap to 4♠ as RKB (1430). What do you lose? A leap to 4♠ would normally be EKB (a jump one level higher than a splinter — see Chapter 16). Is it worth it? For you to decide. In this book, it's worth it — reluctantly.

## OPENER REBIDS HIS MINOR AFTER RESPONDER BIDS THE FOURTH SUIT

| c) **Opener** | **Responder** | d) **Opener** | **Responder** |
|---|---|---|---|
| 1♣ | 1♦ | 1♦ | 1♡ |
| 1♡ | 1♠ | 1♠ | 2♣ |
| 2♣ | ? | 2♦ | ? |

In each sequence opener rebids his original minor facing an unlimited responder. How does responder ask for Keycards in opener's minor? If clubs is the rebid suit, Auction (c), 4◇ is RKB. If diamonds is the rebid suit, Auction (d), 4♡ is RKB. However, if hearts is a first-bid suit, 4♠ is RKB.

### SORTING IT ALL OUT

| Opener | Responder |
|--------|-----------|
| ♠ Q 3 2 | ♠ 8 6 |
| ♡ 7 | ♡ A K 6 3 |
| ◇ A Q J | ◇ K 9 |
| ♣ Q J 10 8 7 4 | ♣ A K 6 5 2 |
| 1♣ | 1♡ |
| 2♣ | ? |

You have a terrific hand but lack a spade control. If you launch into RKB with 4◇ and find you are missing a Keycard, you can't be sure of the spade position. Lacking a control in an unbid suit, it is wiser to go another route. Perhaps a jump to 4♣, a game-forcing slam try, may elicit a spade cuebid, a Keycard ask, or a sign-off. Whatever, you will be better placed. In response to 4♣ opener would like to cuebid 4◇, but that is RKB! (Look back at the chapter on four-level agreement.) When a cuebid conflicts with the RKB ask, the ask takes precedence, and 4NT becomes a cuebid for the lost suit. Here, 4NT is a diamond cuebid, suggesting no spade control. Responder signs off in 5♣.

### HAVING CONTROLS IN BOTH UNBIDS

| Opener | Responder |
|--------|-----------|
| ♠ A J 2 | ♠ 8 6 |
| ♡ 7 | ♡ A K 6 3 |
| ◇ A 6 5 | ◇ K 9 |
| ♣ Q J 10 8 7 4 | ♣ A K 6 5 2 |
| 1♣ | 1♡ |
| 2♣ | 4♣ |
| ? | |

What do your bids mean? 4◇ is RKB (1430), 4♠ is a cuebid and 4NT is a diamond cuebid. If you cuebid one suit, partner will think you don't have a control in the other, unless you cuebid the other one later. You could try 4NT (diamond cuebid) and then cuebid 5♠, or you could cuebid 4♠ and then later 5◇. Or you could pack it all in and jump to 6♣ with your slammish minimum. These practical jumps to slam are recommended when you can't remember what all the other stuff means.

## CLOSE CALL

| Opener | Responder (you) | |
|---|---|---|
| ♠ J | ♠ A K 8 5 | |
| ♡ K J 5 | ♡ A 8 | |
| ◇ Q 4 2 | ◇ K 7 6 3 | 1. RKB (1430) — opener minimum. |
| ♣ K Q 10 6 5 4 | ♣ A J 7 | 2. '1'. |
| | | 3. Queen-ask. |
| 1♣ | 1♠ | 4. Yes, with the ♡K. |
| 2♣ | 4◇¹ | 5. Close call. A bid of 6NT is |
| 4♡² | 4♠³ | possible to protect the ◇K. On |
| 5♡⁴ | 6♣ or 6NT⁵ | the other hand, a heart ruff in |
| pass | | your hand might be critical. |

## LIKE FALLING OFF A LOG

| Opener | Responder (you) | |
|---|---|---|
| ♠ Q 9 3 | ♠ 6 | |
| ♡ 7 | ♡ A K 6 2 | |
| ◇ K Q 9 8 6 3 | ◇ A J 5 2 | |
| ♣ A J 4 | ♣ K Q 5 3 | |
| 1◇ | 1♡ | |
| 2◇ | 4♠¹ | |
| 5♡² | 6◇ | 1. RKB (1430) — opener minimum. |
| pass | | 2. '2 with'. |

In this auction, your leap to 4♠ is RKB (can't use 4♡, your first-bid suit).

## IT WORKS!

| Opener | Responder | |
|---|---|---|
| ♠ A 7 2 | ♠ K 9 | |
| ♡ A J 6 | ♡ K 4 | |
| ◇ K 10 9 8 5 4 | ◇ A 7 3 2 | |
| ♣ 5 | ♣ A K Q 8 2 | |
| | | 1. RKB (1430) — opener minimum. |
| 1◇ | 2♣ | 2. '3' (clearly not '0', please — try |
| 2◇ | 4♡¹ | to construct a '0' Keycard open- |
| 4NT² | 5♣³ | ing bid facing your hand). |
| 6◇⁴ | 7◇ | 3. Queen-ask. |
| pass | | 4. Expecting a ten-card trump fit. |

After an RKB response, the next-ranking side suit at the five-level, even if a previously-bid suit, is the queen-ask.

# NON-AGREEMENT SEQUENCES

Two-level non-agreement sequences that generate an immediate Keycard ask are rare enough after opener rebids his suit, but it's pushing the envelope to ask for Keycards when opener's *second* suit is clubs or diamonds. Nevertheless we stick to our guns: a leap to 4◇ by responder after a second-suit rebid of 2♣, and a leap to 4♡ after a second-suit rebid of 2◇, are both RKB (1430). Of course if hearts is responder's first-bid suit, 4♠ is the substitute RKB ask.

***Note:*** Though it may be tempting to play the jump raise from 2♣ to 4♣ or from 2◇ to 4◇ as RKB asks, those jumps are better played as natural slam tries, typically denying a control in an (or the) unbid suit. Asking for Keycards lacking a control in an unbid suit is usually not the way to go.

### THE JUMP RAISE

| Opener | Responder | |
|---|---|---|
| ♠ 7 | ♠ A K 6 4 3 | |
| ♡ A K 7 5 3 | ♡ 2 | |
| ◇ Q 8 6 | ◇ 5 2 | |
| ♣ K 8 5 4 | ♣ A Q J 7 3 | |
| 1♡ | 1♠ | 1. Game-forcing jump raise — |
| 2♣ | 4♣[1] | usually elicits a cuebid. |
| 4♡[2] | 4♠[2] | 2. Cuebid. |
| 5♣[3] | pass[3] | 3. No diamond control. |

If responder asks for Keycards before dealing with the diamond position, either '2' Keycard response leaves responder with a guess. For our purposes, jump raises and jump preferences are not played as Keycard asks, but rather as suit agreements.

## Opener rebids 2♣ after a 1♡ or 1♠ response

| Opener | Responder |
|---|---|
| 1◇ | 1♡ or 1♠ |
| 2♣ | ? |

If responder wishes to ask for Keycards after 2♣ non-agreement, he leaps to 4◇. Period.

TAKING CHARGE

| Opener | Responder |
|--------|-----------|
| ♠ 5 | ♠ A K 8 3 2 |
| ♡ K J 6 | ♡ A 7 |
| ◇ A J 6 4 3 | ◇ 2 |
| ♣ K 6 3 2 | ♣ Q J 7 5 4 |

| Opener | Responder | |
|--------|-----------|---|
| 1◇ | 1♠ | 1. RKB (1430) — opener hasn't |
| 2♣ | 4◇¹ | jumped or reversed. |
| 4NT² | 6♣³ | 2. '2 without'. |
| pass | | 3. One Keycard missing. |

Responder happens to have a suitable hand for a direct Keycard ask. However, if the hand is not suitable (most hands aren't), there are ways to agree clubs and get partner involved.

## After a 2♣ or 2◇ response to a an opening bid

| Opener | Responder |
|--------|-----------|
| 1◇ or1♡ or 1♠ | 2♣ |
| ? | |

Here we run into a 'systemic' dilemma. If 2♣ is considered a game force, opener can raise to 3♣, considered unlimited, and next bid 4♣ to ask for Keycards. (Three-level agreement sequences were discussed in Chapter 11.)

If 2♣ is not a game force and opener wishes to ask for Keycards, he should jump to 4◇. A raise to 3♣ is considered limited, meaning that a subsequent bid of 4♣ is not even forcing, let alone RKB. Remember, limited hands don't ask for Keycards unless partner splinters or makes a slam try.

A JOLTING RESPONSE

| Opener | Responder |
|--------|-----------|
| ♠ A K 7 6 5 2 | ♠ 4 |
| ♡ 8 | ♡ K 3 2 |
| ◇ 4 | ◇ K Q J 6 |
| ♣ A Q 9 8 4 | ♣ K 10 7 6 3 |

| Opener | Responder | |
|--------|-----------|---|
| 1♠ | 2♣¹ | 1. Not a game force. |
| 4◇² | 4♡³ | 2. RKB (1430) — opener asking. |
| 5♣⁴ | pass | 3. '1'. |
| | | 4. Two Keycards missing, probably |
| | | two aces. |

If 2♣ is a game force, opener can raise to 3♣ and then bid 4♣ to ask for Keycards next round even if responder bids 3NT (see Chapter 11). As it happens, all roads lead to Rome.

## THIS ONE IS EASIER

| Opener | Responder | |
|---|---|---|
| ♠ A K 5 2 | ♠ 7 6 | |
| ♡ 4 | ♡ A Q 7 | |
| ◇ A K Q 3 | ◇ 6 2 | |
| ♣ K 7 6 5 | ♣ A J 10 4 3 2 | |
| | | 1. Not a game force. |
| 1◇ | 2♣[1] | 2. RKB (1430) — opener asking. |
| 4◇[2] | 5♣[3] | 3. '2 with'. Opener expected to |
| 7♣ | pass | have at least four clubs. |

If 2♣ is a game force, opener can bid 3♣ and then 4♣ to ask for Keycards. Those that play Two-over-One can reserve the leap to 4◇ to mean something else as they can ask for Keycards via the raise sequence.

Because of 'heart and spade problems', RKB sequences follow different paths after a 2◇ response to a major-suit opening (see below).

## Opener bids diamonds as a second suit without reversing

| a) Opener | Responder | | b) Opener | Responder |
|---|---|---|---|---|
| 1♡ | 1♠ | | 1♡ or 1♠ | 2♣ |
| 2◇ | ? | | 2◇ | ? |

Say responder has been 'struck' big time and wishes to ask for Keycards right now. How is it done?

Responder (a) can't use either 4♡ or 4♠, first-bid suits, to ask for Keycards, as those bids are natural. That leaves 4NT. But jumps to 4NT when there has been no agreement simply ask for aces (unless you play 'last-bid suit'). This is truly the death sequence of all time. Responder might try leaping to 4◇, and then if possible bid 4NT, RKB (1430), next. Another possibility is to make a jump cuebid of 4♣, also a slam try agreeing diamonds, with the same RKB thought in mind.

Responder (b) has an easier road to RKB. If 2♣ is a game force (not a commercial), (b) can raise to 3◇, creating game-forcing three-level agreement, and then bid 4◇, RKB (1430). If 2♣ is not a game force, Responder (b) can jump to the four of the unbid major to ask for Keycards, diamonds agreed.

| Opener | Responder |
|---|---|
| ♠ J 8 7 | ♠ A 4 |
| ♡ K Q 6 3 2 | ♡ 7 5 |
| ◇ A Q J 3 | ◇ K 10 6 2 |
| ♣ 4 | ♣ A K J 5 3 |
| 1♡ | 2♣ |
| 2◇ | ? |

Here we go again. If 2♣ is a game force, raise to 3◇ and then ask for Keycards via 4◇. If 2♣ is not a game force, a leap to 4♠ is RKB (1430). However, you have other options. You can:

1. Bid 2♠, fourth suit, and then agree diamonds, creating game-forcing agreement.
2. Make a jump reverse to 3♠, a game-forcing diamond agreement slam try. Some play this as a splinter, others as control-showing after partner has bid two suits.
3. Jump raise partner's minor to the four-level, another slam try.

## Opener reverses

| Opener | Responder (you) |
|---|---|
| 1♣ | 1♡ or 1♠ |
| 2◇ | ? |

Say you want to Keycard in diamonds, what can you do? After partner reverses there is no need to jump into outer space to ask for Keycards with a fit. Simply make an unlimited game-forcing raise. Here, a raise to 3◇ (or a preference to 3♣) is an unlimited game force. After that it's a piece of cake to ask for Keycards — use four of the agreed minor. Coming up.

OPENER REVERSES AGAIN

| Opener | Responder | |
|---|---|---|
| ♠ 3 | ♠ K Q 7 5 4 2 | |
| ♡ A K 8 | ♡ 6 | |
| ◇ K J 7 2 | ◇ A Q 8 5 4 | |
| ♣ A Q 5 4 2 | ♣ 7 | |
| 1♣ | 1♠ | 1. Game-forcing three-level |
| 2◇ | 3◇[1] | agreement (heaven on earth). |
| 3NT | 4◇[2] | 2. RKB (3014) — opener has |
| 4NT[3] | 6◇ | reversed. |
| pass | | 3. '2 without'. |

## A 2◇ response to a major-suit opening

| Opener (you) | Responder |
|---|---|
| 1♡ or 1♠ | 2◇ |
| ? | |

Say you wish to Keycard in diamonds. If 2◇ is a game force, you can raise to 3◇ and then bid 4◇. If you don't play 2◇ as a game force, you can leap to four of the unbid major to ask for Keycards.

### TWO WAYS TO GO

| Opener (you) | Responder |
|---|---|
| ♠ K Q 6 3 2 | ♠ A |
| ♡ 7 | ♡ A 6 5 4 |
| ◇ A K 9 8 4 | ◇ Q J 7 6 5 2 |
| ♣ K J | ♣ 8 7 |
| 1♠ | 2◇ |
| ? | |

If 2◇ is a game force, raise to 3◇ and then bid 4◇ (RKB 1430). If 2◇ is not a game force, you have to leap to 4♡ to ask for Keycards directly. Partner responds 5◇, '2 with', and you bid a cheery 6◇. Tell me you're not having fun.

### SAVING TIME

| Opener | Responder | |
|---|---|---|
| ♠ A K Q J 3 | ♠ 7 6 | |
| ♡ A | ♡ 9 7 4 | |
| ◇ 10 9 5 2 | ◇ A K Q 7 3 | |
| ♣ A 6 2 | ♣ Q 5 4 | |
| | | 1. RKB (1430) — not playing 2◇ |
| 1♠ | 2◇ | as a game force. |
| 4♡[1] | 5◇[2] | 2. '2 with'. |
| 7◇[3] | pass | 3. Should be thirteen easy tricks. |

## THE BOTTOM LINE

- After opener rebids 2♣, 4◇ is RKB. Period.
- After opener rebids 2◇, 4♡ is RKB unless hearts is responder's first-bid suit: in that case 4♠ is RKB.
- If an original response of 2♣ or 2◇ is played as a game force, opener can raise to three of the last-bid minor, and follow up by bidding four of the agreed suit as RKB. Players who use this method should consider playing a direct leap to four of the unbid major as an Exclusion ask.
- If the original 2◇ response is not a game force, opener can jump to four of the unbid major to ask for Keycards.
- Jump raises from 2♣ to 4♣ or from 2◇ to 4◇ are slam-invitational raises, not RKB asks.

The good news is that direct Keycard asks at this level are few and far between. Keep the faith.

# CHAPTER 20

# THREE-LEVEL NON-AGREEMENT

Most Keycard asks follow agreement. However, Keycard asks can follow non-agreement. For a Keycard ask to be possible after three-level minor-suit non-agreement, the suit must have been rebid or be a presumed six-card suit. In addition, the asker must be unlimited.

A three-level non-agreement bid is either a one-round force (F), game-forcing (GF), or not forcing (NF).

## SEQUENCES WHERE THE LAST BID IS NOT FORCING

a)
| Opener | Responder |
|--------|-----------|
| 1♣ | 1♡ |
| 2♣ | 2♢ |
| 3♣ | ? |

b)
| Opener | Responder |
|--------|-----------|
| 1♠ | 2♢¹ |
| 2♡ | 3♢(NF) |
| ? | |

1. Not a game force.

c)
| Opener | Responder |
|--------|-----------|
| 1♡ | 1NT |
| 2♢ | 3♣¹ |
| ? | |

d)
| Opener | Responder |
|--------|-----------|
| 1♡ | 1NT |
| 2♠ | 3♣(NF) |
| ? | |

1. Six-card suit presumed.

Some play 3♣ in sequence (d) as forcing for one round. In any event, it is supposed to show a six-card suit, minimum.

e)
| Opener | Responder |
|--------|-----------|
| 1♣ | 1♢ |
| 1♡ | 3♢(NF) |
| ? | |

These sequences all conform. A minor has been bid at the three-level showing a six-card suit (minimum), the last bid is not forcing and partner is unlimited. Although it is unlikely that (c) or (e) will generate an immediate Keycard ask, it's possible with the others.

After a three-level non-forcing-non-agreement sequence, this is the Keycard scene:

1) After 3♣ non-agreement, a leap to 4◇ is RKB.
2) After 3◇ non-agreement, a leap to 4♡ is RKB.
3) A raise to four of the last-bid minor is invitational.

## TWO LIMITED HANDS

| Opener | Responder | |
|--------|-----------|---|
| 1♡ | 2◇ | |
| 2♡ | 3◇¹ | 1. NF. |
| 4♡² | | 2. Natural. |

The 3◇ bid isn't forcing and 4♡ is not RKB. Why? When both hands are limited there is no Keycard ask unless one of them splinters.

## LIKE FALLING OFF A LOG

| Opener | Responder | |
|--------|-----------|---|
| ♠ A K 6 4 3 | ♠ 5 | |
| ♡ K Q J 4 | ♡ 7 2 | |
| ◇ 8 | ◇ A 6 5 2 | |
| ♣ A 8 5 | ♣ K Q J 6 4 3 | 1. Not a game force. |
| | | 2. NF. |
| 1♠ | 2♣¹ | 3. RKB (1430) — a non-forcing |
| 2♡ | 3♣² | three-level non-agreement |
| 4◇³ | 5♣⁴ | sequence. |
| 6♣ | pass | 4. '2 with'. |

Opener has exactly what the doctor ordered for a Keycard ask: 1) a trump fit; 2) controls in the unbid suits; 3) a chunky side suit.

## DON'T GO NUTS

| Opener (you) | Responder | |
|--------------|-----------|---|
| ♠ A Q 5 2 | ♠ 6 4 3 | 1. NF. |
| ♡ 3 | ♡ A 7 6 | 2. RKB (1430) — opener asking. |
| ◇ K J | ◇ A Q 10 7 3 2 | 3. '2 with'. |
| ♣ A K 10 4 3 2 | ♣ 5 | 4. Once partner turns up with both |
| | | red aces plus the ◇Q, don't |
| 1♣ | 1◇ | press your luck. Partner can't also |
| 1♠ | 3◇¹ | have the ♣Q or the ♠K and still |
| 4♡² | 5◇³ | make a non-forcing 3◇ bid. |
| 6◇⁴ | pass | Forget seven; they may lead a |
| | | spade attacking dummy's entry to |
| | | the clubs. |

Here are several other non-forcing non-agreement sequences that could lead to direct Keycard asks. In each sequence opener has made a non-forcing jump rebid, and is facing an unlimited responder:

| a) Opener | Responder | | b) Opener | Responder |
|---|---|---|---|---|
| 1♣ | 1♦ or 1♡ or 1♠ | | 1♦ | 1♡ or 1♠ |
| 3♣ | ? | | 3♦ | ? |

| c) Opener | Responder |
|---|---|
| 1♣ | 1♦ |
| 1♡ | 1♠ |
| 3♣ | ? |

If Responder (a) wants to ask for Keycards, the ask is 4♦ –- 3014, opener has jumped. After opener has jumped, a raise to the four-level is forcing — a debatable agreement.

If Responder (b) wishes to ask for Keycards, the ask is 4♡ — 3014, once again because opener has jumped. In this sequence rebids of 3♡ and 4♦ are both forcing. Now, if only partner remembers!

In (c) 4♦ is RKB (3014 — opener has jumped); a 3♦ rebid is forcing.

## THE BOTTOM LINE

- After three-level club NF non-agreement, an unlimited opener can ask for Keycards by leaping to 4♦. A raise to 4♣ is NF and a leap to 4NT is natural.
- After three-level diamond NF non-agreement, an unlimited opener can ask for Keycards by leaping to 4♡. A raise to 4♦ is NF and a leap to 4NT is natural.
- If opener jump rebids a minor to the three-level, a four-level raise by an unlimited responder is forcing; a leap to 4♦ over 3♣ is RKB, a leap to 4♡ over 3♦ is RKB and 4NT is natural.

## RESPONDER SPLINTERS AFTER OPENER MAKES A NF JUMP REBID

A minimum limited opener cannot ask for Keycards unless responder splinters or makes another sort of slam try. A limited responder also cannot ask for Keycards unless opener splinters or makes another sort of slam try.

## WHOA NELLIE!

| Opener | Responder | |
|---|---|---|
| ♠ K Q 8 | ♠ 4 | 1. Splinter agreeing diamonds (4♡ would be RKB). |
| ♡ K 3 | ♡ A 7 6 5 2 | |
| ◇ A Q 10 9 6 4 3 | ◇ 7 5 2 | 2. Wrong hand for slam, 5 wasted HCP facing a singleton. Furthermore, a Keycard ask of 4NT puts you in la-la land if partner responds 5♡, '2 without'. |
| ♣ 8 | ♣ A J 6 5 | |
| 1◇ | 1♡ | |
| 3◇ | 4♠[1] | |
| 5◇[2] | pass | |

A splinter jump to 4♠, clubs agreed, comes with a reminder, more of a promise, actually an *oath in blood,* of at least one Keycard. After a 4♠ splinter, the only Keycard ask is 4NT (1430). A '0' response of 5◇ is guaranteed to leave a 4NT bidder with three Keycards in a very foul mood.

## A PLETHORA OF TENS

| Opener | Responder | |
|---|---|---|
| ♠ A 10 5 | ♠ 7 | 1. Some would bid 1♡. |
| ♡ 10 | ♡ 8 6 5 4 | |
| ◇ K 4 2 | ◇ A Q J 10 | 2. Splinter to 4♠, clubs agreed, promising at least one Keycard in blood. (4◇ instead is RKB — 3014.) |
| ♣ A K Q 10 5 3 | ♣ 8 7 6 2 | |
| 1♣ | 1◇[1] | 3. RKB (1430) — opener asking. |
| 3♣ | 4♠[2] | 4. The '1'. |
| 4NT[3] | 5♣[4] | 5. Going for it. |
| 6♣[5] | pass | |

## TWO LIMITED HANDS — A SPLINTER STRIKE!

| Opener | Responder | |
|---|---|---|
| ♠ 6 | ♠ A J 4 | |
| ♡ 7 5 3 | ♡ 9 | |
| ◇ A J 6 | ◇ K Q 10 5 4 3 2 | |
| ♣ A K J 6 4 2 | ♣ 5 3 | |
| 1♣ | 1◇ | 1. NF. |
| 2♣ | 3◇[1] | 2. Splinter. |
| 4♠[2] | 4NT[3] | 3. RKB (3014) — opener has jumped. |
| 5♡[4] | 6◇ | 4. '2 without'. |
| pass | | |

Two limited hands — both 2♣ and 3◇ are non-forcing. Neither hand can dream of asking for Keycards unless the other splinters. Sure enough opener splinters, catching responder with the 'right' hand to ask for Keycards: a heart control, the ace of the singleton suit plus good trumps — perfect.

# GF PERK SEQUENCES (THE MINOR HAS BEEN REBID)

***Reminder:*** If partner is unlimited, a leap to 4◇ over 3♣ is RKB, a leap to 4♡ over 3◇ is RKB, a single raise is forcing and a leap to 4NT is natural.

If the opener has a super-strong hand (e.g. he has reversed or jump-shifted), he has a 'perk' — he can use the raise of the known six-card minor as a Keycard ask rather than just a forcing raise. This one of the very few times that the raise is the ask. This low-level ask saves a step and allows for further low-level asks. Other 'perk' sequences were discussed in Chapter 14. Hang in there.

| Opener (you) | Responder |
|---|---|
| 1◇ | 2♣ |
| 2♡ | 3♣ |
| 4♣ | |

RKB (1430). You have reversed and partner has rebid a minor. You are exercising your space-saving privilege.

| Opener (you) | Responder |
|---|---|
| 1♣ | 1◇ |
| 2♠ | 3◇ |
| 4◇ | |

This time you have jump-shifted and partner has rebid a minor; again the raise is the ask.

| Opener (you) | Responder |
|---|---|
| 1♠ | 2◇ |
| 3♣ | 3◇ |
| ? | |

If your agreement is that 3♣ shows extras, then 4◇ is RKB (1430). If 3♣ does not show extras, 4♡ is RKB (1430).

## AFTER OPENER REVERSES

| Opener | Responder | |
|---|---|---|
| ♠ A K 6 5 | ♠ Q 3 | |
| ♡ A K 7 5 2 | ♡ 4 | |
| ◇ K 8 3 | ◇ A Q J 7 6 4 2 | 1. RKB (1430) — opener asking. |
| ♣ 9 | ♣ J 6 5 | 2. '1'. |
| | | 3. Queen-ask. |
| 1♡ | 2◇ | 4. Confirms the ◇Q, denies a |
| 2♠ | 3◇ | side-suit king, but shows an |
| 4◇[1] | 4♡[2] | extra, the seventh diamond. A |
| 4♠[3] | 5NT[4] | 4NT response would deny the |
| 6◇ | pass | queen. |

## LOOKING FOR A HOME RUN, SETTLING FOR A TRIPLE

| Opener | Responder |
|--------|-----------|
| ♠ 6 | ♠ A 8 3 |
| ♡ A Q 6 5 2 | ♡ 4 |
| ◇ K 7 5 | ◇ A Q 10 6 4 3 |
| ♣ A K 7 5 | ♣ 4 3 2 |
| 1♡ | 2◇ |
| 3♣¹ | 3◇ |
| 4◇² | 5♣³ |
| 5NT⁴ | 6◇⁵ |
| pass | |

1. Shows extras.
2. RKB (1430). A perk for a player who has reversed (or jump shifted). If 3♣ does not show extras after a two-level response, 4◇ is a forcing raise and 4♡ is RKB (1430).
3. '2 with'.
4. A grand slam try, not a king-ask. Looking for an undisclosed extra.
5. Can't find one.

A 5NT ask in a minor-suit auction is not a king-ask, it is a grand slam try looking for an 'extra'. In this sequence the ♣Q or extra diamond length qualifies.

## AFTER OPENER JUMP-SHIFTS

| Opener | Responder |
|--------|-----------|
| ♠ A K J 4 | ♠ 6 |
| ♡ 5 | ♡ A 8 6 3 |
| ◇ Q 7 2 | ◇ J 10 9 6 5 4 3 |
| ♣ A K Q 5 2 | ♣ 4 |
| 1♣ | 1◇ |
| 2♠ | 3◇ |
| 4◇¹ | 4♡² |
| 5◇³ | pass |

1. RKB (1430). Noblesse oblige — the jump shifter can ask for Keycards using a raise of a rebid minor.
2. Sorry partner, only '1'.
3. Listen, I'm glad you have '1'.

## AFTER THE FOURTH SUIT

No perks for responder when it comes to RKB asks after the fourth suit followed by opener repeating a minor suit at the three-level. A raise is natural and forcing; a jump to 4◇ over 3♣ or a jump to 4♡ over 3◇ is RKB (1430).

| Opener | Responder |
|--------|-----------|
| 1♡ | 1♠ |
| 2♣ | 2◇¹ |
| 3♣² | ?³ |

1. Fourth suit — not considered natural.
2. Three-level forcing non-agreement facing an unlimited hand.
3. A raise to 4♣ is forcing and a leap to 4◇ is RKB (1430).

## The raise to the four-level

Overlooking 'perk' sequences, the Keycard ask does not vary whether the non-agreement is game-forcing or not (4◇ after 3♣ and 4♡ after 3◇) — all that matters is that the asker is unlimited. What does change is the meaning of the raise to the four-level.

1. If the sequence is not game-forcing, a single raise is invitational.
2. If the sequence is game-forcing, a single raise is forcing.

Then we have this:

OPENER MAKES A NON-FORCING JUMP REBID

| Opener (you) | Responder |
|---|---|
| ♠ K 6 2 | ♠ 5 4 3 |
| ♡ 7 | ♡ A 9 2 |
| ◇ A J 5 | ◇ K Q 10 6 3 |
| ♣ A K Q 6 5 4 | ♣ 3 2 |
| 1♣ | 1◇ |
| 3♣ | 3◇ |
| ? | |

Let's start with the fact that 3◇ is forcing. Whether it is game-forcing or not is a moot point. In any case after opener has jumped, a raise to the four-level (4◇) is forcing and opener can ask for Keycards via a jump to 4♡(1430). A rebid of 4♠ is a splinter. A leap to 4NT should be a heart splinter, the lost splinter, since it can't be natural. But let's not go there, let's not go anywhere near there.

Say you jump to 4♡, then responder bids 5◇, '2 with', and you're at the crossroads. Should you bid 6◇ exposing your ♠K or try 6♣ (or 6NT) to protect the king and hope clubs run?

RESPONDER MAKES A NON-FORCING JUMP REBID

| Opener (you) | Responder | |
|---|---|---|
| ♠ K 6 2 | ♠ 4 3 | |
| ♡ 7 | ♡ K 9 2 | |
| ◇ A J 5 | ◇ K Q 10 6 3 2 | |
| ♣ A K Q 6 5 4 | ♣ 3 2 | |
| 1♣ | 1◇ | |
| 3♣ | 3◇ | |
| 4♡[1] | | 1. RKB 1430. |

On this hand, the response is 4♠ showing '1'. This time you are probably off two aces and have to decide whether to play 5◇ from partner's side or 5♣ from your side. Good luck.

## Raising the last-bid minor to the four-level in a fourth-suit auction

| Opener | Responder | |
|--------|-----------|---|
| 1♠ | 2♣ | 1. Fourth suit |
| 2◊ | 2♡[1] | 2. Three-level forcing non-agreement facing an unlimited hand. |
| 3◊[2] | ?[3] | 3. After the fourth suit, a raise of a rebid minor is forcing and a leap to 4♡ over 3◊ is RKB (1430). |

TWO WAYS TO GO

| Opener | Responder | |
|--------|-----------|---|
| ♠ A J | ♠ K Q 5 3 | |
| ♡ 6 | ♡ A K J 5 2 | 1. Fourth suit. |
| ◊ K Q 10 3 2 | ◊ 4 | 2. RKB (1430) — opener hasn't reversed or jumped; 3◊ would be forcing (if responder had diamonds). A raise to 4♣ here (after bidding the fourth suit) is also considered forcing. |
| ♣ Q 7 6 4 3 | ♣ A J 2 | |
| 1◊ | 1♡ | |
| 2♣ | 2♠[1] | |
| 3♣ | 4◊[2] | |
| 4♡[3] | 5♣[4] | 3. '1'. |
| pass | | 4. To play. |

DOWN TO THE WIRE

| Opener | Responder | |
|--------|-----------|---|
| ♠ 5 3 | ♠ A K 6 2 | |
| ♡ A Q 7 4 3 | ♡ K 5 | 1. Fourth suit. |
| ◊ 7 | ◊ A Q 6 2 | 2. Three-level non-agreement facing an unlimited hand. |
| ♣ A J 4 3 2 | ♣ K 7 6 | 3. RKB (1430) — opener minimum. |
| 1♡ | 1♠ | 4. '2 without'. |
| 2♣ | 2◊[1] | 5. At matchpoints 6NT is clear. At IMPs there is something to be said for 6♣ as a heart ruff(s) may be needed. |
| 3♣[2] | 4◊[3] | |
| 4NT[4] | ?[5] | |
| pass | | |

TOURNAMENT HAND

After three-level diamond non-agreement, game-forcing or not, a leap to
4♡ is RKB. Ditto for 4◇ over 3♣.

| Opener | Responder | |
|---|---|---|
| ♠ 8 7 5 | ♠ A 4 | |
| ♡ — | ♡ A K 6 5 4 2 | |
| ◇ A K 7 6 3 2 | ◇ J 8 4 | 1. Fourth suit. |
| ♣ A Q 5 2 | ♣ K 4 | 2. Three-level non-agreement facing |
| | | an unlimited hand . |
| 1◇ | 1♡ | 3. RKB (1430) — opener hasn't |
| 2♣ | 2♠¹ | jumped or reversed. |
| 3◇² | 4♡³ | 4. '3'. |
| 4NT⁴ | 5♣⁵ | 5. Queen-ask. |
| 5◇⁶ | 6◇ | 6. Negative. |

GOLD CUP FINAL, GREAT BRITAIN

| Opener | Responder | |
|---|---|---|
| ♠ 6 5 | ♠ A K Q 3 | |
| ♡ J 10 5 | ♡ A 4 2 | 1. Three-level non-agreement facing |
| ◇ A K Q 10 6 2 | ◇ J | an unlimited hand. |
| ♣ J 3 | ♣ A K 10 5 2 | 2. RKB (1430) — opener hasn't |
| | | reversed or jumped. |
| 1◇ | 2♣ | 3. '2 with'. |
| 2◇ | 2♠ | 4. Thirteen tricks if opener has |
| 3◇¹ | 4♡² | either seven diamonds, the ♠J, |
| 5◇³ | 7◇⁴ | or the ♣Q, or if the clubs set up |
| pass | | for one extra trick. |

## When a minor is introduced for the first time at the three-level

When either opener or responder introduces a minor as a second-bid suit at
the three-level, no Keycard ask in that suit until the minor has been rebid.

| Opener | Responder |
|---|---|
| 1♠ | 2♡ |
| 3♣ or 3◇ | ? |

| Opener | Responder |
|---|---|
| 1♡ | 1♠ |
| 3♣ or 3◇ | ? |

| Opener | Responder |
|---|---|
| 1♡ | 2◇ |
| 2♡ | 3♣ |
| ? | |

In none of these sequences can '?' ask for Keycards in the last-bid minor. With support for a last-bid minor at the three-level, be patient. Find out more about partner's hand. Partner might even surprise you by having support for your suit. He also might surprise you by having a three-card suit (see below)!

There are several ways to show a fit with slam on the brain.

1) Bid the fourth suit and then support partner.
2) Raise partner's suit to the four-level, forcing.
3) Jump in the fourth suit, a serious slam try.

A jump to 4NT is natural. It is the one strength-showing bid that does not promise support for the last-bid minor — the reason for not being able to use a jump to 4NT to ask for aces or Keycards.

OKBRIDGE SPECIAL

Speaking of having a fit with partner's second suit, this hand was presented to me as a bidding problem. You try it:

As opener you hold:

♠ A 6    ♡ A Q J 10 7 3    ◇ —    ♣ 7 6 4 3 2

You open 1♡, partner responds 2◇, you rebid 2♡, and partner bids 3♣.
Now what?

| Opener | Responder |
|---|---|
| ♠ A 6 | ♠ 7 4 2 |
| ♡ A Q J 10 7 3 | ♡ 4 2 |
| ◇ — | ◇ A K J 10 6 |
| ♣ 7 6 4 3 2 | ♣ A 8 5 |
| 1♡ | 2◇ |
| 2♡ | 3♣ |
| ? | |

I thought a fit-showing jump cuebid of 4♠, a slam try, would fit the bill just right. Hah! Heaven only knows what partner would do. The player who had the hand didn't do much better. He raised to 4♣, forcing, and when partner tried to get out at 4♡, he 'signed off' in 6♣! Clubs broke 4-1, the heart finesse was off, and no game contract could be made!

What does it all mean? It means that it's easier to bid when you can see both hands.

## FAR OUT?

| Opener | Responder |
|---|---|
| ♠ A Q J 5 4 | ♠ 7 |
| ♡ 4 2 | ♡ A Q J 6 5 |
| ◇ A 5 | ◇ K Q J 3 |
| ♣ A K 4 3 | ♣ Q 6 2 |
| 1♠ | 2♡ |
| 3♣ | 4NT[1] |
| 6NT | pass |

1. Natural after three-level non-agreement (14+ to 16 HCP). If interested in a club slam, raise to 4♣ or bid 3◇ and then support clubs. What you can't do is ask for Keycards until the minor has been rebid.

## NEAT BID

| Opener | Responder |
|---|---|
| ♠ Q 6 | ♠ A K J |
| ♡ 4 | ♡ K Q J 5 2 |
| ◇ A K Q J 7 5 3 | ◇ 4 2 |
| ♣ K 8 5 | ♣ Q J 6 |
| 1◇ | 1♡ |
| 3◇ | 4NT[1] |
| pass[2] | |

1. Natural. After the jump rebid, a raise to 4◇ is forcing and a leap to 4♡ is RKB, 3014 (opener has jumped). In this sequence 3♡ is forcing. Notice that the hand is too strong to rebid 3NT.
2. Declines with a minimum point count — a reasonable chance the hand is off two aces.

Even when interference rears its ugly head, the immediate jump to 4NT is natural. For example, as responder, you hold:

♠ K Q 5   ♡ A K J 6 2   ◇ J 8   ♣ Q J 7

| Opener | Oppt. | Responder | Oppt. |
|---|---|---|---|
| 1◇ | 1♠ | 2♡ | pass |
| 3♣ | pass | ? | |

Try 4NT, natural, the bid that best describes your hand. In this sequence 3♣ does not promise extras because your 2♡ response was made in a suit that was higher ranking than your partner's suit. An important bidding point.

# THE BOTTOM LINE

- To ask for Keycards after three-level non-agreement, forcing or not forcing, the last-bid minor having been rebid, or guaranteeing a six-card suit if not rebid, partner must be unlimited. If all of this is in place, the RKB ask is a leap to 4♢ over 3♣ or to 4♡ over 3♢

- If a last bid of 3♣ or 3♢ is not forcing (unless opener has made a jump rebid to 3♣ or 3♢), a raise is also not forcing. After a jump rebid, a raise is forcing.

- If a last bid of 3♣ or 3♢ is forcing, a raise to the four-level is forcing.

- If opener or responder introduces a minor at the three-level as a second-bid suit, partner cannot ask for Keycards in that suit...yet.

- If opener has reversed or opener or responder has jump shifted, and partner rebids a minor at the three-level, a raise of the minor by Mr. Big is RKB. A perk.

- After the fourth suit, a raise of a rebid minor to the four-level is forcing.

# CHAPTER 21

# THE 'BROKEN RECORD': FOUR-LEVEL NON-AGREEMENT

## FOUR-LEVEL NON-AGREEMENT, NOTRUMP NOT IN THE PICTURE

When a player bids and rebids the same minor all the way to the four-level, perhaps mentioning the suit three or four times, perhaps bidding and then jumping in the suit, perhaps sneaking one other suit in there, he is presumed to have a 'reasonable' suit. (Good thinking.) However, it doesn't have to be a solid suit. It could be a one- or two-loser seven- or eight-card suit. If the suit has been bid and then jump rebid, partner should assumes either a solid suit or a seven- or eight-card one-loser suit with an outside entry.

The player who makes a lone ranger venture will henceforth be called 'broken record' (BR). Either opener or responder can be a BR. When BR's last bid of 4♣ or 4♦ is not forcing and partner is limited, there is no Keycard ask. However, if BR's partner is unlimited, a Keycard ask may be available.

The rules are simple and depend upon the number of unbid suits. (A suit bid by an opponent is considered unbid.) If there are no unbid suits, the fourth suit can be used to ask for Keycards. If clubs is the fourth suit and diamonds the BR suit, the asker can use his second suit to ask for Keycards. The idea is not to use 5♣ to ask for Keycards...ever.

| Opener | Responder | |
|--------|-----------|---|
| 1♡ | 2♢ | |
| 2♠ | 3♢ | |
| 4♣ | 4♢[1] | 1. BR in action. |
| ? | | |

There are no unbid suits, but clubs is the fourth suit and since 5♣ cannot be used to ask for Keycards, opener can use his second suit, spades, to ask. So 4♠ in this sequence is Keycard for diamonds, and 4NT is to play.

If there is one unbid suit, that suit is used to ask for Keycards. If clubs is the unbid suit, again the asker can use his second suit as RKB.

| Opener | Responder | |
|--------|-----------|---|
| 1♡ | 2◇ | |
| 2♠ | 4◇¹ | 1. BR suit. |
| ? | | |

The unbid suit is clubs so opener can use his second suit as RKB. Once again 4♠ is RKB (1430) and 4NT is to play.

If there are two unbid suits, there is no RKB ask, just cuebids. Finally, 4NT is to play opposite any BR bid.

Now you try it. Let's look at some BR sequences paying attention to who's limited, who isn't, and the number of unbid suits. Your job is to determine what the RKB ask is, assuming one is available. Hang in there. It'll be over soon.

| a) **Opener** | **Responder** | b) **Opener** | **Responder** |
|---------------|---------------|---------------|---------------|
| 1♣ | 1♡ | 1◇ | 2♣ |
| 2♣ | 3♡ | 2◇ | 2♠ |
| 4♣ | ? | 4◇ | ? |

| c) **Opener** | **Responder** |
|---------------|---------------|
| 1◇ | 2♣ |
| 2◇ | 2♠ |
| 3◇ | 3♡ |
| ? | |

In Auction (a), both hands are limited. Neither 2♣ nor 3♡ (nor 4♣ for that matter) is forcing. When both hands are limited, there are no RKB asks.

In Auction (b), there is one unbid suit, hearts, and responder is unlimited so 4♡ is RKB (1430) — opener not having jumped or reversed.

In Auction (c), all suits have been bid, and responder is still unlimited, so responder's second suit, spades, can be used to ask for Keycards (1430).

Try this one for size: is the last bid in this sequence forcing? If it is, what is the ask?

| Opener | Responder |
|--------|-----------|
| 1◇ | 1♡ |
| 2◇ | 2♠ |
| 3◇ | 4♣ |
| 4◇ | ? |

The sequence is forcing. Responder is trying for slam! All suits have been bid and clubs is the fourth suit so the asker's second suit is used as RKB: 4♠ (1430) is the winner.

After BR makes a forcing 4♣ or 4◇ bid, responses of 4NT and a raise to game are to play. Either may be a plea for mercy.

## 4NT by BR after partner cuebids at the four-level

| Opener | Responder | |
|---|---|---|
| 1♡ | 2◇ | 1. A BR suit. |
| 3♡ | 4◇[1] | 2. Cuebid. Two unbid suits, so no |
| 4♠[2] | 4NT? | Keycard ask available. |

When there are two (or three) unbid suits and BR's partner cuebids, this is the story:

> If BR is limited, 4NT shows the king of the unbid suit.
> If BR is unlimited, 4NT is RKB. In this sequence BR is unlimited so 4NT is RKB (3014)— opener has jumped.

### A TOUGHIE

| Opener | Responder |
|---|---|
| ♠ 7 | ♠ 5 4 3 |
| ♡ 3 2 | ♡ A K Q 6 |
| ◇ A K J 10 6 4 2 | ◇ 5 3 |
| ♣ A 6 2 | ♣ Q J 10 9 |

| Opener | Oppt. | Responder | Oppt. |
|---|---|---|---|
| 1◇ | 1♠ | dbl[1] | 3♠[2] |
| 4◇ | pass | 4♡[3] | pass |
| 4♠[3] | pass | 5◇[4] | pass |
| pass[5] | pass | | |

1. Negative.
2. Preemptive.
3. Cuebid facing a BR suit (three unbid suits including spades).
4. No more to say.
5. Nervous time.

Responder, unlimited, is worth one cuebid. If opener can't take over, it is best to bow out. Opener, minimum, is reluctant to take charge so cuebids and then bows out.

### A VICTORY FOR THE METHODS

| Opener | Responder |
|---|---|
| ♠ A K 5 4 | ♠ 2 |
| ♡ A K 6 4 3 | ♡ 2 |
| ◇ Q J 5 | ◇ 7 6 4 2 |
| ♣ 2 | ♣ A K Q J 5 4 3 |
| 1♡ | 2♣ |
| 2♠ | 4♣[1] |
| 4NT[2] | pass[3] |

1. After opener jumps or reverses, a jump rebid by responder normally shows a solid suit, lacking an outside ace or king, or a one-loser suit with an outside ace.
2. If partner remembers what he is supposed to have, we are off the ◇AK.
3. Insults, insults, insults. When will it ever end?

## TROUBLE FROM A LOCAL TOURNAMENT

| Opener (you) | Responder | |
|---|---|---|
| ♠ A 6 4 3 | ♠ J 5 | |
| ♡ 7 | ♡ A 6 2 | |
| ◇ A K J 10 6 3 2 | ◇ — | |
| ♣ A | ♣ K Q J 10 7 4 3 2 | 1. BR suit if ever there was one. |
| | | 2. The unbid suit — RKB (1430) for |
| 1◇ | 2♣ | clubs. |
| 2♠ | 4♣¹ | 3. '2 with'. |
| 4♡² | 5◇³ | 4. You don't have to play it, partner |
| 7♣⁴ | pass | does. |

Not one pair arrived at 7♣ with this layout. Of course it's not cold with a trump lead.

### EVERYTHING UNDER CONTROL

To ask for Keycards holding '1 without' (don't make a practice of this), at least be sure you can handle responses of '2 with' or '2 without', particularly if you like your present partner.

| Opener | Responder | |
|---|---|---|
| ♠ A 7 2 | ♠ 6 | |
| ♡ 5 | ♡ A Q J 3 | |
| ◇ K Q J 8 7 6 4 3 | ◇ 10 2 | |
| ♣ 4 | ♣ A K 7 6 5 3 | |
| | | |
| 1◇ | 2♣ | |
| 2◇ | 2♡ | |
| 4◇¹ | ? | 1. BR diamonds, minimum hand. |

Responder can afford to use 4♠, the unbid suit, as RKB (1430). A '2 without' 5◇ response can be passed. A '2 with' 5♡ response can be converted to 6◇.

### NOTHING UNDER CONTROL

| Opener | Responder | |
|---|---|---|
| ♠ A 7 2 | ♠ 6 | |
| ♡ 5 | ♡ K Q J 3 | |
| ◇ K Q J 8 7 6 4 3 | ◇ 10 2 | |
| ♣ 4 | ♣ A K 7 6 5 3 | |
| | | |
| 1◇ | 2♣ | |
| 2◇ | 2♡ | |
| 4◇¹ | ? | 1. BR diamonds, minimum hand. |

Here responder cannot afford to use 4♠ as RKB (1430) because a '2 with' 5♡ response puts the partnership overboard.

# THE ETERNAL STRUGGLE

| Opener | Responder |
|--------|-----------|
| ♠ — | ♠ A Q J 10 5 3 2 |
| ♡ K 7 | ♡ A J 4 3 2 |
| ◇ Q 6 3 | ◇ 8 |
| ♣ A Q J 7 6 4 3 2 | ♣ — |
| 1♣ | 1♠ |
| 2♣ | 2♡ |
| 4♣[1] | 4♠[2] |
| ?[3] | |

1. Great clubs, minimum hand. I want clubs to be trumps, do you hear me?
2. Yes, I hear you, but I want spades to be trumps, do you hear me?
3. The moment of truth!

After you have shown a BR suit and partner stubbornly rebids his first-bid suit at the game-level, he is trying to tell you something — like he thinks his suit is as good or better than yours. And when his suit is a major and yours a minor he is reminding you that game in his suit is one level lower. From such sequences come partnership breakups, divorces, murders and worse.

It is rare and courageous, very courageous, to overrule a BR suit. If you do, you had better be right!

## CLOSE CALL
Works out well to play a 4NT bid after a BR bid as natural. (Of course it does, I made up the hand.)

| Opener | Responder |
|--------|-----------|
| ♠ K J 7 5 3 2 | ♠ 4 |
| ♡ K 6 | ♡ A J |
| ◇ K 5 3 | ◇ 8 4 |
| ♣ A 6 | ♣ K Q J 8 7 4 3 2 |
| 1♠ | 2♣ |
| 2♠ | 4♣[1] |
| 4NT[2] | pass |

1. Forcing.
2. Expecting one-loser clubs with an outside ace.

## LET ME OFF THIS SHIP!

| Opener | Responder |
|--------|-----------|
| ♠ K Q 7 5 2 | ♠ — |
| ♡ A J 4 3 | ♡ K 6 2 |
| ◇ — | ◇ A Q 10 7 5 4 3 2 |
| ♣ Q 6 4 2 | ♣ K 7 |
| 1♠ | 2◇¹ |
| 2♡ | 4◇² |
| ?³ | |

1. Not a game force but promises another bid.
2. BR suit, forcing.
3. You want out, big time, but dare not pass a forcing bid; Big Brother may be watching. There are four ways to get out of this mess: 1) pass and lose partner's confidence forever; 2) bid 4NT and actually play this abomination; 3) Raise to 5◇ and let partner play it; 4) excuse yourself from the table and never come back. Option (4) is clearly best, but if you decide to stay, raising with a void shows real class. Disregard all snickers and raised eyebrows when you table this disease.

Playing Two-over-One game-forcing, unless you have a mechanism to stop in four of a minor after a two-level response, you are doomed on hands like this.

### ONE LAST LOOK

What do you think is the Keycard ask in the following BR sequences — and is it a 1430 or a 3014 ask?

| Opener | Responder |
|--------|-----------|
| 1♠ | 2◇ |
| 2♠ | 4◇ |
| ? | |

Trick question. There is no ask — two unbid suits. The best opener can do is cuebid one suit denying a control in the other. After a cuebid, if responder (BR) is unlimited he can, if he wishes, pick up the ball and bid 4NT RKB (1430).

| Opener | Responder |
|--------|-----------|
| 1♠ | 2◇ |
| 2♡ | 4◇ |
| ? | |

RKB is 4♡ (1430). When the unbid (or fourth) suit is clubs facing BR diamonds, the asker's second suit, hearts in this case, is used to ask for Keycards.

And what if the opener has five hearts and wants to bid 4♡ naturally? Why did I know you would ask that question? Well, you can't have everything. Besides, a hand usually plays more comfortably when the seven- or eight-card suit is the trump suit. At least that is what you plan to tell opener when he turns up with 6-6 in the majors.

| Opener | Responder |
|--------|-----------|
| 1♢ | 2♣ |
| 2♠ | 3♣ |
| 3♢ | 4♣ |
| ? | |

This is easy: RKB is 4♡ (1430) — the unbid suit, opener asking.

| Opener | Responder |
|--------|-----------|
| 1♡ | 2♢ |
| 3♡ | 4♢ |
| ? | |

Here there is no ask — two unbid suits. So 4♠ and 5♣ are cuebids, while 4NT and 5♢ are to play.

| Opener | Responder |
|--------|-----------|
| 1♢ | 1♡ |
| 3♢ | 4♣ |
| 4♢ | ? |

Again, RKB is 4♠, the unbid suit. This time it is 3014, because opener has jumped.

| Opener | Responder | |
|--------|-----------|---|
| 1♢ | 2♣ | |
| 2♢ | 3♣[1] | 1. Not forcing. |
| 4♢ | ? | |

Here there is no ask, as both hands are limited.

## GAME-FORCING FOUR-LEVEL BR SEQUENCES AFTER A 3NT BID

A player who bids 3NT is limited. If BR is also limited and removes 3NT to four of his long minor, the bid is not forcing; another cry for mercy.

## A DISEASED RESPONDER

| Opener | Responder | |
|--------|-----------|---|
| 1♠ | 1NT | 1. Not forcing. |
| 2NT | 3◇[1] | 2. Should have a diamond fit. |
| 3NT[2] | 4◇[3] | 3. Even a fit is not enough to make |
| pass[4] | | game with this hand. |
| | | 4. Can't wait to see this disease. |

When the player with the BR minor suit is unlimited, a four-level takeout of 3NT is not only forcing, but is also a slam try. Facing a slam try, the 3NT bidder has options. He can:

1. Cuebid to show slam interest.
2. Bid 4NT to play.
3. Raise the minor to game or slam.

What the 3NT bidder can't do is ask for Keycards or pass!

### ACBL BULLETIN BIDDING COMPETITION

| Opener | Responder | |
|--------|-----------|---|
| ♠ A K 6 5 3 | ♠ Q 2 | 1. Not played as a game force. |
| ♡ K 5 4 2 | ♡ A 7 | 2. Fourth suit at the three-level, |
| ◇ Q | ◇ A K J 10 8 4 | game force. |
| ♣ Q 6 3 | ♣ A 5 2 | 3. Presumed minimum. |
| | | 4. A BR slam-try suit. |
| 1♠ | 2◇[1] | 5. Cuebid — 4NT would be natu- |
| 2♡ | 3♣[2] | ral. The 3NT bidder cannot ask |
| 3NT[3] | 4◇[4] | for Keycards. |
| 4♠[5] | 4NT[6] | 6. RKB (1430). An unlimited |
| 5♣[7] | 5♡[8] | responder can ask for Keycards |
| 5♠[9] | 5NT[10] | after the 3NT bidder cuebids. |
| 6♡[11] | 7◇[12] | 7. '1'. |
| pass | | 8. Queen-ask; 5◇ is to play. |
| | | 9. Yes, with the ♠K. |
| | | 10. After a king-showing response |
| | | to a queen-ask, a follow-up bid |
| | | of 5NT, a grand slam try, asks |
| | | for any other king. |
| | | 11. How does the ♡K grab you? |
| | | 12. Just fine, thank you. Expecting to |
| | | set up a spade for trick thirteen. |

## ESCAPE HATCH

| Opener | Responder |
|--------|-----------|
| ♠ Q J 7 6 4 3 | ♠ 2 |
| ♡ A Q J | ♡ 9 8 |
| ◇ 6 | ◇ A K Q 10 5 4 |
| ♣ Q J 2 | ♣ A K 4 3 |

| Opener | Responder | |
|--------|-----------|--|
| 1♠ | 2◇ | 1. Four-level slam try with a BR suit. |
| 2♠ | 3♣ | 2. Natural. Not interested. Too |
| 3NT | 4◇[1] |     much secondary strength, too |
| 4NT[2] | pass |     little primary strength. |

## THE BOTTOM LINE

- If a 3NT bidder cuebids after a four-level BR slam try, 4NT by BR is RKB
  — 1430 if opener hasn't jumped or reversed, 3014 if he has.

Keep the faith.

# CHAPTER 22

# RKB FOR MINORS IN NOTRUMP SEQUENCES

Notrump bids are limit bids, so if slam is in the air it is usually the partner of the notrump bidder who makes the Keycard ask. Nonetheless, if the notrump bidder has an incredible fitting hand facing a game-forcing two-suiter or has been invited to slam, he can break ranks and ask for Keycards.

## AFTER A 1NT OPENING BID

Assuming your partnership can show one or both minors after a 1NT or 2NT opening bid, you should also have a way to make a low-level Keycard ask if there is a fit and slam is looking good.

But first a couple of reminders:

1) When responding to a Keycard ask with a balanced hand facing a known two-suiter, or vice versa, the kings of both long suits are counted in the response. In effect, 6 Keycards are in play.

2) 3014 asks when the responder to a strong 1NT or a 2NT opening bid does the asking, 1430 asks when the notrump bidder does the asking.

There are several methods currently in vogue when it comes to showing either one or both minors in response to an opening bid of 1NT.

1) A 2♠ response that shows both minors, strong or weak.

2) A direct jump to 3♣ or 3♦ that is played as a one-suited slam try. (Most play these jumps as invitational. If they are invitational, RKB asks are not in the picture.)

3) Four suit transfers — the most popular method.

Before looking at some examples, check out these responder guidelines after a 1NT opening bid:

1) After three-level game-forcing minor-suit agreement, four of the agreed minor (by either player) is RKB: 3014 if responder asks, 1430 if opener asks.

2) After three-level non-game-forcing agreement, four of the agreed minor is invitational. To ask for Keycards after non-forcing club agreement, leap to 4◇ (3014). To ask for Keycards after non-forcing diamond agreement, leap to 4♡ (3014).

## WHEN TWO ARE MISSING

| Opener | Responder |
|---|---|
| ♠ K Q 5 | ♠ 9 |
| ♡ Q 10 7 | ♡ 3 |
| ◇ A J 6 2 | ◇ K Q 10 5 4 |
| ♣ K 7 4 | ♣ A Q J 6 5 3 |
| 1NT | 2♠¹ |
| 3◇² | ? |

1. Minor-suit Stayman, so to speak (shows both minors).
2. 4+ diamonds.

If this is played as a game-forcing sequence and responder wishes to ask for Keycards, he can raise gently to 4◇. If this is not a game-forcing sequence, responder must leap to 4♡ as a raise to 4◇ is invitational.

If 3◇ is not game-forcing, responder leaps to 4♡, RKB (3014). The response here will be 5♣, '2 without', and responder signs off in 5◇ as two Keycards are missing.

### FACING A TWO-SUITER

Although most RKB asks are made by the responder, a notrump opener has a little leeway facing a game-forcing two-suiter. Once there has been three-level agreement in a game-forcing auction, opener can use four of the agreed minor as RKB (1430).

| Opener | Responder |
|---|---|
| ♠ A J 4 | ♠ 6 |
| ♡ A Q 3 | ♡ 4 2 |
| ◇ Q 8 6 4 3 | ◇ K J 7 5 2 |
| ♣ A 6 | ♣ K Q J 5 3 |
| 1NT | 2♠¹ |
| 3◇² | 3♠³ |
| 4◇⁴ | 4NT⁵ |
| 6◇⁶ | pass |

1. Both minors (not a game force).
2. 4+ diamonds (not the ask).
3. Singleton, now a game force.
4. RKB (1430).
5. '2 without' (including the ♣K).
6. 1 Keycard missing.

Opener has a phenomenal hand for diamonds and partner has shown game-forcing values. Given this scenario, either player can use four of the agreed minor to ask for Keycards.

FACING A BALANCED SLAM TRY (RENO NATIONALS, 2004)

Here opener is limited, but facing a balanced slam try, opener can ask for Keycards.

| Opener | Responder |
|--------|-----------|
| ♠ A K 6 3 | ♠ 10 2 |
| ♡ A 5 | ♡ K J |
| ◇ K 4 2 | ◇ A Q 7 5 3 |
| ♣ Q 7 6 5 | ♣ K J 10 2 |

| Opener | Responder | |
|--------|-----------|---|
| 1NT | 2♠¹ | 1. Minors (not a game force). |
| 3♣² | 3NT³ | 2. 4+ clubs. |
| 4♣⁴ | 4♠⁵ | 3. Balanced slam try (14-15 HCP). |
| 6♣ | pass | 4. RKB (1430) — nothing wasted. |
| | | 5. '2 without'. |

## *If a 3♣ or 3◇ response is a one-suited slam try*

*When responder's suit is clubs:*

| Opener | Responder | |
|--------|-----------|---|
| 1NT | 3♣¹ | 1. One-suited slam try. |

Possible continuations are:

| 3◇, 3♡ or 3♠ | Ambiguous cuebids showing strength in the bid suit — could be an effort to get to 3NT or could be an effort to get to slam. |
|---|---|
| 3NT | No slam interest. |
| 4♣ | The agreement, not the ask. |
| 4◇ | RKB (1430). |

Opener has many options after partner makes a one-suited slam try. What about the responder? If the opener bids 4♣ over 3♣ (the agreement), responder can bid 4◇ — RKB (3014). If the opener bids anything else, 4♣ by responder is RKB (3014).

*When responder's suit is diamonds:*

| Opener | Responder | |
|--------|-----------|---|
| 1NT | 3◇¹ | 1. One-suited slam try. |

Possible continuations are:

| 3♡, 3♠ or 4♣ | Ambiguous cuebids showing strength in the bid suit — could be an effort to get to 3NT or could be an effort to get to slam. |
|---|---|
| 3NT | No slam interest. |
| 4◇ | The agreement, not the ask. |
| 4♡ | RKB (1430). |

If opener raises to 4♦, the agreement not the ask, 4♥ by responder is RKB (3014). If opener bids anything else, 4♦ by the responder is RKB (3014).

WHAT, YOU WANT IT ALL?
Some slams aren't 100% even in this book!

| Opener | Responder | |
|---|---|---|
| ♠ A 5 | ♠ 8 | |
| ♥ A 6 3 | ♥ K J 7 | |
| ♦ A 8 2 | ♦ K 5 | |
| ♣ J 7 6 2 | ♣ K Q 10 8 5 4 3 | |
| 1NT | 3♣ | |
| 4♣[1] | 4♦[2] | 1. The agreement. |
| 4♥[3] | 6♣ | 2. The ask — RKB (3014). |
| pass | | 3. '3'. |

## Four-suit transfers that could lead to RKB asks

Playing four-suit transfers, 2♦ is a transfer to hearts, 2♥ is a transfer to spades, 2♠ is a transfer to clubs and 2NT is a transfer to diamonds. We are concerned with the 2♠ and the 2NT transfers only. These two transfers might conceal weak or strong hands.

Opener, for his part, can show a suitable or unsuitable hand for responder's minor with a two-step response:

| Opener | Responder | | Opener | Responder |
|---|---|---|---|---|
| 1NT | 2♠[1] | | 1NT | 2NT[1] |
| 2NT[2] or 3♣[3] | | | 3♣[2] or 3♦[3] | |

| 1. Transfer to clubs. | 1. Transfer to diamonds. |
|---|---|
| 2. Max for clubs. | 2. Max for diamonds. |
| 3. Mini for clubs. | 3. Mini for diamonds. |

If responder is interested in slam and wishes to Keycard directly after opener's rebid, this is what he does: holding clubs, he jumps to 4♦ and holding diamonds he jumps to 4♥. If either player bids responder's suit at the four-level, even with a jump, it is invitational.

| Opener | Responder | |
|---|---|---|
| ♠ K Q 7 4 | ♠ 5 | |
| ♡ Q J 8 | ♡ K 3 | 1. Transfer to clubs (weak or strong). |
| ◇ K Q 6 2 | ◇ A 5 4 | |
| ♣ K 4 | ♣ A Q J 6 5 3 2 | 2. Non-fitting hand for clubs. |
| | | 3. RKB (3014). |
| 1NT | 2♠[1] | 4. '1' (can't be '4', responder has |
| 3♣[2] | 4◇[3] | '2'). |
| 4♠[4] | 5♣[5] | 5. 2 Keycards missing (could be two |
| pass | | aces). |

In 3014 sequences when the strong hand (in this case the opener) turns up with an unsettling '1' (or an even more unsettling '0'), it makes sense to play that a return to 4NT by the asker is to play. Period. That agreement is now in place. Playing matchpoints it is essential to get out in 4NT on many hands where two Keycards are missing.

A HAPPIER ENDING

| Opener | Responder | |
|---|---|---|
| ♠ A J 5 3 | ♠ K 6 | |
| ♡ K 6 4 | ♡ A Q 2 | |
| ◇ A J 6 | ◇ K Q 8 7 4 3 2 | 1. Transfer to diamonds. |
| ♣ A 6 5 | ♣ 3 | 2. Good hand for diamonds. |
| | | 3. RKB (3014) — 3◇ would be to |
| 1NT | 2NT[1] | play, 4◇ invitational. |
| 3♣[2] | 4♡[3] | 4. '3'. |
| 4♠[4] | 5♡[5] | 5. SSA in hearts. |
| 6♣[6] | 7NT[7] | 6. Kxx(x). |
| pass | | 7. Bingo! Can count thirteen tricks. |

Some play their transfers a little differently. They play that a 2NT response is a transfer to 3♣ and a 3♣ response is a transfer to diamonds, which leads to these possibilities:

| Opener | Responder | |
|---|---|---|
| 1NT | 2NT[1] | 1. Transfer to clubs (weak or strong). |
| 3♣ | | |

Now 4♣ is invitational, and 4◇ is RKB (3014).

| Opener | Responder | |
|---|---|---|
| 1NT | 3♣[1] | |
| 3◇ | | 1. Transfer to 3◇. |

And now 4◇ is invitational and 4♡ is RKB (3014).

## Double transfer sequences

Double transfer sequences (responder shows two suits) may lead to a Keycard ask — usually by the responder, the unlimited hand. However, if opener has a fitting hand to die for, he can take charge.

### AGREEMENT MAKES THE WORLD GO ROUND

| Opener | Responder | |
|---|---|---|
| ♠ K 6 | ♠ A Q 5 3 2 | 1. Transfer. |
| ♡ A 8 7 4 | ♡ 3 | 2. Natural, game force. |
| ◇ J 7 3 | ◇ A | 3. The agreement (presumed 4+ |
| ♣ A K 8 2 | ♣ J 10 7 6 5 4 | clubs). |
| 1NT | 2♡¹ | 4. RKB (3014). After four-level game-forcing club agreement, |
| 2♠ | 3♣² | 4◇ is RKB. |
| 4♣³ | 4◇⁴ | 5. '4' including the ♠K. |
| 4♠⁵ | 7♣⁶ | 6. Knowing of the ♣AKxx plus the |
| pass | | ♠K, not bidding a grand is off-the-board cowardly. |

After a double transfer sequence ending in 3♣ or 3◇, the opener, with a great hand plus a fit for the minor, can ask for Keycards directly by leaping to 4◇ over 3♣ or to 4♡ over 3◇. Both are 1430 asks.

### 2003 COUPE DE FRANCE CHAMPIONSHIPS

| Opener | Responder | |
|---|---|---|
| ♠ K 5 | ♠ A Q 7 3 2 | |
| ♡ A 9 4 | ♡ 6 | |
| ◇ A K 3 | ◇ Q 7 2 | |
| ♣ Q 9 7 5 3 | ♣ K J 10 6 | |
| | | 1. Transfer. |
| 1NT | 2♡¹ | 2. Game-force, usually a 5-card |
| 2♠ | 3♣² | suit. |
| 4◇³ | 4NT⁴ | 3. RKB (1430). |
| 6♣ | pass | 4. '2 without' including the ♠K. |

**The exception:** Rather than agree clubs (4♣), opener takes the bull by the horns and asks for Keycards. It's rare for the opener to do something like this, but if ever there was a hand to do it, this is it.

THE RIGHT SINGLETON

| Opener | Responder | |
|--------|-----------|---|
| ♠ J 7 3 | ♠ 2 | |
| ♡ K 6 | ♡ A Q 8 4 3 | |
| ◇ A K J 5 | ◇ 7 2 | |
| ♣ A J 6 2 | ♣ K Q 8 4 3 | |
| | | 1. Transfer to hearts. |
| 1NT | 2◇¹ | 2. Natural. |
| 2♡ | 3♣² | 3. The agreement, not the ask — |
| 4♣³ | 4♠⁴ |    4◇ would be RKB (1430). |
| 5◇⁴ | 6♣⁵ | 4. Cuebid. |
| pass | | 5. Enough already!. |

# RESPONDING TO 2NT WITH BOTH MINORS

It's easy enough for a 2NT opener to agree a minor suit when partner's response has shown both minors. At times he can do more than agree the suit, he can bypass the agreement and ask for Keycards straight away. *Noblesse oblige.*

If a response of 3♠ shows both minors with at least game-going values, these scenarios are possible:

| Opener | Responder | |
|--------|-----------|---|
| 2NT | 3♠¹ | 1. Minors, GF. |
| ? | | |

| 4♣ or 4◇ | 4+ clubs or 4+ diamonds. Not the ask. |
|-----------|----------------------------------------|
| 4♡ | RKB clubs (1430). |
| 4♠ | RKB diamonds (1430). |

The 2NT opener may not have the right hand to ask for Keycards directly. He might need a cuebid first. Therefore 4♣ and 4◇ are agreements, not asks. If the 2NT opener has all the controls plus a nice fit, he can ask for Keycards directly via 4♡ (for clubs) or 4♠ (for diamonds). If opener agrees a minor, responder may wish to ask for Keycards. After four-level club agreement, 4◇ is RKB. After four-level diamond agreement, 4♡ is RKB. Both asks are 3014.

## WHAT A FIND!

| Opener | Responder | |
|---|---|---|
| ♠ A K 8 | ♠ 4 | |
| ♡ Q 6 3 | ♡ 2 | |
| ◇ K J 5 | ◇ A Q 8 6 2 | 1. Minors. |
| ♣ A K 4 3 | ♣ Q J 7 6 5 2 | 2. 4+ clubs. The agreement (can't ask for Keycards with that heart |
| 2NT | 3♠[1] | holding). |
| 4♣[2] | 4◇[3] | 3. RKB (3014). |
| 4♠[4] | 6♣[5] | 4. '4' including the ◇K — don't |
| pass | | forget the ◇K! |

## SAVING TIME

| Opener | Responder | |
|---|---|---|
| ♠ K Q | ♠ 6 5 | |
| ♡ A 7 3 | ♡ 8 | |
| ◇ A Q J 8 4 | ◇ K 9 7 5 2 | |
| ♣ K J 2 | ♣ A 7 6 5 4 | |
| 2NT | 3♠[1] | 1. Minors. |
| 4♠[2] | 5◇[3] | 2. RKB (1430). |
| 6◇[4] | pass | 3. '2 without'. |

Opener bypasses the agreement (4◇), and takes control with a direct Keycard ask (4♠), based on his minor-suit fillers plus controls in both majors. Slam is on a finesse.

# OPENER MAKE A JUMP REBID OF 2NT AND RECEIVES A GAME-FORCING THREE-LEVEL MINOR-SUIT PREFERENCE

| Opener | Responder |
|---|---|
| 1◇ | 1♠ |
| 2NT | 3◇ (GF) |
| ? | |

Although 3◇ is game-forcing agreement (some play it as an artificial check-back) it is not a slam try. It would be rare for a limited hand, even a strong limited hand, to ask for Keycards without knowing partner's intentions. But if the opener thinks he has the 'right' hand to make an ask, the raise to 4◇ is RKB (1430). Had responder wanted to make a clear-cut slam try, he could have leaped to 4◇, a jump-preference agreement, not the ask. Something opener should think about.

TAKING YOUR TIME

| Opener | Responder | |
|---|---|---|
| ♠ K 6 | ♠ A Q 7 4 2 | 1. Cuebid — probably weak in clubs. |
| ♡ A K J | ♡ 9 6 3 | 2. Singletons can be cuebid beneath the level of the Keycard ask. |
| ◇ A K 10 7 2 | ◇ Q 6 5 4 | |
| ♣ J 8 3 | ♣ 7 | |
| | | 3. RKB (1430); 4♣ is a slam-try cuebid so the opener is within himself to ask for Keycards. |
| 1◇ | 1♠ | |
| 2NT | 3◇ | |
| 3♡[1] | 4♣[2] | 4. '1'. |
| 4◇[3] | 4♡[4] | 5. Queen-ask. |
| 4♠[5] | 5◇[6] | 6. Yes, with no side-suit king (4NT would deny the ◇Q). |
| 6◇[6] | pass | |

What if responder wants to ask for Keycards in diamonds after the 2NT rebid? He should bid 3◇, creating game-forcing agreement and then bid 4◇, RKB (3140). A planned sequence. Jumping directly to 4◇, a jump preference, is not a Keycard ask, but it is a slam try.

Here are two more examples of planned RKB sequences involving notrump. The first after a reverse, the second after the fourth suit.

| Opener | Responder | Opener | Responder |
|---|---|---|---|
| 1♣ | 1♡ | 1♡ | 1♠ |
| 2◇ | 3◇[1] | 2♣ | 2◇ |
| 3NT | 4◇[2] | 2NT | 3♣[1] |
| | | 3♡ | 4♣[2] |

1. Game-forcing three-level agreement.
2. RKB — (3014) in the first sequence, (1430) in the second. In the first, opener has reversed so when responder asks it is a 3014 ask. In the second, opener has not jumped or reversed so the ask is 1430. Responder is unlimited in both sequences.

WRESTING CONTROL FROM THE BIG HAND

| Opener | Responder | |
|---|---|---|
| ♠ A K Q | ♠ 8 | |
| ♡ J 7 | ♡ A Q 6 4 2 | |
| ◇ A Q 6 5 3 | ◇ J 10 7 4 | |
| ♣ Q 5 2 | ♣ A 8 3 | |
| 1◇ | 1♡ | |
| 2NT | 3◇[1] | 1. Game force. |
| 3♠[2] | 4◇[3] | 2. Cuebid. |
| 5♣[4] | 6◇ | 3. RKB (3014). |
| pass | | 4. '2 with'. |

On this layout responder has to decide whether to take control (3◇ followed by 4◇) or give up control (4◇ directly), or cuebid 4♣ after partner's 3♠ cuebid. If responder elects to cuebid, 4◇ by the opener will be RKB (1430).

## SIMPLE GERBER OVER AN OPENING BID OF 1NT OR 2NT

A direct leap to 4♣ after an opening bid of 1NT or 2NT is simple Gerber, no agreed suit. Since the king and queen of responder's long suit are unknown, the responses show aces — just aces, like the good old days.

| Opener | Responder | |
|---|---|---|
| 1NT or 2NT | 4♣[1] | 1. Simple Gerber. |

These are the ace-showing responses to simple Gerber, no suit(s) having been bid.

| | |
|---|---|
| 4◇ | 0 or 4 aces |
| 4♡ | 1 ace |
| 4♠ | 2 aces |
| 4NT | 3 aces |

### A SIMPLE PLAN

| Opener | Responder | |
|---|---|---|
| ♠ K Q 6 3 | ♠ 4 | |
| ♡ K Q J 5 | ♡ 2 | |
| ◇ K Q 2 | ◇ A J 5 | |
| ♣ A 6 | ♣ K Q J 8 7 5 4 3 | 1. Simple Gerber, no agreed suit — just aces, please. |
| 2NT | 4♣[1] | 2. One ace. |
| 4♡[2] | 4NT[3] | 3. What kind of partner are you? To play. |
| pass | | |

After a simple or a Keycard Gerber ask, a follow-up bid of 4NT is to play. A follow up bid of 5♣ is the king-ask by number. Responses are 1st step = 0, 2nd step = 1, etc. If responder's unknown suit is clubs, and two Keycards are missing, responder had better sign off in 4NT because 5♣ is a king-ask! Help!

## MAJOR-MINOR DOUBLE TRANSFER SEQUENCES AFTER A 2NT OPENING

If responder has a major-minor two-suiter in response to a 2NT opening bid, the normal approach is to transfer into the major and then bid the minor at the four-level:

| Opener | Responder | |
|--------|-----------|---|
| 2NT | 3♢[1] | 1. Transfer to hearts. |
| 3♡ | 4♣[2] | 2. Presumably a 5-card suit. |
| ? | | |

What does opener's next bid mean in this double transfer sequence ending in 4♣? Let's try this:

| 4♢ | RKB for clubs (1430) |
|----|----------------------|
| 4♡, 4NT and 5♣ | To play |
| 4♠ | Cuebid, probably lacking a diamond control |

The reason 4♢ is an RKB ask for clubs (♡K included) is that opener has shown no great interest in hearts. (Could have shown good hand for hearts in response to 3♢). When diamonds is responder's second suit, opener uses the unbid major to ask for keycards:

| Opener | Responder | |
|--------|-----------|---|
| 2NT | 3♡[1] | 1. Transfer to spades. |
| 3♠ | 4♢[2] | 2. Natural. |
| 4♡[3] | | 3. The unbid major — RKB 1430 for diamonds. |

but in these sequences 4NT is best played as natural.

SEE IT ALL IN ACTION

| Opener | Responder | |
|--------|-----------|---|
| ♠ A 5 | ♠ K 10 6 4 2 | |
| ♡ A J 7 3 | ♡ 4 | 1. Transfer. |
| ♢ K Q 8 6 | ♢ A 7 5 3 2 | 2. Natural — game force. |
| ♣ A Q 4 | ♣ J 3 | 3. The unbid major — RKB 1430 for diamonds. |
| 2NT | 3♡[1] | 4. '2 without' including the ♠K. |
| 3♠ | 4♢[2] | 5. SKA. |
| 4♡[3] | 5♣[4] | 6. Nothing cooking here. |
| 5NT | 6♢[6] | 7. Rats — would have bid a grand if you had a king. |
| pass[7] | | |

| Opener | Responder | |
|---|---|---|
| ♠ A 6 2 | ♠ K 9 | |
| ♡ A 5 | ♡ Q 10 7 3 2 | |
| ◇ A K Q 6 | ◇ 5 | |
| ♣ A 7 5 4 | ♣ Q J 8 6 2 | |
| | | |
| 2NT | 3◇[1] | 1. Hearts. |
| 3♡ | 4♣[2] | 2. Clubs. |
| 4◇[3] | 4♠[4] | 3. RKB (1430). |
| 5♣ | | 4. '0'. |
| | | 5. Opener knows both the ♣K and the ♡K are missing. Even so, there is a good chance of only one loser between the two suits if responder has the queen-jacks of both suits. |

# AFTER A MINOR-SUIT OPENING AND A 2NT RESPONSE

| Opener | Responder | Opener | Responder |
|---|---|---|---|
| 1♣ | 2NT | 1◇ | 2NT |
| 4♣[1] | | 4◇[1] | |

1. RKB for clubs (1430).    1. RKB for diamonds (1430).

This agreement also assumes that a rebids of 3♣ and 3◇ are forcing. If you play that the 2NT response shows 11-12 and therefore rebids of 3♣ or 3◇ are not forcing, this agreement may not be for you.

GET A LOAD OF THIS

| Opener | Responder | |
|---|---|---|
| ♠ 5 | ♠ A 7 2 | |
| ♡ A J 8 3 | ♡ K Q 5 | |
| ◇ A K Q J 8 6 4 | ◇ 7 5 2 | |
| ♣ 3 | ♣ A J 6 5 | |
| | | 1. 13-15 HCP. |
| | | 2. RKB (1430), diamonds agreed. |
| 1◇ | 2NT[1] | 3. '2 without'. |
| 4◇[1] | 4NT[3] | 4. SSA in hearts. |
| 5♡[4] | 6♡[5] | 5. The KQ, any length. |
| 7NT[6] | | 6. Can count thirteen tricks. |

Opener can risk a 5♡ SSA in hearts because the responses are:

| 5♠ | xx or the queen. Opener bids 6♢. |
|----|----|
| 5NT | Kxx(x). Opener bids 6♢ unless he wants to gamble on a grand knowing a heart finesse is probably going to be needed (not to mention the problem of the fourth heart). |
| 6♣ | Kx. Opener bids 7♢. |
| 6♢ | A return to the trump suit denies second- or third-round control. Opener passes. |

## AN 'OUT OF THE BLUE' CUE

Sometimes even a severely limited hand will 'come alive' and make a slam try.

| Opener | Responder | |
|--------|-----------|--|
| ♠ 4 | ♠ A 10 6 | |
| ♡ A J 7 5 4 | ♡ 3 2 | |
| ♢ A Q 6 5 | ♢ K J 8 4 3 2 | 1. Spade control with a huge dia- |
| ♣ A K 3 | ♣ 6 4 |    mond fit. |
| | | 2. If 3♠ is played as a game force, |
| 1♡ | 1NT |    4♢ by opener is RKB. If it is not |
| 2♢ | 3♠[1] |    played as a game force, 4♢ is to |
| 4NT[2] | 5♠[3] |    play and 4NT is RKB (1430). |
| 5NT[4] | 6♢[5] | 3. '2 with' — a ten-card fit is |
| pass | |    assumed. |
| | | 4. Anything else over there? I'm |
| | |    getting greedy! |
| | | 5. No, nothing. |

# THE BOTTOM LINE

- After a 1NT opening bid followed by game-forcing three-level minor-suit agreement, four of the agreed minor by the responder, the unlimited hand, is RKB (3014). Opener can sometimes use four of the agreed minor in a game-forcing auction to ask for keycards, but it is rare.
- If the three-level agreement is not game-forcing, the responder must jump to 4◇ over 3♣ or to 4♡ over 3◇ to create a Keycard ask (3014).
- After a 1NT opening bid followed by a double transfer ending in 3♣ or 3◇, a raise by the opener agrees the minor, but a leap to 4◇ over 3♣ or a leap to four of the unbid major when diamonds is the last-bid suit is RKB (1430).
- After a 2NT opening bid and a 3♠ response showing both minors, opener can agree the minor at the four-level or can bypass the agreement and ask for Keycards directly. A jump to 4♡ is RKB for clubs and a jump to 4♠ is RKB for diamonds.
- After a 2NT opening bid followed by a double transfer ending in four of a minor, 4◇ by the opener is RKB (1430) for clubs and four of the unbid major is RKB (1430) for diamonds. In all double transfer sequences, the kings of both suits are included in the Keycard response, but only the queen of the agreed suit is counted.
- After a 2♣ response to an opening bid followed by a 2NT rebid, 4♣ by the responder is RKB for clubs (1430). After a 2◇ response to an opening bid followed by a 2NT rebid, 4◇ by responder is RKB for diamonds (1430). A jump to 4♣ is a slam try in clubs.
- After a 1♣ or 1◇ opening bid and a natural 2NT response, if opener's suit is clubs, a jump to 4♣ is RKB for clubs (1430). If opener's suit is diamonds, a jump to 4◇ is RKB for diamonds (1430) and a jump rebid of 4♣ is a natural slam try.
- A direct jump to 4♣ after a 1NT or 2NT opening bid is simple Gerber asking for aces, no agreed suit. After the ace-showing response, 4NT by the Gerber bidder is to play, and 5♣ asks for kings by steps starting with '0'.

# THE WRAP-UP

## PART FOUR

# CHAPTER 23

## SECOND-SUIT OPTIONS

This chapter deals with follow-up bids by the RKB bidder at the five- and six-level. We start with follow up bids at the five-level.

## FOLLOW-UP BIDS AT THE FIVE-LEVEL AFTER A '0' RESPONSE

Follow-up bids in a non-agreed suit are always some sort of an ask: either the queen-ask (next step) or a SSA (not the next step). However, after a '0' response, it's generally all over but the signing off. The most likely follow-up bid is a return to either player's first-bid suit, which is to play.

> BELIEVING IN YOUR METHODS
> After game-forcing four-level diamond agreement, 4♠ is RKB when hearts is the asker's first-bid suit.

| Opener | Responder | |
|---|---|---|
| ♠ 2 | ♠ K J 3 | |
| ♡ A K Q J 10 8 | ♡ 4 | |
| ◇ A K 6 2 | ◇ Q 7 5 3 | |
| ♣ K Q | ♣ 10 8 6 5 4 | |
| 2♣ | 2◇[1] | 1. Waiting. |
| 2♡ | 2NT[2] | 2. Scattered values. |
| 3◇ | 4◇ | 3. RKB (1430). |
| 4♠[3] | 5♣[4] | 4. '0'. |
| 5♡[5] | pass | 5. To play (asker's first-bid suit). |

## FOLLOW-UP BIDS AT THE FIVE-LEVEL AFTER A '1' RESPONSE

Now something might be cooking:

1) A return to the asker's first-bid major is to play. A return to a first-bid minor, if the next step, is the queen-ask.
2) A return to the agreed suit is to play.
3) A return to the responder's first-bid suit is to play — if the suit has been rebid or supported. If not and it's the next step, it's the queen-ask; if it's not the next step, it's a SSA.
4) A follow-up bid in an unbid suit that is not a first-step queen-ask is a SSA.

## USING RESPONDER'S FIRST-BID SUIT AS THE QUEEN-ASK

Asker can use responder's first-bid suit, a suit that has not been supported or rebid, as the queen-ask when it is the next step.

| Opener | Responder |
|---|---|
| ♠ A Q 7 | ♠ 5 2 |
| ♡ A J 10 8 6 4 3 | ♡ Q 5 |
| ◇ 6 | ◇ A Q 7 4 3 |
| ♣ A 2 | ♣ K 8 5 4 |

| Opener | Responder | |
|---|---|---|
| 1♡ | 2◇ | 1. 1430 — opener asking. |
| 3♡ | 4♡ | 2. '1'. |
| 4NT[1] | 5♣[2] | 3. Queen-ask. |
| 5◇[3] | 6♣[4] | 4. Yes, with the ♣K. |
| 6♡[5] | pass | 5. Missing a Keycard. |

## SOME SUITS ARE BETTER THAN OTHERS

| Opener | Responder |
|---|---|
| ♠ A K Q J 10 6 | ♠ 3 |
| ♡ A J 7 2 | ♡ K 8 6 5 4 |
| ◇ 8 | ◇ K Q J 2 |
| ♣ K 3 | ♣ Q 6 5 |

| Opener | Responder |
|---|---|
| 1♠ | 2♡ |
| 4◇[1] | 4♡[2] |
| 4NT[3] | 5♣[4] |
| 5♠[5] | |

1  Splinter agreement for hearts.
2. Not interested.
3. A stubborn RKB (1430).
4. '1'.
5. To play, asker's first-bid major. Even if responder has the ♡Q, spades will play as well as hearts. However, if responder doesn't have the ♡Q, spades could be a safer trump suit.

## HITTING THE JACKPOT

| Opener | Responder |
|---|---|
| ♠ A 6 3 | ♠ K Q 4 2 |
| ♡ A K 8 3 | ♡ 6 |
| ◇ A Q 7 6 2 | ◇ K 9 8 5 4 3 |
| ♣ A | ♣ 10 8 |

| Opener | Responder |
|---|---|
| 1◇ | 1♠ |
| 2♡ | 4◇[1] |
| 4♡[2] | 4♠[3] |
| 5♠[4] | 6♠[5] |
| 7◇ | pass |

1. Game-forcing jump preference, not the ask.
2. RKB (1430). After four-level diamond agreement, 4♡ is RKB unless hearts is a first-bid suit. If it is, 4♠ is RKB.
3. '1'
4. SSA in spades, an unsupported suit — besides, there has been jump agreement to a first-bid suit solidifying that as the agreed suit.
5. The KQ. The raise of a SSA shows the KQ with any length.

Review of responses to that SSA of 5♠ (keep in mind that neither the ace nor length is an issue when responding to a SSA in a previously-bid suit):

> A return to the agreed suit (6♢), denies the king or the queen — and does not count as a step. No denial response counts as a step.

| | | |
|---|---|---|
| 1st step (5NT) | = | Q |
| 2nd step (6♣) | = | K |
| Raise of the ask suit (6♠) | = | KQ |

## '2', '3' AND '4' RESPONSES

After a '2' or '3' response to a 1430 ask, the future looks bright, very bright. A '2' or '3' response to a 1430 (strong asking weak) is a big response and usually leads to a small or a grand slam. If hearts is the agreed suit and the 1430 response to 4NT is 5♢ showing '3', 5♡ is the queen-ask. It is not to play!

By contrast, a '2' or '3' response to a 3014 (weak asking strong) ask is no big deal. In fact '3' and '4' are expected responses; '2' means partner has miscounted his points. After a '2' or '3' response, a return to the agreed suit or to the asker's first-bid suit is to play. A return to responder's unsupported first-bid suit is to play if it has been rebid. If it hasn't, it is the queen-ask (if it's the next step) or a SSA (if it's not the next step).

There is no way to get off the bus after a '4' response in a 5-Keycard scenario. When hearts is the agreed suit and the RKB response is 5♢ showing '4', 5♡ is the queen-ask.

## FOLLOW-UP BIDS AT THE SIX-LEVEL IN PREVIOUSLY-BID SUITS, BUT NOT THE AGREED SUIT

1) If there has been jump agreement to a first-bid suit, that suit is considered the agreed suit. If the RKB bidder follows up the response by bidding a lower-ranking suit at the six-level, it is a SSA.

2) If there has been no jump agreement to the agreed suit, follow-up bids at the six-level in lower-ranking previously-bid suits, supported or not, are either to play or at the very least 'choice of contract'. The asker may have shown a two-suiter, having rebid the second suit, and wants to give partner a final choice in selecting the better trump suit.

To overrule a six-level bid in the asker's first-bid suit takes courage — it also takes great trumps! Overruling partner's first-bid suit to play in an eight-card fit requires that you hold the AKQJ between the two hands — and you had better be the one with the jack! Overruling partner's first-bid suit to play in a nine-card trump fit requires holding the AKQ between the two hands. If you aren't 100% sure these conditions exist, pass, so the partnership can continue. However, if you don't like your partner...

## AN OVERRULE?

| Opener | Responder |
|---|---|
| ♠ A 8 6 3 | ♠ K Q 5 2 |
| ♡ K Q | ♡ A 9 7 2 |
| ◇ 6 | ◇ 8 5 4 3 |
| ♣ A K Q J 7 4 | ♣ 5 |

| | |
|---|---|
| 1♣ | 1♡ |
| 2♠ | 4♠[1] |
| 4NT[2] | 5♠[3] |
| 6♣[4] | pass[5] |

1. Strong spades — not regressive.
2. RKB (1430).
3. '2 with'.
4. To play.
5. This responder knows the spades aren't solid. If opener had ♠AJxx, he would know the spades were solid.

| Opener | Responder |
|---|---|
| ♠ A 8 6 3 | ♠ K Q J 2 |
| ♡ K Q | ♡ A 9 7 2 |
| ◇ 6 | ◇ 8 5 4 3 |
| ♣ A K Q J 7 4 | ♣ 5 |

| | |
|---|---|
| 1♣ | 1♡ |
| 2♠ | 4♠[1] |
| 4NT[2] | 5♠[3] |
| 6♣[4] | 6♠[5] |

1. Strong spades — not regressive.
2. RKB (1430.)
3. '2 with'.
4. To play.
5. Knows spades *are* solid and that 6♠ should be as safe as 6♣.

## TOUCHY, TOUCHY, TOUCHY

| Opener | Responder |
|---|---|
| ♠ A 7 4 | ♠ K Q 9 3 2 |
| ♡ K Q J | ♡ 7 |
| ◇ 5 | ◇ A 10 8 6 2 |
| ♣ A K Q J 9 6 | ♣ 4 2 |

| Opener | Oppt. | Responder | Oppt. |
|---|---|---|---|
| 1♣ | 2♡ | 2♠ | 4♡ |
| 4NT[1] | pass | 5♠[2] | pass |
| 6♣[3] | all pass | | |

1. RKB (1430) — presumably for spades, but not clear.
2. '2 with' (♠KQ and the ◇A).
3. To play — opener's first-bid suit at the six-level.

This one is scary. Opener has had no chance to support spades and may not have a spade fit. Opener may have just wanted to ask for aces. Even if your 'last-bid suit' is the agreed suit, you must make allowances when there has been high-level competition. Responder should pass 6♣

THE TEST

| Opener | Responder (you) |
|--------|-----------------|
| ♠ A Q 6 3 | ♠ 8 7 5 2 |
| ♡ 4 | ♡ A K J 6 3 2 |
| ◇ A K Q J 8 6 4 | ◇ — |
| ♣ A | ♣ 6 5 4 |
| 2♣[1] | 2♡[2] |
| 3◇[2] | 3♡ |
| 3♠ | 4♠ |
| 4NT[3] | 5♣[4] |
| 6◇[5] | ?[6] |

1. Strong and artificial.
2. Natural.
3. RKB (1430).
4. '1'. (Do not count a void in partner's first-bid suit for anything. It's a minus!)
5. To play.
6. Pass. Your spades have to be mighty strong to bid 6♠, mighty strong.

HONOR THE DOUBLER

Playing from the short side builds character.

| | Partner | | You |
|--|---------|--|-----|
| | ♠ 5 | | ♠ 7 3 2 |
| | ♡ K Q 4 | | ♡ A 8 6 3 2 |
| | ◇ A K 7 | | ◇ Q 8 5 2 |
| | ♣ A K Q J 6 3 | | ♣ 4 |

| Oppt. | Partner | Oppt. | You |
|-------|---------|-------|-----|
| 2♠ | dbl | 3♠ | 4♡ |
| pass | 4NT[1] | pass | 5♣[2] |
| pass | 6♣[3] | pass | ? |

1. RKB — apparently for hearts (1430).
2. '1'.
3. To play.

Competition has made it impossible for the doubler to show his suit and ask for Keycards at the same time. After a takeout double, responder's suit is assumed to be the agreed suit. However, if interference has ruined your party, responder should defer to the doubler's suit at the six-level. You should pass 6♣ with your singleton club and expect a lead out of turn. By the way, it builds character to declare a slam with a singleton trump.

GIVING PARTNER A CHOICE

The asker may have a two-suiter and, having bid and rebid a second suit, might have received simple preference to his first suit (which could be a doubleton). It is possible that the second suit (perhaps a 5-3 fit) offers a better fit than the agreed suit (perhaps a 5-2 fit). The RKB bidder must be given the opportunity to explore that option.

| Opener | Responder | |
|---|---|---|
| ♠ A Q 10 7 2 | ♠ K 5 | |
| ♡ 8 | ♡ A K 6 4 3 | |
| ◇ A K Q 10 4 | ◇ J 3 2 | 1. Simple preference — could be |
| ♣ K Q | ♣ J 7 6 | honor doubleton. |
| | | 2. Natural. |
| 1♠ | 2♡ | 3. Cuebid. |
| 3◇ | 3♠[1] | 4. RKB (1430) — spades agreed. |
| 4◇[2] | 4♡[3] | 5. '2 without'. |
| 4NT[4] | 5♡[5] | 6. Choice of contract. |
| 6◇[6] | pass[7] | 7. I have chosen. |

If the response to 4NT is 5♣ ('1'), a follow up bid of 5◇ (or 6◇) is passable because the suit has been rebid. 5♡ would be the queen-ask; how can the opener have heart support and wait until his sixth bid to show it? Give me a break.

## WHEN RESPONDER HAS A TWO-SUITER

| Opener | Responder | |
|---|---|---|
| ♠ K Q | ♠ A 6 5 3 2 | |
| ♡ A 8 4 | ♡ Q 6 | |
| ◇ A 7 3 | ◇ K Q 6 5 2 | 1. Simple preference; usually three |
| ♣ A J 6 4 2 | ♣ 5 | spades but not written in stone. |
| | | 2. Two-suiter. |
| 1♣ | 1♠ | 3. Cuebid. |
| 2NT | 3◇ | 4. RKB (3014) — opener has |
| 3♠[1] | 4◇[2] | jumped. |
| 4♡[3] | 4NT[4] | 5. '4'. |
| 5◇[5] | 6◇[6] | 6. Choice of contract. |
| pass[7] | | 7. I have chosen...(and correctly). |

## WHEN THEY ARE IN YOUR FACE... AGAIN

Interference may make it impossible for you to support partner's suit and make a Keycard ask in the agreed suit. When that happens and you use RKB and then bid partner's suit at the six-level, that is a choice of contract bid, not some sort of an ask.

| Opener | | Responder | |
|---|---|---|---|
| ♠ J 8 4 | | ♠ A K 7 3 2 | |
| ♡ 6 | | ♡ A 10 | |
| ◇ A Q J 8 4 | | ◇ K 10 7 3 2 | |
| ♣ A Q 4 3 | | ♣ 2 | |

| Opener | Oppt. | Responder | Oppt. |
|---|---|---|---|
| 1◇ | 2♡ | 2♠ | 4♡ |
| 4♠ | pass | 4NT[1] | pass |
| 5♡[2] | pass | 6◇[3] | pass |
| pass[4] | pass | | |

1. RKB (1430) — opener hasn't jumped. Even though opener should have extras, by our rules if the opener hasn't jump-raised, he is presumed to be minimum.
2. '2 without'.
3. Choice of contract.
4. An easy choice.

Competition has precluded early support. Of course, responder might have leaped to 6◇ over 4♠, but that's a bit practical for this book. Besides, the ♠Q is an important card.

### DONE IN BY THE 'RULES'

While we're discussing auctions following a takeout double, consider the following hand reported by Chip Martel. It concerns a sequence he and his partner, Lew Stansby, both three-time World Champions as of this writing, had to deal with. Look at the auction before peeking at their hands.

| Chip | Oppt. | Lew | Oppt. |
|---|---|---|---|
| | 2♡[1] | pass | 4♡ |
| dbl | pass | 4♠ | pass |
| 4NT[2] | pass | 5♣[3] | pass |
| ? | | | |

1. Weak.
2. RKB (3014) — they haven't read this book, or worse, they have!
3. '0' or '3'.

What does 5◇ mean at this point? It looks like a queen-ask, spades agreed. Here are the actual hands:

| Chip | Lew |
|---|---|
| ♠ A J 5 | ♠ Q 10 6 2 |
| ♡ A | ♡ 8 7 |
| ◇ K Q J 8 7 4 | ◇ 10 9 |
| ♣ A K 9 | ♣ 10 7 6 3 2 |

Chip wanted 5◇ to be natural, but fearing it would be interpreted as the queen-ask, he bid 6◇ which did not fare well. He suggested that when the opponents are in the auction at a high level, their suit should be the queen-ask liberating other suits to be natural. Is this a good rule? It is if you've made a takeout double with a strong suit that is lower ranking than both partner's and the opponents' suit. But what if you really want to make a queen-ask and the opponents' suit is higher ranking than the agreed suit? You can't use a lower-ranking unbid suit as the queen-ask because now that's natural!

Maybe just bidding your suit (5◇) over 4♠ is the answer when you aren't thrilled with the suit partner will think is the agreed suit. After all, 5◇ is a big bid in this sequence. Strangely, had they been playing 1430 responses, Lew would have responded 5◇ ('0 or 3') and Chip could have passed!

### WORLD CHAMPIONS IN ACTION
The following hand was bid by Christian Mari and Alain Levy, both former world champions, in international competition.

| Mari | Levy | |
|------|------|---|
| ♠ 10 | ♠ A K 7 6 5 4 3 | |
| ♡ K J 7 3 2 | ♡ 6 | |
| ◇ A 7 3 | ◇ 5 | |
| ♣ A 8 6 3 | ♣ K Q 4 2 | 1. Fourth suit forcing. |
| 1♡ | 1♠ | 2. Felt he was too weak to bid 2NT. |
| 2♣ | 2◇[1] | 3. RKB, spades agreed — 1430, |
| 2♡[2] | 3♠ | opener minimum. |
| 4♠ | 4NT[3] | 4. '2 without'. |
| 5♡[4] | 6♣[5] | 5. Choice of contract. |
| pass[6] | | 6. Knows spades *aren't* solid. |

An example of responder giving opener a choice of contract at the six-level. This one is a bit far out because Levy didn't support clubs a 'bit' sooner. Nonetheless, it does not pay to mess with six-level bids in previously-bid suits unless you know the agreed trump suit is solid or there has been jump agreement to a first-bid suit. Read on.

### THE TABLE IS SET
After a jump raise or jump preference to the asker's first-bid suit, that suit is considered the trump suit. Period. Any follow-up bid at the six-level in a lower-ranking suit, previously-bid or not, is a SSA grand slam try. It is *not* 'choice of contract'.

| Opener (you) | Responder |
|---|---|
| ♠ A | ♠ Q 7 5 3 2 |
| ♡ K Q J 5 4 3 | ♡ A 7 6 |
| ◇ 2 | ◇ A 7 5 |
| ♣ A K 10 9 4 | ♣ 6 3 |
| 1♡ | 1♠ |
| 3♣ | 4♡[1] |
| 4NT[2] | 5♡[3] |
| 6♣[4] | 6◇[5] |
| 7♡[6] | pass[7] |

1. Jump preference to a first-bid suit — the table is set.
2. RKB (1430) — jump-shifter asking.
3. '2 without'.
4. SSA in clubs.
5. Third-round control — queen or doubleton.
6. Going for it.
7. In the first and second edition of this madness, Kantar used this example and gave me ♡A10x to more or less assure the grand. In the third edition, he gave me the ♡A9x because he lives with guilt. This time I don't have either the nine or the ten. Has he gone mad? We could go down!

It is close whether to settle for six or go for gold by bidding a grand. Facing the ♣Q you are in great shape, but facing a doubleton club you may have to trump two clubs in dummy and the contract may depend upon the size of the second highest trump in dummy. Most partners find it easier to deal with bidding six and making seven as opposed to you know what. Amen.

# THE BOTTOM LINE

- After a '0' response, follow-up bids at the five-level are always some sort of ask: the next step is the queen-ask, any other (except the agreed suit, which is to play) is a SSA.
- After a '1' response, a return to the asker's first-bid major is to play. A return to a first-bid minor, if the next step, is the queen-ask. A return to the agreed suit is to play. A return to the responder's first-bid suit is to play — if the suit has been rebid or supported. If not and it's the next step, it's the queen-ask; if it's not the next step, it's a SSA. A follow-up bid in an unbid suit that is not a first-step queen-ask is a SSA.
- After a '2' or '3' response (1430) or a '3' response (3014), you are usually headed to slam. All the asks are available. After a '4' response, there is no way out short of slam.
- If there has been jump agreement to a first-bid suit, that suit is agreed; a six-level bid in a lower-ranking suit is a SSA.
- If there has been no jump agreement to a first-bid suit, a six-level bid in a lower-ranking previously-bid suit is either to play or a choice of contracts.

# CHAPTER 24

# THE LAST ROUND-UP

This (almost) final chapter is going to deal with some miscellaneous topics that haven't yet been covered (hard to believe there are any, isn't it?).

## RKB WHEN PARTNER PREEMPTS

### Responding to a Weak Two with a lower-level RKB ask

When partner opens a Weak Two, it makes sense to use a lower RKB ask. If you are missing two Keycards it is far safer to stop in 4♡ or 4♠ rather than put the contract at risk at the five-level.

One possibility is to use a leap to 4♣ (1430) to ask for Keycards (some use it to ask for trump honors), opener's suit agreed. However, the responses are different because responses of '3' and '4' are not in the game.

| Opener | Responder | |
|--------|-----------|--|
| 2♡[1] | 4♣[2] | 1. Weak. |
| | | 2. RKB (1430), hearts agreed. |

Say the opening bid is a weak 2♡ bid and responder jumps to 4♣, RKB (1430). The responses are:

| | | | |
|------|----------|---|------------|
| 4♢ | 1st step | = | 0 |
| 4♡ | 2nd step | = | 1 without |
| 4♠ | 3rd step | = | 1 with' |
| 4NT | 4th step | = | 2 without |
| 5♣ | 5th step | = | 2 with |

After a 1st step response of zero, the other major is the queen-ask. After any other response the queen is a known quantity and new suits are Specific Suit Asks; 4NT is the Specific King Ask.

THE 4♣ RESPONSE IN ACTION

| Opener | Responder | |
|--------|-----------|--|
| ♠ Q J 9 5 3 2 | ♠ A 7 6 | |
| ♡ 8 4 3 | ♡ 5 | |
| ♢ A 7 | ♢ K Q J 6 2 | |
| ♣ Q 2 | ♣ A K J 4 | 1. RKB. |
| 2♠ | 4♣[1] | 2. '1 with'. |
| 4♠[2] | pass[3] | 3. Two Keycards missing (could be two aces). |

## RKB over higher-level preempts

The 4♣ ask and similar responses can also be used after opening bids of 3◊, 3♡ and 3♠ (and you can use 4◊ over after a 3♣ opening). The loss factor is giving up a natural 4♣ response.

| Opener | Responder |
|---|---|
| ♠ A 6 | ♠ K 9 |
| ♡ K 10 9 7 5 3 2 | ♡ A Q 6 |
| ◊ 4 | ◊ A Q 7 6 5 3 |
| ♣ 8 7 6 | ♣ A 3 |
| | |
| 3♡ | 4♣[1] |
| 4NT[2] | 5◊[3] |
| 6♡[4] | 7♡[5] |
| pass | |

1. RKB 1430.
2. 4th step response = '2 without'.
3. SSA in diamonds.
4. Jump in trump suit = singleton.
5. Figuring to dump losing clubs on diamonds.

## THE BOTTOM LINE

- When partner opens with a Weak Two-bid or a three-level preempt, you can use 4♣ as RKB (1430).
- There are five step responses: '0', '1 without', '1 with', '2 without' and '2 with'.

## WHEN OPPONENTS INTERFERE OVER RKB

When the opponents interfere over an RKB ask, thank them. They have presented you with two extra bids, 'double' and 'pass'. After an RKB ask, interference might come above or beneath six of the agreed suit. If it comes above, a positive response commits the partnership to a grand slam (or 6NT). Very risky.

### Interference is below six of the agreed suit

If the ask is 1430 (strong asking weak), the more common ask, and the interference comes below six of the agreed suit, responses are:

| | | |
|---|---|---|
| dbl | = | 0 |
| pass | = | 1 |
| 1st step | = | 2 |
| 2nd step | = | 3 |

If you can remember the acronym DOPI (pronounced DOPEY, as in the Snow White story, it should be easy.

| DO | Double | = | 0 |
|----|--------|---|---|
| P1 | Pass | = | 1 |

If the ask is 3014 (weak asking strong) and the interference is below six of the agreed suit, responses are a bit different — and with good reason ('0' or '1' responses are not in the ballpark):

| dbl | = | 2 |
|-----|---|---|
| pass | = | 3 |
| 1st step | = | 4 |

Suppose you hold:  ♠ Q J 5 3   ♡ 6 5   ◇ K 7 4  ♣ K J 3 2

| Partner | Oppt. | You | Oppt. |
|---------|-------|-----|-------|
| 1♠ | 2♡ | 3♠[1] | pass |
| 4NT | 5◇ | ? | |

1. Limit raise.

Double to show '0'. With '1' you would pass, with '2' you would bid 5♡.
   Try another:  ♠ A J 10 6   ♡ A Q 4   ◇ 7 3   ♣ A K 8 4

| You | Oppt. | Partner | Oppt. |
|-----|-------|---------|-------|
| 1♣ | 1◇ | 1♠ | 2♡ |
| 4♠ | pass | 4NT | 5◇ |
| ? | | | |

This is a 3014 ask, interference below six of the agreed suit. 'Double shows '2' 'pass' shows '3', what you have and what you should bid. A 1st step response of 5♡ shows '4'.

## Interference is above six of the agreed suit

This time there are only two steps: they show an even or an odd number of Keycards.

*In a 1430 (strong asking weak) scenario:*

| dbl | = | 0 or 2 (even) |
|-----|---|---------------|
| pass | = | 1 or 3 (odd) |

*In a 3014 (weak asking strong) scenario*

| dbl | = | 2 or 4 (even) |
|-----|---|---------------|
| pass | = | 3 (odd) |

Suppose you hold:

♠ 5 2    ♡ A Q J 7 6    ◇ A 8    ♣ J 10 4 2

| You | Oppt. | Partner | Oppt. |
|-----|-------|---------|-------|
| 1♡ | pass | 2NT[1] | 2♠ |
| pass | 4♠ | 4NT[2] | 6♠ |
| ? | | | |

1. Jacoby 2NT agreeing hearts.

Here you have '2', an even number, so 'double'.

## The queen-ask after interference

After an RKB response to 'interference Blackwood', a next step rebid by the RKB bidder, including 5NT, is the queen-ask, a grand slam try. With the queen, jump in the trump suit; without the queen, sign off in the trump suit.

LOOKING FOR MY FAIR LADY

| You | | Partner | |
|-----|---|---------|---|
| ♠ A 10 6 4 3 | | ♠ K 8 5 2 | |
| ♡ K Q J 7 4 | | ♡ A 6 3 2 | |
| ◇ 10 | | ◇ A | |
| ♣ A K | | ♣ 6 5 4 3 | |

| You | Oppt. | Partner | Oppt. |
|-----|-------|---------|-------|
| 1♠ | 2NT[1] | 4◇[2] | pass |
| 4NT[3] | 5◇ | 5♠[4] | pass |
| 5NT[5] | pass | 6♠[6] | all pass |

1. Minors.
2. Splinter for spades.
3. RKB (1430).
4. '3'. Dbl = '0', Pass = '1', 5♡ = '2'.
5. Queen-ask (next step, including 5NT).
6. Queen denial.

More practice:

♠ K 6 4 3 2    ♡ 8    ◇ 6 5 3    ♣ A K 8 7

| Partner | Oppt. | You | Oppt. |
|---------|-------|-----|-------|
| 1♠ | 2♡ | 4♡[1] | pass |
| 4NT[2] | 5◇[3] | ?[4] | |

1. Strong spade raise with heart shortness.
2. RKB (1430).
3. Interference below six of the agreed suit.
4. Bid 5♡. Dbl = '0', Pass = '1', 5♡ = '2'.

♠ 4 3    ♡ K 2    ◇ K J 6    ♣ A J 7 6 3 2

| Partner | Oppt. | You | Oppt. |
|---------|-------|-----|-------|
| 1♣ | 1♡ | 2♡[1] | pass |
| 4♣[2] | 4◇[3] | ?[4] | |

1. Limit or better in clubs.
2. RKB (1430) after two-level agreement.
3. Interference below six of the agreed suit — pass to show '1'. Double shows '0', and 4♡, the next step, shows '2'; 4♠ would show '3'.

♠ A K 4 2    ♡ 6 5    ◇ 4 3    ♣ A Q J 6 3

| You | Oppt. | Partner | Oppt. |
|-----|-------|---------|-------|
| 1♣ | 1♡ | 1♠ | 3♡ |
| 4♠ | pass | 4NT[1] | 5◇[2] |
| ?[3] | | | |

1. RKB 3014. Opener has jumped.
2. Interference below six of the agreed suit.
3. Double shows '2' and Pass shows '3'. You have three Keycards so you should pass.

♠ A K 6 5    ♡ 9    ◇ Q 7    ♣ A K Q 4 3 2

| You | Oppt. | Partner | Oppt. |
|-----|-------|---------|-------|
| 1♣ | pass | 1♠ | 2♡ |
| 4♡ | pass | 4NT[1] | 6◇[2] |
| ?[3] | | | |

1. A 3014 ask, opener has jumped.
2. Interference below six of the agreed suit
3. Pass. This is a 3014 ask with interference beneath six of the agreed suit: Dbl = '2', Pass = 3, 6♡ = 4.

# THE BOTTOM LINE

If opponents interfere over your Keycard ask, you can use 'Double' and 'Pass' as part of your responses:

- If the interference is below six of the agreed suit, use DOPI responses. If the ask is 1430, dbl = '0', pass = '1', 1st step = '2', 2nd step = '3'. If the ask is 3014, dbl = '2', pass = '3', and 1st step = '4'.
- If the interference is above six of the agreed suit, use DEPO responses. Double = even (1430 '0 or 2', 3014 '2 or 4'), Pass = odd (1430 '1 or 3', 3014 '3').
- After the RKB response over interference, the next step is a queen-ask. Jump in the trump suit with the queen, or sign off in the trump suit without it.

# KEYCARD ASKS IN TAKEOUT DOUBLE SEQUENCES

Without agreements, sticky RKB sequences can arise after a takeout double. Perhaps the simplest agreements are these:

1) If the last bid is a major suit, a jump to 4NT is RKB for that major.
2) If the last bid is 3♣ and a bid of 3◇ is played as forcing, then a leap to 4◇ is RKB for clubs.
3) If the last bid is 3◇ and a bid of 3♡ is played as forcing, then a leap to 4♡ is RKB for diamonds. Be sure partner has read this page!

| Oppt. | Partner | Oppt. | You |
|-------|---------|-------|-----|
| 1♠ | dbl | pass | 2♠¹ |
| pass | 3◇² | pass | 4♡³ |

1. Cuebid: creates a force until there has been suit agreement below game.
2. Forcing.
3. RKB (3014) for diamonds.

In this sequence 3♡ is clearly forcing so 4♡ is RKB (3014) for diamonds and 4◇ would be invitational. The doubler is considered the strong hand in RKB sequences.

| Oppt. | You | Oppt. | Partner |
|-------|-----|-------|---------|
| 1♡ | dbl | pass | 2♡¹ |
| pass | 2♠² | pass | 3♣² |
| pass | 4◇³ | | |

1. Cuebid: creates a force until there has been suit agreement below game.
2. Forcing.
3. RKB (3014) for clubs.

In this sequence 3◇ by you is forcing so 4◇ can be used as RKB for clubs; a raise to 4♣ is invitational. These last two sequences can both be considered three-level non-agreement situations.

| Oppt. | You | Oppt. | Partner |
|-------|-----|-------|---------|
| 1♡ | dbl | pass | 3♣ |
| pass | ? | | |

A 3◇ rebid by you is forcing, so if you want to ask partner for Keycards in clubs, leap to 4◇. A raise to 4♣ would be invitational.

# THE BOTTOM LINE

- After a takeout double, if the response is 3♣ or 3♦ and that is the first time the suit has been bid, jumps by the doubler from 3♣ to 4♦ (when 3♦ is forcing) or from 3♦ to 4♥ (when 3♥ is forcing) are RKB asks, not splinter jumps.
- The takeout doubler is considered the strong hand in RKB ask sequences. If the doubler does the asking, it is a 1430 ask; if the partner of the doubler does the asking, it is a 3014 ask.

## RKB AFTER PARTNER OVERCALLS

What about asking for Keycards after partner overcalls? Even though it is rare, it happens. With a fit for partner's major-suit overcall, the only RKB ask is 4NT, but with a fit for a minor-suit overcall, maybe we can do better. In this book, 'better' means 'lower'.

| Oppt. | Partner | Oppt. | You |
|---|---|---|---|
| 1♥ | 2♣ or 2♦ | pass | ? |

If you wish to make a *direct* Keycard ask after a 2♣ or 3♣ overcall, try 4♦ (assuming diamonds is an unbid suit). After a 2♦ or 3♦ overcall, try 4NT (jumps to 4♥ or 4♠ are considered natural). In overcall sequences, the partner of the overcaller (called 'the advancer') is considered the strong hand.

If there has been splinter agreement after a two-level minor suit overcall, four of the agreed minor can be used to ask for Keycards.

| Oppt. | You | Oppt. | Partner |
|---|---|---|---|
| 1♥ | 2♣ | pass | 3♥¹ |
| pass | 4♣² | | |

1. Game-forcing splinter.
2. RKB 3014.

| West | East |
|------|------|
| ♠ K J 10 6 5 3 | ♠ A |
| ♡ Q J | ♡ 9 |
| ◇ A | ◇ 8 6 5 3 2 |
| ♣ A 9 5 4 | ♣ K Q J 7 6 2 |

| West | North | East | South |
|------|-------|------|-------|
| | | | 1◇ |
| 1♠ | pass | 2♣ | pass |
| 3◇¹ | pass | 4♣² | pass |
| 4♠³ | pass | 6♣ | all pass |

1. Game-forcing splinter. .
2. RKB (3014) after game-forcing agreement (overcaller is the strong hand).
3. '2 without'.

# RKB AFTER A PASSED HAND MAKES A FIT-SHOWING JUMP

What does the last bid in this sequence mean?

| Opener | Responder |
|--------|-----------|
| | pass |
| 1♣ | 2♡? |

For years most people played it to show an 'almost opening bid' with almost any distribution. Modern methods are that a passed-hand jump shift shows a big fit with opener's suit plus length in the jump suit. The jump usually shows ten cards between the two suits, or possibly nine with at least five cards in partner's first-bid minor, and 8-10 HCP. In the above sequence responder shows hearts and clubs; opener can Keycard by leaping to 4♣ (1430).

| Opener | Responder | |
|--------|-----------|--|
| ♠ A K 8 | ♠ 6 4 | 1. Passed-hand jump shift promising at least five diamonds, usually with five hearts, and 8-10 HCP. |
| ♡ K 5 | ♡ A J 4 3 2 | |
| ◇ A 9 8 6 4 | ◇ K 7 5 3 2 | 2. RKB (1430). |
| ♣ A 3 2 | ♣ 7 | 3. '2 without'. |
| | pass | 4. If opener can be sure responder has ten red cards, he can bid 7◇. However, it's possible that responder has only nine and there will be no play for 7◇. |
| 1◇ | 2♡¹ | |
| 4◇² | 4NT³ | |
| ?⁴ | | |

After a fit-showing jump shift, opener may not wish to to use RKB until he hears a further cuebid.

## TWO WILD HANDS!

| Opener | Responder | |
|---|---|---|
| ♠ — | ♠ A K 9 7 2 | |
| ♡ A Q 10 5 4 | ♡ 5 2 | |
| ◇ A K J 10 6 3 | ◇ Q 7 5 4 2 | |
| ♣ 8 6 | ♣ 9 | |
| | | 1. Passed-hand jump shift. |
| | pass | 2. Ambiguous force. |
| 1◇ | 2♠¹ | 3. Cuebid (singletons are often cue- |
| 3♡² | 4♣³ | bid below game in the agreed |
| 6◇ | | suit). |

How forcing is a passed-hand jump shift? It is forcing to three of the agreed minor. If either player bids three of the agreed minor at any time, partner is allowed to pass.

## THE BOTTOM LINE

- After a 2♣ or 3♣ overcall, 4◇ is RKB (assuming diamonds is an unbid suit). After a 2◇ or 3◇ overcall, 4NT is RKB. In overcall sequences, the partner of the overcaller (called 'the advancer') is considered the strong hand.
- If there has been splinter agreement after a two-level minor-suit overcall, four of the agreed minor can be used to ask for Keycards.
- After a fit-showing jump shift by a passed hand over opener's minor, a jump rebid of four of the minor is RKB (1430).

# CHAPTER 25

# 52 QUICK RKB TIPS

**1**  Don't even think of playing this version of RKB until you are sure of your asks, your agreement sequences and your partner!

**2**  Not every slam problem can be solved by using RKB; cuebidding, perhaps followed by RKB, is also an option.

**3**  Agreement makes the world go round, the world go round. Try to clarify the agreed suit before making an RKB ask.

**4**  When opener asks for Keycards, it is 1430 unless responder has jump-shifted. If he has and opener asks, it's a 3014 ask.

**5**  When responder asks it is 1430 — unless opener has jumped, reversed, opened 1NT, 2NT, or 1♣ or 2♣, strong.  If he has, it is 3014.

**6**  After a 5♣ response to RKB, a major agreed, 5♢ is the queen ask; after a 5♢ response to RKB, spades agreed, 5♡ is the queen-ask.

**7**  After a 5♢ response to RKB (1430) hearts agreed, 5♡ is the queen-ask facing '3' and to play facing '0'.

**8**  After a 5♢ response to RKB (3014), hearts agreed, 5♡ is the queen-ask facing '4' (the usual case) and to play facing '1'.

**9**  When your response to 4NT is 5♣ or 5♢ after major-suit agreement, assume partner knows how many Keycards you have (the difference is three!). If he doesn't know, shop around for a new you-know-what!

**10**  When responding to a queen-ask after a major-suit agreement, the denial response is a return to the trump suit.

**11** When responding to the queen-ask knowing of a ten-card fit, show the queen even if you don't have it!

**12** When responding to the queen-ask holding the queen of the agreed suit plus an outside king, bid the king-suit; with two outside kings, bid the cheaper king-suit first.

**13** A 5NT response to a queen-ask, hearts or spades agreed, shows the queen and denies a side-suit king, but shows an extra, usually the queen of partner's first-bid suit or extra trump length in the long-trump hand.

**14** After partner preempts, 4♣ by you is RKB with specialized responses.

**15** When the response to 4NT is 5♣ or 5◇, a major suit agreed, assume partner *knows* how many Keycards you have. There is no such animal as a sign-off after a '3' response to a 1430 ask (strong asking weak) or a '4' response to a 3140 ask (weak asking strong). Please.

**16** After a Keycard response to a 4NT ask, hearts or spades agreed, 5NT asks for specific kings up the line. With two kings, bid the lower-ranking first; with three kings, bid 6NT (or seven of the agreed suit with a nine-card fit).

**17** After a king-showing response to a 5NT ask, a new suit by the asker is a subsequent king-ask, a grand slam try. Responder signs off without the asked-for king, but bids on with it. A first-step response, excluding the sign-off response, shows Kxx(x). A second-step response shows Kx.

**18** Any ask made above five of the agreed suit is a grand slam try. Responder is encouraged to bid a grand if thirteen tricks can be counted.

**19** The Specific Suit Ask comes with two faces: (1) after the RKB response, a new suit that is not the queen-ask; (2) a new suit by the asker after a king-showing response to a queen-ask.

**20** In most Keycard sequences the stronger (unlimited) hand makes the ask. A limited hand cannot ask for Keycards unless partner has splintered or made a slam try.

**21**    Most Keycard asks come directly after the agreement. First the agreement, then the ask. Yes, there are exceptions where four-level agreement is the ask: if a 2♣ opener, a jump-shifter or a reverser agrees partner's minor at the four level, that is RKB. *Noblesse oblige.*

**22**    Forget slam if you are off two Keycards unless you know they are both kings; then you have choices.

**23**    After a game-forcing three-level splinter, clubs or diamonds agreed, a bid of four of the agreed suit by either hand is RKB. If cuebidding takes the partnership beyond four of the agreed suit, 4NT is the next RKB off-ramp.

**24**    After a four-level splinter, clubs or diamonds agreed, the cheapest unbid (or the fourth) suit can be used to ask for Keycards. If diamonds is the agreed suit and clubs is the fourth suit or the unbid suit, the asker can use a second-bid major to ask for Keycards.

**25**    After a splinter to 4♠, clubs agreed, 4NT is RKB. The player who makes the splinter to 4♠ promises at least one Keycard... *in blood!*

**26**    No suit the opponents have bid can ever be used as an RKB ask. Ditto for 4♣ and 5♣ when diamonds is the agreed suit.

**27**    After minor-suit agreement, if an RKB ask can be made at the four-level in a non-agreed suit, bidding 4NT instead is a replacement cuebid in the RKB ask-suit.

**28**    When four of the agreed minor can be used to ask for Keycards, leaping to 4NT is natural; 4NT after the fourth suit is also natural.

**29**    After two-level minor-suit agreement or after game-forcing three-level minor-suit agreement, four of the agreed minor by an unlimited hand is RKB.

**30**    After three-level non-forcing minor-suit agreement, four of the agreed suit is RKB if there are two or three unbid suits (if they have bid a suit, that is considered unbid). If there are fewer than two unbid suits, leaps to 4♦ over 3♣ or to 4♥ over 3♦ are RKB asks.

**31** After four-level club agreement, 4♢ is RKB; after four-level diamond agreement, 4♡ is RKB unless hearts is a first-bid suit. If it is, then 4♠ is RKB. If both majors are first-bid suits, 4NT is RKB.

**32** The negative response to a 4♡ or 4♠ queen-ask is 4NT.

**33** After a non-zero response to a RKB ask, 4NT is the queen-ask if it is the next step. If 4NT is not the next step it is the SKA; 4NT is the only SKA available after minor suit agreement.

**34** After a response to RKB, a minor suit agreed, the next step, including 4NT (see previous tip) is the queen-ask. If the asker follows up with a suit that is not the next step, it is a SSA.

**35** If the response to a RKB ask is '0', clear the decks; any follow-up in a previously-bid suit or 4NT is to play.

**36** After minor-suit agreement, 5NT by the asker is *not* the Specific King Ask. It is a grand slam try looking around for some extra that the responder has not been able to show, particularly the queen of the asker's first-bid suit, etc. If the responder has an extra, responder bids the grand.

**37** In double-agreement sequences, the kings and queens of both suits are included in the responses.

**38** When a balanced hand faces a two-suiter, the kings of both suits as well as the queen of the agreed suit are included in the RKB response.

**39** After minor-suit agreement, a leap one level beyond a splinter jump is Exclusion Keycard Blackwood (EKB). The jump is made in the void suit and responder does not count the ace of the void suit in the response. However, the king of the agreed suit is counted (but not the queen). Responses start with a first step '0'.

**40** After major-suit agreement, a leap above game is EKB.

**41** A strong 2♣ opener, a jump-shifter or an opener who reverses cannot splinter. Their jump after partner rebids a suit or after agreement is EKB.

**42** Any ask beneath five of the agreed suit should be considered a small slam try; any ask above five of the agreed suit should be considered a grand slam try.

**43** After *jump* agreement to a first-bid suit, that suit is the agreed suit. Period.

**44** After non-jump *preference* agreement to a first-bid suit, there is still the possibility of playing in the asker's second suit if the asker has shown a two-suiter.

**45** When an RKB ask follows agreement to the asker's *second*-bid suit and the asker returns to his first-bid *major* at the five- or six-level, it is to play.

**46** If you know in your heart of hearts that partner is not going to be able to field one of your brilliant asking bids, shelve it.

**47** Do not let these minor suits asks throw you: most of them occur after three- or four-level agreement. Few come after two-level agreement or after the dreaded non-agreement.

**48** Just play the stuff that you feel comfortable with, perhaps adding a bit here and there once you are satisfied with your comfort level. Don't over-tax your partner!

**49** After a takeout double, 1430 if the doubler asks, 3014 if partner does.

**50** After an overcall, 3014 if the overcaller asks, 1430 if the advancer does.

**51** When making a 1430 ask, be prepared for a possible discouraging response, particularly a '2 without' 3rd step response. If you can't handle it, cuebid instead.

**52** Don't go out of your way to ask for Keycards holding '0' or '1' Keycard; think 'cuebid'!

# CHAPTER 26

# THE GRAND FINALE

## SIXTY HANDS TO BID WITH YOUR FAVORITE PARTNER

This last chapter of the book contain sixty hands for you to bid with your favorite partner — take turns being Opener and Responder, if you like. Use your own bidding methods but try to incorporate some, most, or all of the asks outlined in this book. Then look at the section headed 'My Auctions', which will be my suggested path to the 'correct' contract. (Of course I have the advantage of seeing both hands!) I will try to be fair — but it's tough! Also I will try to mention various ways to bid the hand, keeping in mind that no two pairs play all the same conventions. Assume IMP scoring, though mention will be made if the hand might be bid differently at matchpoint scoring.

Let it be known that players who use a strong 1♣ system have a decided advantage on slam hands because they start one level lower. Also players who play Two-over-One are better placed on slam hands because they can make game-forcing agreements at a lower level.

Having said that, the following are the agreements being used in my suggested auctions, trying to cater to Standard players:

1. 1NT = 15-17 HCP; 2NT = 20-22 HCP; Transfers.
2. Strong 2♣ opening; 2♢ response is waiting.
3. Inverted minors: a raise from 1♣ to 2♣ or from 1♢ to 2♢ is game-forcing.
4. Crisscross: jumps from 1♣ to 2♢ or 1♢ to 3♣ are limit raises. Jump raises are preemptive. Limit raises will be mentioned in conjunction with Crisscross.
5. 4NT after the fourth suit is natural.
6. Limit raises in the majors.
7. Two-over-one not a game force, but does promise another bid.
8. After a two-over-one initial response, a jump by the opener to a lower-ranking suit is a splinter agreeing partner's suit.
9. Strong jump shifts at the two-level, excluding 2♢ which is Crisscross.
10. All asks in the book including both 1430 and 3140 RKB asks.
11. Exclusion Keycard Blackwood.

# OPENER'S HANDS

HAND 1

&spades; A K J 6 2
&hearts; A K Q J
&diams; A K J
&clubs; 3

HAND 2

&spades; 7 5 4
&hearts; K Q 8 3
&diams; A 7 5 2
&clubs; A 9

HAND 3

&spades; K J 10 8 4 3
&hearts; K 6 2
&diams; 4 3
&clubs; 5 4

HAND 4

&spades; A J 5 2
&hearts; Q 8
&diams; K Q J 6 5
&clubs; K 8

HAND 5

&spades; K Q 8 7 5 2
&hearts; 4
&diams; A Q 6 4
&clubs; A 3

HAND 6

&spades; K Q J 6
&hearts; 8
&diams; Q 7 6
&clubs; A 7 5 3 2

HAND 7

&spades; 5 4
&hearts; A Q
&diams; K 7 6 3
&clubs; A K 6 5 4

HAND 8

&spades; A K 5 4
&hearts; K 7
&diams; A K Q 10 6 2
&clubs; 7

HAND 9

&spades; A K J 5 2
&hearts; 4 2
&diams; A Q 8
&clubs; 10 8 5

HAND 10

&spades; Q 8
&hearts; A Q 7 6 2
&diams; K Q 5 3
&clubs; K 4

HAND 11

&spades; A K 10 8 6 4
&hearts; 8
&diams; Q
&clubs; A J 10 5 2

HAND 12

&spades; A K 7 5 4
&hearts; A Q 6
&diams; 9 5 2
&clubs; 10 3

HAND 13

&spades; K Q 8 6 5
&hearts; —
&diams; A K J 5 3 2
&clubs; K 6

HAND 14

&spades; A 6 3
&hearts; 9 8 4
&diams; A Q J 2
&clubs; K Q 5

HAND 15

&spades; A 6
&hearts; A 8 4
&diams; K J 10 6 2
&clubs; A J 7

HAND 16

&spades; A Q 6 4 3
&hearts; 5
&diams; A K 4 2
&clubs; K J 7

HAND 17

&spades; A K 8
&hearts; 6
&diams; A K 7 4
&clubs; A K 10 6 5

HAND 18

&spades; 6
&hearts; A 8 7 4 2
&diams; A K Q 6
&clubs; K Q 2

HAND 19

&spades; A K J 6 3 2
&hearts; K 4
&diams; 2
&clubs; A 6 4 3

HAND 20

&spades; 5 3
&hearts; A K
&diams; A 10 5 2
&clubs; A K Q 6 4

HAND 21

&spades; 5
&hearts; A K Q 6 3
&diams; K 10 8 7 4
&clubs; 9 3

HAND 22

&spades; J 10 7
&hearts; A K Q
&diams; A K 8 2
&clubs; 5 4 2

HAND 23

&spades; A K Q
&hearts; 7
&diams; A J 8 7 5 2
&clubs; K 6 4

HAND 24

&spades; 5
&hearts; K 5 4 3
&diams; A K Q 6 4
&clubs; K Q 8

HAND 25

    ♠ A 6 3
    ♡ A J 8 6 4 2
    ◇ K 5 4
    ♣ 7

HAND 26

    ♠ 4
    ♡ A Q 10 4 3
    ◇ A Q 2
    ♣ K 10 6 5

HAND 27

    ♠ 6 4 2
    ♡ A K J
    ◇ 4
    ♣ K 10 7 5 3 2

HAND 28

    ♠ A Q 7
    ♡ A 4 2
    ◇ A 7 6 4
    ♣ Q 6 3

HAND 29

    ♠ A J
    ♡ A 7
    ◇ A Q J 9 5 4
    ♣ 4 3 2

HAND 30

    ♠ A K 2
    ♡ A 7 6 5
    ◇ K Q 8
    ♣ A K 4

HAND 31

    ♠ A Q 10 9
    ♡ A K 6
    ◇ 8
    ♣ Q 8 7 6 4

HAND 32

    ♠ —
    ♡ A Q 8 7 5 2
    ◇ K Q 7
    ♣ A Q 10 3

HAND 33

    ♠ A K J 7
    ♡ K Q
    ◇ A K Q 8 2
    ♣ 5 4

HAND 34

    ♠ Q 5
    ♡ A 6 5
    ◇ K 6 3 2
    ♣ K Q J 7

HAND 35

    ♠ A Q J 10 6
    ♡ A K
    ◇ A K J 3 2
    ♣ 5

HAND 36

    ♠ 5
    ♡ A 9 8 4
    ◇ A Q J 10 8 6 3
    ♣ 6

RHO opens 3♡ in front of you.

HAND 37

♠ K Q 5
♡ A K 8 6 3
◇ A 7 6 5
♣ 2

HAND 38

♠ 3
♡ Q 6 5
◇ K Q 4
♣ A J 10 6 5 3

HAND 39

♠ 4
♡ A Q J 8 4 3 2
◇ 7 6
♣ 5 4 2

HAND 40

♠ A Q J 5
♡ 10 8 7 4
◇ —
♣ K Q J 6 2

HAND 41

♠ —
♡ K 8 4
◇ A K J 6 4
♣ Q J 8 3 2

You open 1◇, LHO overcalls 1♠, and partner bids 2♣. Take it from here.

HAND 42

♠ A Q J 4 2
♡ 8
◇ A K 8 6 3
♣ 5 4

HAND 42

♠ A Q 7 6 3
♡ —
◇ K 3
♣ A K Q 5 4 2

HAND 44

♠ 6 5 4
♡ A K J 6 4 2
◇ 7
♣ Q J 8

HAND 45

♠ —
♡ A K J 5
◇ K Q 6
♣ A Q 9 7 5 2

HAND 46

♠ K J 6
♡ 4
◇ A K 5 3
♣ A Q J 4 2

HAND 47

♠ A 6
♡ K Q 4 2
◇ 5 4
♣ A Q 10 3 2

HAND 48

♠ A Q J 9 8 5
♡ K J 5 4
◇ A K
♣ A

HAND 49

♠ 6 3
♡ A Q 7 3
◇ A J 4 2
♣ K Q 6

HAND 50

♠ A K J 5 2
♡ 3
◇ J 7 2
♣ A K 6 3

HAND 51

♠ Q J
♡ K Q 7 4 3
◇ K 8
♣ Q J 5 2

HAND 52

♠ A J 7
♡ A K Q 6 3
◇ 6
♣ 8 6 5 2

HAND 53

♠ A Q J 8 3
♡ 9
◇ A 8 5
♣ A 6 4 2

HAND 54

♠ A 6 5 4
♡ 4
◇ A Q J 3 2
♣ K J 8

HAND 55

♠ A K Q 6
♡ A K 6 4 3
◇ 2
♣ Q J 6

HAND 56

♠ A K 6 3
♡ A
◇ A J 6
♣ A K Q 7 6

HAND 57

♠ Q J 5 4
♡ J 7
◇ K J 6 2
♣ A K 4

HAND 58

♠ A 3
♡ A K 8 5
◇ A Q 5 2
♣ A 8 6

HAND 59

♠ A K 9 4
♡ A 5
◇ K Q 10 7
♣ 9 8 7

HAND 60

♠ A Q J 5
♡ A Q J 7 4
◇ A Q
♣ 6 2

# RESPONDER'S HANDS

## HAND 1

♠ 8 7 5 4 3
♡ 9 4
◇ 7 6 5
♣ A Q 2

## HAND 2

♠ A K 6 2
♡ A J 7 6 4 2
◇ 4
♣ K 7

## HAND 3

♠ Q 6 5
♡ 9
◇ A K 7 6 2
♣ A K J 7

## HAND 4

♠ K 7 4 3
♡ K 6
◇ A 4 2
♣ A Q 6 5

## HAND 5

♠ A J 3
♡ A J 7
◇ 5 2
♣ K J 6 4 2

## HAND 6

♠ 3
♡ K Q J 4
◇ A K J 5 4 3 2
♣ 4

## HAND 7

♠ A 10 6 2
♡ K 8
◇ A Q J 5 4 2
♣ 3

## HAND 8

♠ 7 6 3 2
♡ A J 5 3
◇ 5
♣ A 6 5 4

## HAND 9

♠ 6
♡ A K Q 5
◇ K J 10 6 4 2
♣ 3 2

## HAND 10

♠ 6 3
♡ 4
◇ A J 10 6
♣ A Q 7 6 3 2

## HAND 11

♠ 9 7 5 3 2
♡ A Q 6
◇ 9 8 4
♣ K 3

## HAND 12

♠ Q J 2
♡ K 8 5 4 3 2
◇ A 8
♣ A 7

## HAND 13

- ♠ J 10 4 2
- ♡ A K J
- ◇ —
- ♣ Q J 7 5 4 3

## HAND 14

- ♠ K Q J 9 5 4
- ♡ 6
- ◇ K 6 5
- ♣ A 9 2

## HAND 15

- ♠ K 7 5 3 2
- ♡ 2
- ◇ A Q 5 4 3
- ♣ 3 2

## HAND 16

- ♠ J 2
- ♡ K Q 10 7 4
- ◇ Q 6
- ♣ A Q 10 3

## HAND 17

- ♠ Q 4
- ♡ K Q 5 3 2
- ◇ J 6 3 2
- ♣ Q 3

## HAND 18

- ♠ A K Q 5 3
- ♡ Q J 6 3
- ◇ 5 4
- ♣ 4 3

## HAND 19

- ♠ Q 8 5
- ♡ A Q 8
- ◇ A 9 7
- ♣ K J 7 2

## HAND 20

- ♠ K J 7 4 2
- ♡ 8 6
- ◇ K Q J 6 3
- ♣ 2

## HAND 21

- ♠ A K 7 2
- ♡ 5 4
- ◇ A Q J 6 5
- ♣ Q 7

## HAND 22

- ♠ 4
- ♡ 7
- ◇ Q J 7 6 5 3
- ♣ A K 7 6 3

## HAND 23

- ♠ 8 6
- ♡ K Q 5
- ◇ K Q 6 4 3
- ♣ J 3 2

## HAND 24

- ♠ K Q J 6 2
- ♡ A J 7 2
- ◇ J 3
- ♣ A J

HAND 25

♠ 4
♡ K Q 5
◇ A 8 7 2
♣ A Q J 6 3

HAND 26

♠ A 9 6
♡ K
◇ 8 6 5
♣ A Q J 7 4 2

HAND 27

♠ K 8 5
♡ 7
◇ A 10 9 6 5 2
♣ A Q 4

HAND 28

♠ K 6 3
♡ K Q 10 7 5 3
◇ 3
♣ A 10 2

HAND 29

♠ K Q 6 3
♡ Q J 10 4
◇ 6
♣ A K J 7

HAND 30

♠ 6 4 3
♡ 4
◇ A 6 2
♣ Q J 10 7 5 2

HAND 31

♠ 5
♡ 5 3 2
◇ A J 6 3 2
♣ A K J 10

HAND 32

♠ Q 7 6 3
♡ K 6 4 3
◇ A 4
♣ 6 5 2

HAND 33

♠ Q 4 2
♡ A 10 6 3
◇ 6 5 4 3
♣ J 8

HAND 34

♠ A K J 7 4 3
♡ 8
◇ A J 10
♣ 5 4 2

HAND 35

♠ K 5 4 3
♡ Q 7 4 2
◇ 6
♣ Q 7 6 3

HAND 36

♠ A K Q 10 6
♡ —
◇ K 7 5 2
♣ K 7 4 3

LHO opens 3♡ in front of your partner.

## HAND 37

&spades; A J 8
&hearts; J 7 5 4 2
&diams; 4
&clubs; A J 4 3

## HAND 38

&spades; A K J 7 4 2
&hearts; A
&diams; A 9 7
&clubs; Q 4 2

## HAND 39

&spades; A 10 7 6
&hearts; K 6
&diams; A K J 5 2
&clubs; A 8

## HAND 40

&spades; K 3
&hearts; K Q J 5 2
&diams; A K J 4 3
&clubs; 5

## HAND 41

&spades; A J 6 3
&hearts; 7 5 2
&diams; 2
&clubs; A K 7 6 4

Partner opens 1&diams;, RHO overcalls 1&spades; and you bid 2&clubs;. Take it from here.

## HAND 42

&spades; —
&hearts; A J 6 3
&diams; Q J 9 5 4 2
&clubs; Q J 2

## HAND 43

&spades; 8 5 4 2
&hearts; A 9 4
&diams; Q 10 9 6 5 2
&clubs; —

## HAND 44

&spades; K Q J 2
&hearts; 3
&diams; A K Q J 6 3 2
&clubs; A

## HAND 45

&spades; A J 6
&hearts; 6 3 2
&diams; 8 4
&clubs; K J 8 6 3

## HAND 46

&spades; 8 3
&hearts; A K 6 5 2
&diams; Q J 7 4 2
&clubs; 6

## HAND 47

&spades; K 8 3
&hearts; A J 7 5 3
&diams; A K 6 2
&clubs; 7

## HAND 48

&spades; K 10 7 4 3 2
&hearts; —
&diams; J 6 3 2
&clubs; Q 9 4

HAND 49

    ♠ K Q J 10 7 4 2
    ♡ 5
    ♢ K Q 7 6
    ♣ 4

HAND 50

    ♠ 6 3
    ♡ A K 10 6 4
    ♢ A K 5
    ♣ J 4 2

HAND 51

    ♠ A K 6
    ♡ 5
    ♢ A J 4
    ♣ K 9 7 6 4 3

HAND 52

    ♠ K Q 9
    ♡ 4
    ♢ A 7 4 2
    ♣ Q J 7 4 3

HAND 53

    ♠ K 6 4 2
    ♡ A 6 3 2
    ♢ 6
    ♣ K Q 7 3

HAND 54

    ♠ 10 2
    ♡ A J 9 3 2
    ♢ K 10 8 6
    ♣ Q 3

HAND 55

    ♠ 3
    ♡ 7 2
    ♢ A K Q J 5 4
    ♣ 8 4 3 2

HAND 56

    ♠ Q 7 5 4
    ♡ 10 3 2
    ♢ 3
    ♣ J 9 8 4 2

HAND 57

    ♠ A
    ♡ A K 6 5 4 3
    ♢ 3
    ♣ Q J 8 5 2

HAND 58

    ♠ Q J 6 4 2
    ♡ 4 3
    ♢ K J 7 6 3
    ♣ 3

HAND 59

    ♠ Q 10 6 3 2
    ♡ K 10 6 4 3
    ♢ A 5 2
    ♣ —

HAND 60

    ♠ K 2
    ♡ 5 2
    ♢ 9 6
    ♣ A Q J 7 5 4 3

# MY AUCTIONS

### 1.

| Opener | Responder | |
|---|---|---|
| ♠ A K J 6 2 | ♠ 8 7 5 4 3 | 1. Waiting. |
| ♡ A K Q J | ♡ 9 4 | 2. Positive response. |
| ◇ A K J | ◇ 7 6 5 | 3. RKB 1430. |
| ♣ 3 | ♡ A Q 2 | 4. '1'. |
| | | 5. Queen-ask. |
| 2♣ | 2◇[1] | 6. Confirms the queen (ten-card fit |
| 2♠ | 3♠[2] | known) and denies a side-suit king. |
| 4NT[3] | 5♣[4] | 7. At worst 7♠ is on a diamond |
| 5◇[5] | 6♠ [6] | finesse, but there are so many |
| 7♠[7] | pass | winning scenarios aside from a |
| | | last-ditch diamond finesse that |
| | | the grand should be bid. This is |
| | | not a high-risk grand. |

### 2.

| Opener | Responder | |
|---|---|---|
| ♠ 7 5 4 | ♠ A K 6 2 | |
| ♡ K Q 8 3 | ♡ A J 7 6 4 2 | |
| ◇ A 7 5 2 | ◇ 4 | |
| ♣ A 9 | ♣ K 7 | 1. Four hearts with a maximum |
| | | raise. |
| 1◇ | 1♡ | 2. RKB (1430). The 2♡ raise makes |
| 2♡ | 2♠ | responder the strong hand. |
| 4♡[1] | 4NT[2] | 3. '3'. |
| 5◇[3] | 5♠[4] | 4. SSA in spades. |
| 6♡ | pass | 5. Denies third-round spade control. |

After a '3' response to a 1430 ask, hearts agreed, 5♡ is the queen ask. It is not to play. Therefore, 5♠ can be used as a SSA ask. If opener held two small spades, opener would make a 1st step response of 5NT leading to a grand.

### 3.

| Opener | Responder | |
|---|---|---|
| ♠ K J 10 8 4 3 | ♠ Q 6 5 | |
| ♡ K 6 2 | ♡ 9 | |
| ◇ 4 3 | ◇ A K 7 6 2 | |
| ♣ 5 4 | ♣ A K J 7 | |
| 2♠ | 4♣[1] | 1. RKB. |
| 4♡[2] | 4♠ | 2. '1 without'. |
| pass | | |

Give opener the ♠AK, and the response is 4NT, leading to 6♠.

**4.**

| Opener | Responder | |
|---|---|---|
| ♠ A J 5 2 | ♠ K 7 4 3 | |
| ♡ Q 8 | ♡ K 6 | |
| ◇ K Q J 6 5 | ◇ A 4 2 | |
| ♣ K 8 | ♣ A Q 6 5 | |
| 1◇ | 1♠ | 1. RKB 3014 (opener has jumped). |
| 3♠ | 4NT[1] | 2. '1 or 4', but almost always '4'. |
| 5◇[2] | 5♡[3] | 3. Queen-ask. |
| 5♠[4] | pass | 4. Negative. |

Strange hand: 5♠ could go down with a bad spade break and 6♠ makes on a good spade break, but 6◇ or 6NT are the best slams. Did you get there?

**5.**

| Opener | Responder | |
|---|---|---|
| ♠ K Q 8 7 5 2 | ♠ A J 3 | |
| ♡ 4 | ♡ A J 7 | |
| ◇ A Q 6 4 | ◇ 5 2 | |
| ♣ A 3 | ♣ K J 6 4 2 | 1. RKB (1430). |
| 1♠ | 2♣ | 2. '2 without'. |
| 2◇ | 3♠ | 3. SKA. A grand slam try. |
| 4NT[1] | 5♡[2] | 4. ♣K. |
| 5NT[2] | 6♣[3] | 6. Do you have the ◇K (or a single- |
| 6◇[4] | 6♠[5] | ton?). |
| pass | | 7. Negative. |

After a positive response to a SKA, a new suit by the asker is a second king-ask. Responder accepts with the king and 'sometimes' with a singleton. With a singleton, it depends whether the ask is in a previously-bid suit (the case here) or in an unbid suit. In a bid suit responder needs four trumps to accept. In an unbid suit, three will do. Playing Two-over-One, the game-forcing agreement can take place at the two-level leaving opener more room for exploration. As it happens, the same contract will be reached.

**6.**

| Opener | Responder | |
|---|---|---|
| ♠ K Q J 6 | ♠ 3 | 1. If 3◇ is considered a game |
| ♡ 8 | ♡ K Q J 4 | force, 4◇ is RKB. If 3◇ is not a |
| ◇ Q 7 6 | ◇ A K J 5 4 3 2 | game force, since there is only |
| ♣ A 7 5 3 2 | ♣ 4 | one unbid suit 4◇ would be invi- |
| | | tational and responder would |
| 1♣ | 1◇ | have to leap to 4♡ to ask for |
| 1♠ | 2♡ | Keycards. 'With zero or one, the |
| 3◇[1] | 4◇[2] | jump is fun.' Remember? |
| 4♡[3] | 5◇[4] | 2. RKB (1430) — opener has not |
| pass | | jumped, etc. |
| | | 3. '1'. |
| | | 4. Two aces missing. If the ask is |
| | | 4♡, the reply is 4♠ and |
| | | responder signs off in 5◇. |

7. | Opener | Responder |
|---|---|
| ♠ 5 4 | ♠ A 10 6 2 |
| ♡ A Q | ♡ K 8 |
| ◇ K 7 6 3 | ◇ A Q J 5 4 2 |
| ♣ A K 6 5 4 | ♣ 3 |
| | |
| 1♣ | 1◇ |
| 3◇ | 4◇[1] |
| 4♡[2] | 4NT[3] |
| 5♣[4] | 5♠[5] |
| 6◇[6] | pass |

1. RKB (3014). After three-level-non-forcing agreement, when there are two or three unbid suits, the raise is the ask. Bidding an unbid suit is temporarily considered a game try though it might be a concealed slam try.
2. '3'.
3. SKA after minor-suit agreement,
4. The ♣K.
5. Do you have the ♠K or a singleton?
6. Negative.

After a SKA, a new suit asks for the king, looking for a grand. If it is impossible that responder can have that king (not the case here), then it is an ask for third-round control for the grand.

8. | Opener | Responder |
|---|---|
| ♠ A K 5 4 | ♠ 7 6 3 2 |
| ♡ K 7 | ♡ A J 5 3 |
| ◇ A K Q 10 6 2 | ◇ 5 |
| ♣ 7 | ♣ A 6 5 4 |
| | |
| 1◇ | 1♡ |
| 2♠ | 3♠ |
| 4NT[1] | 5♡[2] |
| 6◇[3] | pass[4] |

1. RKB (1430).
2. '2 without'.
3. To play.
4. Okay, okay.

After an RKB ask, a return to opener's first-bid suit is to play even if there has been agreement in another suit.

9. | Opener | Responder |
|---|---|
| ♠ A K J 5 2 | ♠ 6 |
| ♡ 4 2 | ♡ A K Q 5 |
| ◇ A Q 8 | ◇ K J 10 6 4 2 |
| ♣ 10 8 5 | ♣ 3 2 |
| | |
| 1♠ | 2◇ |
| 3◇ | 3♡[1] |
| 3♠[2] | 5◇[3] |
| pass[4] | |

1. Strength-showing bid, probably looking for 3NT.
2. Reasonable spades, probably.
3. I give up.
4. I wonder what they are going to lead?

RKB should not be used with two or more quick losers in an unbid suit — until partner cuebids that suit or takes over with an RKB ask of his own.

**10. Opener**

♠ Q 8
♡ A Q 7 6 2
◇ K Q 5 3
♣ K 4

**Responder**

♠ 6 3
♡ 4
◇ A J 10 6
♣ A Q 7 6 3 2

| Opener | Responder | |
|---|---|---|
| 1♡ | 2♣ | 1. Jump agreement, not the ask. |
| 2◇ | 4◇¹ | 2. Cuebid suggesting no spade control. |
| 5♣² | 5◇³ | 3. Well, if you don't have one, I don't either. |
| pass | | |

If responder had a singleton spade and a doubleton heart, slam would be a great proposition. However, the bidding would have gone differently. Responder would have jumped to 3♠ over 2◇, a fit-showing, control-showing cuebid: a singleton or the ace if you are of that persuasion. It is so important to agree the suit with a game-forcing bid that in my opinion either control is acceptable.

**11. Opener**

♠ A K 10 8 6 4
♡ 8
◇ Q
♣ A J 10 5 2

**Responder**

♠ 9 7 5 3 2
♡ A Q 6
◇ 9 8 4
♣ K 3

| Opener | Responder | |
|---|---|---|
| 1♠ | 3♠¹ | 1. Limit raise. |
| 4♣² | 4♡³ | 2. A slam try cuebid. |
| 4♠⁴ | 5♣⁵ | 3. Cuebid. |
| 6♠⁶ | pass | 4. Having made a slam try, 4♠ is enough. |
| | | 5. Cuebid. |
| | | 6. Willing to gamble slam facing the ♣K. |

A player who makes a limit raise with two important cards (♡A, ♣K) facing a partner who makes a slam try should show both cards even though it may mean going beyond game. The ♣K is worth its weight in gold. Notice that the ♡Q is valueless and the hand is still cold for 6♠ .

**12. Opener**

♠ A K 7 5 4
♡ A Q 6
◇ 9 5 2
♣ 10 3

**Responder**

♠ Q J 2
♡ K 8 5 4 3 2
◇ A 8
♣ A 7

| Opener | Responder | |
|---|---|---|
| 1♠ | 2♡ | 1. Double agreement now in place. |
| 3♡ | 3♠¹ | 2. Would rather the lead came up to partner's hand. |
| 4♡² | 4NT³ | 3. RKB (1430) — double agreement, opener has not jumped or reversed. |
| 5◇⁴ | 5♡⁵ | 4. '3 or 0' (surely '3'). |
| 5NT⁶ | 7NT⁷ | 5. Queen-ask facing '3', to play facing '0'. |
| | | 6. 2nd step response = the lower-ranking queen (1st step = neither queen, 3rd step = higher-ranking queen, 4th step= both queens). |
| | | 7. Can count thirteen tricks. |

After a '3' response to a 1430 ask, hearts agreed or hearts one of the agreed suits, a 5♡ rebid by the asker is the queen-ask facing '3', to play facing '0'. A '3' response to a 1430 ask is about the most the asker can hope for so it is 'highly' unlikely he will want to sign off.

13. **Opener**       **Responder**

♠ K Q 8 6 5     ♠ J 10 4 2

♡ —            ♡ A K J

◇ A K J 5 3 2   ◇ —

♣ K 6         ♣ Q J 7 5 4 3

| 1◇ | 2♣¹ | 1. Strong enough to bid both suits |
|---|---|---|
| 2♠ | 3♠ | in the proper order. |
| 5♡² | 5♠³ | 2. EKB — a jump above game. |
| pass | | 3. '0'. The ♡A doesn't count. |

Here Exclusion keeps you out of a slam off two cashing aces.

14. **Opener**      **Responder**

♠ A 6 3      ♠ K Q J 9 5 4

♡ 9 8 4     ♡ 6

◇ A Q J 2    ◇ K 6 5

♣ K Q 5     ♣ A 9 2

| 1NT | 2♡¹ |
|---|---|
| 2♠ | 4♡² |
| 4NT³ | 5♠⁴ |
| 6♠ | pass |

1. Transfer.
2. Singleton slam try — at least six spades, 12+ to 14+ HCP. With more, responder carries on if partner signs off.
3. RKB 1430. A 'perfecto' — three small facing a singleton.
4. '2 with'.

15. **Opener**      **Responder**

♠ A 6       ♠ K 7 5 3 2

♡ A 8 4    ♡ 2

◇ K J 10 6 2   ◇ A Q 5 4 3

♣ A J 7     ♣ 3 2

| 1NT | 2♡¹ |
|---|---|
| 2♠ | 3◇² |
| 4♡³ | 5◇⁴ |
| 5NT⁵ | 6◇⁶ |
| pass | |

1. Transfer.
2. Second suit — game force.
3. RKB 1430 for diamonds.
4. '2 with'.
5. Anything else over there I don't know about?
6. No, nothing.

When a balanced hand asks a two-suiter for Keycards, or vice versa, the kings of both suits are included in the response. After minor-suit agreement, 5NT is not the SKA, it is a grand slam try looking for unmentioned extras.

16. **Opener**        **Responder**

&spades; A Q 6 4 3    &spades; J 2
&hearts; 5           &hearts; K Q 10 7 4
&diams; A K 4 2      &diams; Q 6
&clubs; K J 7        &clubs; A Q 10 3

1&spades;            2&hearts;
3&diams;[1]          4NT[2]
pass[3]

1. Shows reversing values; after a two-level response the range is 15+ on up.
2. Natural. The range is approximately 14-15 HCP.
3. Too many negatives: 1) no fit in partner's long suit; 2) no intermediate spot card in your own long suit; 3) chances are there are only about 31-32 HCP between the two hands with no suit to run.

After opener bids a new suit at the three-level after a two-level response, 4NT by the responder is natural. If responder has a fit for diamonds or spades, he should agree the suit below game and go from there.

17. **Opener**        **Responder**

&spades; A K 8        &spades; Q 4
&hearts; 6           &hearts; K Q 5 3 2
&diams; A K 7 4      &diams; J 6 3 2
&clubs; A K 10 6 5   &clubs; Q 3

1&clubs;             1&hearts;
2&diams;             3&diams;[1]
4&diams;[2]          4&spades;[3]
5&diams;[4]          pass

1. Game-forcing three-level agreement.
2. RKB (1430).
3. The big '0'.
4. Opener has the option of bidding 4NT, to play, after a '0' response to RKB. At matchpoints, that seems a viable option.

18. **Opener**        **Responder**

&spades; 6           &spades; A K Q 5 3
&hearts; A 8 7 4 2   &hearts; Q J 6 3
&diams; A K Q 6      &diams; 5 4
&clubs; K Q 2        &clubs; 4 3

1&hearts;            1&spades;
2&diams;             4&hearts;[1]
4NT[2]               5&clubs;[3]
5&hearts;[4]         pass

1. Played as showing opening-bid values with concentrated strength in hearts and spades.
2. RKB (1430).
3. '1'.
4. When two Keycards are missing, even though one may be the king of trumps, it is better to sign off at the five-level. If partner has &hearts;QJ10x, 6&hearts; will be on a finesse, but you never know about missing tens and jacks (unless you are the one that is looking at them) so in the long run it is better to play safe when you are not looking at them.

**19.**

| Opener | Responder |
|--------|-----------|
| ♠ A K J 6 3 2 | ♠ Q 8 5 |
| ♡ K 4 | ♡ A Q 8 |
| ◇ 2 | ◇ A 9 7 |
| ♣ A 6 4 3 | ♣ K J 7 2 |
| 1♠ | 2♣¹ |
| 3◇² | 3♠³ |
| 4♣⁴ | 4♡⁵ |
| 4♠⁶ | 5◇⁷ |
| 6♠ | pass |

1. Not a game force.
2. Splinter in diamonds with four clubs.
3. Natural (double agreement now in place).
4. RKB (1430) after minor-major double agreement.
5. '0 or 3' (should be '3').
6. To play facing '0', queen-ask facing '3'.
7. Higher-ranking queen only.

Lots going on here:
a) Using 3◇ as a splinter rather than natural.
b) Double agreement after the 3♠ bid.
c) Using four of the agreed minor to ask for 'double Keycard' after major-minor double agreement.
d) 6 Keycards included in the response as the kings and queens of both suits are counted.
e) The return to 4♠, one of the agreed suits, is to play facing '0', but the queen-ask facing '3' after a 1430 ask.
f) When responding to a double agreement queen-ask, there are four steps: neither, lower, higher, both.

**20.**

| Opener | Responder |
|--------|-----------|
| ♠ 5 3 | ♠ K J 7 4 2 |
| ♡ A K | ♡ 8 6 |
| ◇ A 10 5 2 | ◇ K Q J 6 3 |
| ♣ A K Q 6 4 | ♣ 2 |
| 1♣ | 1♠ |
| 2◇ | 4◇¹ |
| 4♡² | 4♠³ |
| 4NT⁴ | 5♠⁵ |
| 6◇⁶ | pass |

1. Game-forcing jump agreement, supposedly a slammish-type hand with strong diamonds.
2. RKB 1430 after game-forcing four-level diamond agreement — hearts not a first-bid suit.
3. '1'.
4. Queen-ask.
5. Yes, with the ♠K.
6. Well, I'm glad you've got that card. I'd hate to be off the ♠AK.

A little shaky, but 4◇ is supposed to show a good hand as well as strong diamonds, so opener really shouldn't have to worry about being off the ♠AK. However, a really good partner would have the ♠KQ to relieve anguish!

**21. Opener**          **Responder**

♠ 5                      ♠ A K 7 2
♡ A K Q 6 3              ♡ 5 4
◇ K 10 8 7 4            ◇ A Q J 6 5
♣ 9 3                    ♣ Q 7

| | | |
|---|---|---|
| 1♡ | 2◇ | 1. Game-forcing splinter. |
| 3♠¹ | 4♠² | 2. Cuebid denying a club control (no 4♣ bid). |
| 5◇³ | pass | 3. Also no club control. |

After a game-forcing three-level splinter, four of the agreed suit is RKB. A cuebid suggests a lack of control in the unbid suit.

**22. Opener**          **Responder**

♠ J 10 7                 ♠ 4
♡ A K Q                  ♡ 7
◇ A K 8 2               ◇ Q J 7 6 5 3
♣ 5 4 2                  ♣ A K 7 6 3

| | | |
|---|---|---|
| 1NT | 2♠¹ | 1. Minors — not a game force. |
| 3◇ | 4♡² | 2. RKB (3014) including the ♣K. If 2♠ were game-forcing, 4◇ would be RKB. |
| 4♠³ | 5♣⁴ | 3. '3'. |
| 5◇⁵ | pass | 4. SSA. |
| | | 5. Denies as little as third-round. |

Here the SSA keeps you out of an impossible slam.

**23. Opener**          **Responder**

♠ A K Q                  ♠ 8 6
♡ 7                      ♡ K Q 5
◇ A J 8 7 5 2          ◇ K Q 6 4 3
♣ K 6 4                  ♣ J 3 2

| | | |
|---|---|---|
| 1◇ | 3♣¹ | 1. Crisscross, showing limit raise values. Those who play limit raises bid 3◇ instead. |
| 4♡² | 5◇³ | 2. Splinter; 4◇ would be RKB. |
| pass | | 3. Not interested with so much wasted heart strength. |

In order even to think about a slam facing a limit raise you should have a singleton or void. Even a 19-point balanced hand facing a limit raise seldom produces slam. If you could see both hands, 3NT is best, so congratulations if you got there. Playing limit raises, responder bids 3◇. If opener wishes to ask for Keycards, 4◇ is the ask ('When there are two or three, the raise is free') and 4♡ is a splinter.

24. **Opener** | **Responder**

| Opener | Responder |
|---|---|
| ♠ 5 | ♠ K Q J 6 2 |
| ♡ K 5 4 3 | ♡ A J 7 2 |
| ◇ A K Q 6 4 | ◇ J 3 |
| ♣ K Q 8 | ♣ A J |

| Opener | Responder |
|---|---|
| 1◇ | 1♠ |
| 2♡ | 3♡[1] |
| 3NT[2] | 4NT[3] |
| 5♡[4] | 6NT[5] |
| pass | |

1. Game-forcing three-level agree-ment — has big things in mind.
2. Natural, descriptive.
3. RKB (3014) — opener has reversed, showing extras.
4. '2 without'.
5. Hoping to make it on power alone without having to worry about the missing ♡Q.

After eight-card major-suit agreement, 4NT over 3NT by an unlimited hand is RKB.

25. **Opener** | **Responder**

| Opener | Responder |
|---|---|
| ♠ A 6 3 | ♠ 4 |
| ♡ A J 8 6 4 2 | ♡ K Q 5 |
| ◇ K 5 4 | ◇ A 8 7 2 |
| ♣ 7 | ♣ A Q J 6 3 |

| Opener | Responder |
|---|---|
| 1♡ | 2♣ |
| 2♡ | 3♠[1] |
| 4NT[2] | 5♠[3] |
| 7♡ | pass |

1. Slam invitational splinter.
2. RKB (1430) — opener asking.
3. '2 with'.

Declarer intends to pitch a possible losing diamond on dummy's fifth (or sixth) club. Of course if dummy turns up with the ♣K or the ◇Q, that won't be necessary. The ◇J wouldn't hurt either. All in all, a bit risky.

26. **Opener** | **Responder**

| Opener | Responder |
|---|---|
| ♠ 4 | ♠ A 9 6 |
| ♡ A Q 10 4 3 | ♡ K |
| ◇ A Q 2 | ◇ 8 6 5 |
| ♣ K 10 6 5 | ♣ A Q J 7 4 2 |

| Opener | Responder |
|---|---|
| 1♡ | 2♣ |
| 3♠[1] | 4♣[2] |
| 4◇[3] | 7♣ |
| pass | |

1. Slam-invitational splinter.
2. RKB (3014) — opener has jumped.
3. '3'.

Although it is unusual to ask for Keycards with two or more quick losers in an unbid suit, it is justified here. Opener is known to have at most 10 HCP between clubs and hearts, so at the very least opener must have the ◇K and probably more. Splinter jumps show very strong helping hands. And yes, if opener has

♠ 4    ♡ A Q J 4 3    ◇ K 4 2    ♣ K 10 6 5

the best contract is 6NT from opener's side. As it is, opener plans to discard diamond losers on dummy's hearts.

If responder doesn't relish asking for Keycards with three small diamonds, he can cuebid 4♠ . This might encourage opener to bid 4NT (1430). The response is 5♠, '2 with', and if opener follows that up with a bid of 5NT, a grand slam try looking for extras (not a king-ask), responder is right there with a 7♣ bid. He has two extras: the ♡K and club length.

27. **Opener**          **Responder**

| ♠ 6 4 2 | ♠ K 8 5 |
| ♡ A K J | ♡ 7 |
| ◇ 4 | ◇ A 10 9 6 5 2 |
| ♣ K 10 7 5 3 2 | ♣ A Q 4 |

| 1♣ | 1◇ | 1. Game-forcing splinter. |
| 2♣ | 3♡¹ | 2. Should be interpreted as looking |
| 3♠² | 3NT | for a spade stopper holding a |
| pass | | heart stopper. |

28. **Opener**          **Responder**

| ♠ A Q 7 | ♠ K 6 3 |
| ♡ A 4 2 | ♡ K Q 10 7 5 3 |
| ◇ A 7 6 4 | ◇ 3 |
| ♣ Q 6 3 | ♣ A 10 2 |

| 1NT | 2◇¹ | 1. Transfer. |
| 2♡ | 4◇² | 2. Slam-try splinter with long hearts. |
| 5♣³ | 6♡ | 3. '3 without'. |
| pass | | |

After a slam-try splinter in this sequence, it was suggested that opener can sign off in 4♡, ask for Keycards via 4NT (1430) or show Keycards via step responses excluding four of the agreed suit (which is to play) and 4NT (which is RKB). The 1st step, 4♠ in this sequence, would show '2 with'. The 2nd step response of 5♣ shows '3 without'. A more than reasonable slam is reached. Even if responder does not have the 'convenient' ♣10, the slam is still playable.

29. **Opener**          **Responder**

| ♠ A J | ♠ K Q 6 3 |
| ♡ A 7 | ♡ Q J 10 4 |
| ◇ A Q J 9 5 4 | ◇ 6 |
| ♣ 4 3 2 | ♣ A K J 7 |

| | | 1. Natural; 4♡ would be RKB for |
| 1◇ | 1♡ | diamonds (3014). |
| 3◇ | 4NT¹ | 2. Gambling the diamonds will |
| 6NT² | pass | come in. |

After three-level diamond non-agreement, the suit having been rebid or jump rebid, a leap to 4♡ is RKB for diamonds — even if hearts is a first-bid suit. A bid of 3♡ is forcing in these sequences.

30. 

| Opener | Responder |
|---|---|
| ♠ A K 2 | ♠ 6 4 3 |
| ♡ A 7 6 5 | ♡ 4 |
| ◇ K Q 8 | ◇ A 6 2 |
| ♣ A K 4 | ♣ Q J 10 7 5 2 |
| 2♣ | 3♣ |
| 4♣[1] | 4◇[2] |
| 5♡[3] | 7♣[4] |
| pass | |

1. RKB (1430) — a perk for the 2♣ opener when responder bids a minor naturally at the three-level.
2. '1'
3. A scary SSA in hearts. Logical, but scary. As mentioned earlier, don't pull this one out of the hat on an unsuspecting and perhaps unforgiving partner. In these sequences it doesn't pay be 'right', if you know what I mean.
4. With a singleton in the ask suit, the long trump hand is asked to jump in the trump suit.

31. 

| Opener | Responder |
|---|---|
| ♠ A Q 10 9 | ♠ 5 |
| ♡ A K 6 | ♡ 5 3 2 |
| ◇ 8 | ◇ A J 6 3 2 |
| ♣ Q 8 7 6 4 | ♣ A K J 10 |
| 1♣ | 1◇ |
| 1♠ | 2♡[1] |
| 3NT[2] | 4♣[3] |
| 4♡[4] | 6♣[5] |
| pass | |

1. Too strong for a non-forcing jump to 3♣.
2. 15-17 HCP, usually with a 5-4-3-1 pattern. If balanced, he would have opened 1NT.
3. Slam try.
4. Cuebid; 4◇ and 4♠ are also cuebids and 4NT is to play.
5. Looks promising facing a slam try with a likely singleton diamond.

After a 3NT jump rebid followed by a slam-try agreement, opener may only cuebid to express slam interest, unless he has previously jumped in the agreed suit,

32. 

| Opener | Responder |
|---|---|
| ♠ — | ♠ Q 7 6 3 |
| ♡ A Q 8 7 5 2 | ♡ K 6 4 3 |
| ◇ K Q 7 | ◇ A 4 |
| ♣ A Q 10 3 | ♣ 6 5 2 |
| 1♡ | 3♡[1] |
| 4♠[2] | 5◇[3] |
| 6♣[4] | 6♡[5] |
| pass | |

1. Limit raise.
2. EKB (jump over game after agreement).
3. '2' keycards including the ♡K, but excluding the ♠A.
4. SSA in clubs. Looking for magic, either the ♣K or a singleton.
5. Denies second- or third-round club control.

**33. Opener**

♠ A K J 7
♡ K Q
♢ A K Q 8 2
♣ 5 4

| | |
|---|---|
| 1♢ | 1♡ |
| 2♠ | 3♢ |
| 3♡[1] | 3♠[2] |
| 4♠[3] | pass |

**Responder**

♠ Q 4 2
♡ A 10 6 3
♢ 6 5 4 3
♣ J 8

1. Strapped for a bid. If responder bids 4♡, opener is planning to bid 5♢. Opener is still angling for 3NT.
2. Probably honor-third and surely denies a club stopper.
3. Going for the 4-3 fit with strong trumps; 5♢ is surely another option. The idea is to stay out of slam on this one. Also if partner has something like:
   ♠Q42 ♡J1063 ♢J1043 ♣Q8
   you have just hit a home run!

**34. Opener**

♠ Q 5
♡ A 6 5
♢ K 6 3 2
♣ K Q J 7

| | |
|---|---|
| 1NT | 2♡[1] |
| 2♠ | 4♡[2] |
| 4NT[3] | 5♢[4] |
| 6♠ | pass |

**Responder**

♠ A K J 7 4 3
♡ 8
♢ A J 10
♣ 5 4 2

1. Transfer.
2. Singleton slam-try with at least six spades, typically 13-15 HCP.
3. RKB (1430) — notrump bidder asking.
4. '3'.

Opener elects to ask for Keycards having the perfect holding in hearts as well as a KQJ suit which should provide discard(s) if needed. However, if a singleton club is led, call 911.

**35. Opener**

♠ A Q J 10 6
♡ A K
♢ A K J 3 2
♣ 5

| | |
|---|---|
| 2♣[1] | 2♢[2] |
| 2♠ | 4♢[3] |
| 4NT[4] | 5♣[5] |
| 6♠ | pass |

**Responder**

♠ K 5 4 3
♡ Q 7 4 2
♢ 6
♣ Q 7 6 3

1. Too heavy for 1♠.
2. Waiting.
3. Splinter agreeing spades.
4. RKB (1430).
5. '1'.

Don't tell me you came home lame on this one!

36. **Opener**          **Responder**
    ♠ 5               ♠ A K Q 10 6
    ♡ A 9 8 4         ♡ —
    ◇ A Q J 10 8 6 3  ◇ K 7 5 2
    ♣ 6               ♣ K 7 4 3

*The opponents open 3♡ in front of 'Opener', but pass throughout from there on in.*

| Oppt. | Opener | Oppt. | Responder |
|-------|--------|-------|-----------|
| 3♡ | 4◇ | pass | 5♡¹ |
| pass | 5NT² | pass | 6◇³ |
| all pass | | | |

1. Exclusion Keycard Blackwood.
2. '1' Keycard excluding the ♡A.
3. One ace missing.

If opener shows two Keycards outside of hearts, meaning opener has both minor-suit aces, responder bids 7◇.

37. **Opener**      **Responder**          1. Game-forcing splinter with 4+
    ♠ K Q 5         ♠ A J 8                   hearts.
    ♡ A K 8 6 3     ♡ J 7 5 4 2            2. RKB (1430).
    ◇ A 7 6 5       ◇ 4                    3. '2 with' — knows of a ten-card
    ♣ 2             ♣ A J 4 3                 heart fit.
                                           4. Should be manageable facing
    1♡              4◇¹                       four hearts as opener has
    4NT²            5♠³                       multiple hand entries to ruff
    7♡⁴             pass                      diamonds.

38. **Opener**      **Responder**
    ♠ 3             ♠ A K J 7 4 2
    ♡ Q 6 5         ♡ A
    ◇ K Q 4         ◇ A 9 7
    ♣ A J 10 6 5 3  ♣ Q 4 2

    1♣              2♠¹                     1. Strong.
    3♣              4♣²                     2. RKB (1430).
    4◇³             6♣                      3. '1'.

After a strong jump shift, if opener rebids a minor, a raise to four of that minor is RKB. This is a 'perk' given a strong jump-shifter (doesn't have to agree the suit first and then ask, the usual scenario). If the original response is 1♠, opener rebids 2♣ and responder can ask for Keycards via a jump to 4◇ (1430).

39. **Opener**    **Responder**

  ♠ 4           ♠ A 10 7 6
  ♡ A Q J 8 4 3 2  ♡ K 6
  ◇ 7 6        ◇ A K J 5 2
  ♣ 5 4 2     ♣ A 8

| Opener | Responder | |
|---|---|---|
| 3♡ | 4♣[1] | 1. RKB (by agreement, after a |
| 4♠[2] | 6♡ | preempt). |
| pass | | 2. '1 with'. |

Expecting to set up the diamonds if necessary..

40. **Opener**    **Responder**

  ♠ A Q J 5    ♠ K 3
  ♡ 10 8 7 4   ♡ K Q J 5 2
  ◇ —        ◇ A K J 4 3
  ♣ K Q J 6 2  ♣ 5

| Opener | Responder | |
|---|---|---|
| 1♣ | 1♡ | 1. RKB 1430 — opener limited. |
| 2♡ | 4NT[1] | 2. '1' (or '3') with a diamond void. |
| 6◇[2] | 6♡[3] | 3. To play facing '1'. This is so sad. |
| pass[4] | | 4. You're telling me. |

This one illustrates one of the pitfalls of jumping in your void suit with
only one Keycard. It could be right, but not on this hand. It is near impossible for opener to anticipate this turn of events, but there you are — in a
slam off two cashing aces. I'd like to think you did better.

Could opener have '3' Keycards on this auction? Of course it is possible, but a player with three aces, four-card support and a void usually does
more than screw up his courage and raise to 2♡.

41.    **Opener**             **Responder**

     ♠ —                ♠ A J 6 3
     ♡ K 8 4         ♡ 7 5 2
     ◇ A K J 6 4    ◇ 2
     ♣ Q J 8 3 2    ♣ A K 7 6 4

| Opener | Oppt. | Responder | Oppt. |
|---|---|---|---|
| 1◇ | 1♠ | 2♣ | pass |
| 4♠[1] | pass | 5◇[2] | pass |
| 6♣ | all pass | | |

1. EKB. One level higher than a splinter.
2. '2' excluding the ♠A.

The bidding calls for a heart lead so the slam will probably go down.

**42. Opener**    **Responder**

| Opener | Responder | |
|---|---|---|
| ♠ A Q J 4 2 | ♠ — | |
| ♡ 8 | ♡ A J 6 3 | |
| ◇ A K 8 6 3 | ◇ Q J 9 5 4 2 | |
| ♣ 5 4 | ♣ Q J 2 | 1. Splinter for diamonds; jumping to |
| | | 4◇ is another possibility, particu- |
| 1♠ | 2◇ | larly if you don't play 3♡ as a |
| 3♡¹ | 4♡² | splinter. |
| 4♠² | 5◇³ | 2. Cuebid. |
| pass | | 3. Nobody has a club control. |

**43. Opener**    **Responder**

| Opener | Responder | |
|---|---|---|
| ♠ A Q 7 6 3 | ♠ 8 5 4 2 | |
| ♡ — | ♡ A 9 4 | |
| ◇ K 3 | ◇ Q 10 9 6 5 2 | |
| ♣ A K Q 5 4 2 | ♣ — | |
| 1♣ | 1◇ | |
| 2♠ | 3♠ | 1. EKB. |
| 5♡¹ | 5♠² | 2. '0' Keycards outside of hearts. |
| pass | | |

You may not want to write home about this one.

**44. Opener**    **Responder**

| Opener | Responder | |
|---|---|---|
| ♠ 6 5 4 | ♠ K Q J 2 | |
| ♡ A K J 6 4 2 | ♡ 3 | |
| ◇ 7 | ◇ A K Q J 6 3 2 | |
| ♣ Q J 8 | ♣ A | |
| 1♡ | 4NT¹ | 1. Regular Blackwood, mystery suit. |
| 5◇² | 6◇³ | 2. One ace. |
| pass | | 3. Mystery solved. |

It is usually right to agree a suit before asking for Keycards or aces, particularly when you are missing the king and/or queen of your long suit. However, if you have a solid suit and are not playing 'last-bid suit' or that strong jump shifts followed by 4NT agree the jump-shift suit, a direct 4NT looks like a good bet. Of course, you must consider partner's physical condition, as he or she is expected to pass 6◇ holding a singleton or void in diamonds.

45. **Opener**          **Responder**

| Opener | Responder |
|---|---|
| ♠ — | ♠ A J 6 |
| ♡ A K J 5 | ♡ 6 3 2 |
| ◇ K Q 6 | ◇ 8 4 |
| ♣ A Q 9 7 5 2 | ♣ K J 8 6 3 |
| 1♣ | 2◇¹ |
| 4♠² | 5♣³ |
| 6♣ | pass |

1. Crisscross, the equivalent of a limit raise. Those that don't play Crisscross respond 3♣, limit, or 1NT.
2. EKB (3♠ would be a splinter).
3. '1' (does not count the ♠A).

After a limit raise to 3♣, a leap to 4♠ is a splinter and a leap to 5♠ is EKB. After a 1NT response, opener would bid 2♡. Responder now has a choice of actions: perhaps 2♠, possibly 4♣. All roads should lead to 6♣.

46. **Opener**          **Responder**

| Opener | Responder |
|---|---|
| ♠ K J 6 | ♠ 8 3 |
| ♡ 4 | ♡ A K 6 5 2 |
| ◇ A K 5 3 | ◇ Q J 7 4 2 |
| ♣ A Q J 4 2 | ♣ 6 |
| 1♣ | 1♡ |
| 2◇ | 4◇¹ |
| 4♠² | 4NT³ |
| 5♣⁴ | 5♡⁵ |
| 6◇⁶ | pass |

1. More descriptive than 3◇.
2. RKB (1430); 4♡ would be natural.
3. '1'.
4. Queen-ask.
5. Yes, with the ♡K.
6. All very nice and pretty, but we are missing an ace.

A queen-ask made beneath game in the agreed suit is considered a small slam try, but any ask above game in the agreed suit is a grand slam try.

47. **Opener**          **Responder**

| Opener | Responder |
|---|---|
| ♠ A 6 | ♠ K 8 3 |
| ♡ K Q 4 2 | ♡ A J 7 5 3 |
| ◇ 5 4 | ◇ A K 6 2 |
| ♣ A Q 10 3 2 | ♣ 7 |
| 1♣ | 1♡ |
| 3♡ | 4◇¹ |
| 4♠² | 4NT³ |
| 5♣⁴ | 5◇⁵ |
| 5NT⁶ | 7♡⁷ |
| pass | |

1. Slam-try cuebid. Not a bad idea to bid (or cuebid) a side four-card suit headed by the AK before using RKB. Partner should realize that third-round control in that suit may be important.
2. Deciding to let partner take charge.
3. RKB (3014) — opener has jumped.
4. '3'.
5. Queen-ask.
6. Yes, with a third-round extra — either the queen of partner's first-bid suit, or third-round control in a second-bid suit.
7. It must be third-round control in diamonds.

Notice that if opener does the asking, the bidding should go like this after the 4◇ cuebid:

| Opener | Responder | |
|---|---|---|
| | ... | 1. RKB (1430). |
| 4NT[1] | 5♡[2] | 2. '2 without'. |
| 5NT[3] | 7♡[4] | 3. SKA. |
| pass | | 4. Can't be any losers. |

From responder's point of view, opener must have both black-suit aces, the ♡KQ, plus nine cards between clubs and hearts. (If opener has a balanced hand with 15-17 HCP he opens 1NT.) So where is there a loser?

48. 
| Opener | Responder |
|---|---|
| ♠ A Q J 9 8 5 | ♠ K 10 7 4 3 2 |
| ♡ K J 5 4 | ♡ — |
| ◇ A K | ◇ J 6 3 2 |
| ♣ A | ♣ Q 9 4 |

| Opener | Responder | |
|---|---|---|
| 1♠ | 4♠ | 1. RKB (1430). |
| 4NT[1] | 6♡[2] | 2. '1' (or '3') with a heart void. |
| 7♠[3] | pass | 3. Should be a no-brainer. |

This time it is right to show the void with one Keycard. Of course, this time the responder is known to have a weak hand.

49. 
| Opener | Responder |
|---|---|
| ♠ 6 3 | ♠ K Q J 10 7 4 2 |
| ♡ A Q 7 3 | ♡ 5 |
| ◇ A J 4 2 | ◇ K Q 7 6 |
| ♣ K Q 6 | ♣ 4 |

| Opener | Responder | |
|---|---|---|
| 1NT | 4♣[1] | 1. Gerber with simple ace responses, no agreed suit: 4◇ = 0 or 4 aces, 4♡ = 1 ace, 4♠ = 2 aces, 4NT = 3 aces. |
| 4♠[2] | pass | 2. Two aces. |

50. 
| Opener | Responder |
|---|---|
| ♠ A K J 5 2 | ♠ 6 3 |
| ♡ 3 | ♡ A K 10 6 4 |
| ◇ J 7 2 | ◇ A K 5 |
| ♣ A K 6 3 | ♣ J 4 2 |

| Opener | Responder | |
|---|---|---|
| 1♠ | 2♡ | 1. Extras. |
| 3♣[1] | 4NT[2] | 2. Natural in this sequence. |
| pass[3] | | 3. Singleton in partner's first-bid suit, no intermediates in the long suits. |

On a bad day, you could actually go down in 4NT with 31 HCP between the two hands!

**51. Opener**     **Responder**

| Opener | Responder |
|--------|-----------|
| ♠ Q J | ♠ A K 6 |
| ♡ K Q 7 4 3 | ♡ 5 |
| ◇ K 8 | ◇ A J 4 |
| ♣ Q J 5 2 | ♣ K 9 7 6 4 3 |
| 1♡ | 2♣ |
| 3♣ | 4♣[1] |
| 4♡[2] | 4NT[3] |
| pass | |

1. RKB 1430 (two unbid suits).
2. '3 or 0' (must be '0' as responder has '3').
3. After a '0' response, 4NT is to play. Responder could also bid 5♣, but 4NT is surely the right bid at matchpoints.

**52. Opener**     **Responder**

| Opener | Responder |
|--------|-----------|
| ♠ A J 7 | ♠ K Q 9 |
| ♡ A K Q 6 3 | ♡ 4 |
| ◇ 6 | ◇ A 7 4 2 |
| ♣ 8 6 5 2 | ♣ Q J 7 4 3 |
| 1♡ | 2♣ |
| 3◇[1] | 4♣[2] |
| 4♠[3] | 5♣[4] |
| pass | |

1. GF splinter for clubs — this is about as weak as a splinter jump gets.
2. RKB (four of the agreed suit in a game-forcing auction).
3. '2 without'.
4. Two Keycards missing.

**53. Opener**     **Responder**

| Opener | Responder |
|--------|-----------|
| ♠ A Q J 8 3 | ♠ K 6 4 2 |
| ♡ 9 | ♡ A 6 3 2 |
| ◇ A 8 5 | ◇ 6 |
| ♣ A 6 4 2 | ♣ K Q 7 3 |
| 1♠ | 4◇[1] |
| 4NT[2] | 5♡[3] |
| 6♣[4] | 7♣[5] |
| 7♠ | pass |

1. Splinter.
2. RKB (1430).
3. '2 without'.
4. Specific Suit Ask.
5. KQ(x).

The 6♣ ask is not all that risky. These are the responses:

| | | |
|---|---|---|
| 6◇ (1st step) | = | third-round control (queen or xx) |
| 6♡ (2nd step) | = | Kxx(x) |
| 6♠ (trump suit) | = | no second- or third-round control |
| 6NT (third step) | = | Kx |
| Raise of the ask suit | = | KQ(x) |

After a 1st or 2nd step response, opener signs off in 6♠. Facing any other positive response, opener is willing to bid a grand.

**54. Opener**

♠ A 6 5 4
♡ 4
◇ A Q J 3 2
♣ K J 8

| | |
|---|---|
| 1◇ | |
| 1♠ | |
| 4♡² | |
| 6◇ | |

**Responder**

♠ 10 2
♡ A J 9 3 2
◇ K 10 8 6
♣ Q 3

| | |
|---|---|
| 1♡ | |
| 3◇¹ | |
| 5♣³ | |
| pass | |

1. NF three-level agreement.
2. RKB 1430 — one unbid suit so opener has to jump. Since 3♡ would agree hearts, it is okay to use 4♡ as the RKB ask here.
3. '2 without'.

**55. Opener**

♠ A K Q 6
♡ A K 6 4 3
◇ 2
♣ Q J 6

| | |
|---|---|
| 1♡ | |
| 2♠ | |
| 4NT² | |

**Responder**

♠ 3
♡ 7 2
◇ A K Q J 5 4
♣ 8 4 3 2

| | |
|---|---|
| 2◇ | |
| 4◇¹ | |
| pass | |

1. A 'broken record'. After responder has bid and then jumped in diamonds, opener assumes either a solid suit or a one-loser suit with an outside entry.
2. To play.

After a BR sequence ending at the four-level, 4NT is to play. The unbid suit is RKB. However, when clubs is the unbid suit, opener can use his second suit to ask for keycards. In the sequence above, 4♠ would be RKB (1430).

**56. Opener**

♠ A K 6 3
♡ A
◇ A J 6
♣ A K Q 7 6

| | |
|---|---|
| 2♣ | |
| 3♣ | |
| 4♡³ | |
| 5♠⁵ | |
| 7♣ | |

**Responder**

♠ Q 7 5 4
♡ 10 3 2
◇ 3
♣ J 9 8 4 2

| | |
|---|---|
| 2◇¹ | |
| 4◇² | |
| 4NT⁴ | |
| 5NT⁶ | |
| pass | |

1. Waiting. Those who play 2♡ as a double negative would bid 2♡.
2. Splinter.
3. RKB (1430). The cheapest unbid suit can be used as RKB after a four-level splinter bypasses the agreed suit.
4. '0' — checking to see if partner can be trusted. Opener has all five keycards!
5. Specific Suit Ask in spades.
6. 1st step response showing the queen or a doubleton — probably the queen since responder is known to have a singleton diamond.

The only way to make a SSA in spades is to go through 4NT first.

**57. Opener**      **Responder**

| Opener | Responder | |
|---|---|---|
| ♠ Q J 5 4 | ♠ A | |
| ♡ J 7 | ♡ A K 6 5 4 3 | |
| ◇ K J 6 2 | ◇ 3 | 1. Transfer. |
| ♣ A K 4 | ♣ Q J 8 5 2 | 2. Natural, game-forcing; usually a five-card suit. |
| 1NT | 2◇¹ | 3. Probably 6-5 or 5-5, slammish. |
| 2♡ | 3♣² | 4. Clearly a doubleton. |
| 3NT | 4♣³ | 5. RKB (1430), both kings and the |
| 4♡⁴ | 4NT⁵ | ♡Q included. |
| 5♡⁶ | 6♣⁷ | 6. '2 without'. |
| pass | | 7. Choice of contract. |

When the asker has a two-suited hand and receives delayed simple preference to the first suit, usually showing a doubleton, he can give his partner one more chance to play in the other lower-ranking suit by bidding that suit at the six-level.

**58. Opener**      **Responder**

| Opener | Responder | |
|---|---|---|
| ♠ A 3 | ♠ Q J 6 4 2 | |
| ♡ A K 8 5 | ♡ 4 3 | 1. Transfer. |
| ◇ A Q 5 2 | ◇ K J 7 6 3 | 2. Second suit — usually five. |
| ♣ A 8 6 | ♣ 3 | 3. The unbid major — RKB for diamonds including the ♠K and |
| 2NT | 3♡¹ | the ◇Q. |
| 3♠ | 4◇² | 4. '1'. |
| 4♡³ | 4♠⁴ | 5. One Keycard missing. This is a |
| 6◇⁵ | pass | 6-Keycard auction. |

After a 2NT opening and a double transfer ending in 4◇, opener can ask for Keycards by bidding the unbid major. Responder includes the kings of both suits in the response as well as the queen of the last-bid minor.

**59. Opener**      **Responder**

| Opener | Responder | |
|---|---|---|
| ♠ A K 9 4 | ♠ Q 10 6 3 2 | |
| ♡ A 5 | ♡ K 10 6 4 3 | |
| ◇ K Q 10 7 | ◇ A 5 2 | |
| ♣ 9 8 7 | ♣ — | 1. Transfer. |
| 1NT | 2♡¹ | 2. Four spades with a side-suit |
| 3♠² | 5♣³ | doubleton. |
| 5NT⁴ | 6♠ | 3. Exclusion Keycard Blackwood. |
| pass | | 4. '3' (outside of clubs). |

This hand came up in a strong French tournament. Nonetheless, most pairs played in game on a hand that might easily make a grand. Of course, responder is lucky to catch opener with no strength in clubs, but even if you reverse opener's minors, 6♠ still has a play. It is tempting for responder to break ranks and bid 7♠ over 5♣ holding what is sure to be the perfect dummy.

60. **Opener**      **Responder**

| Opener | Responder | |
|---|---|---|
| ♠ A Q J 5 | ♠ K 2 | |
| ♡ A Q J 7 4 | ♡ 5 2 | |
| ◇ A Q | ◇ 9 6 | |
| ♣ 6 2 | ♣ A Q J 7 5 4 3 | 1. Not played as game force. |
| | | 2. Forcing and unlimited after |
| 1♡ | 2♣¹ |     opener reverses. |
| 2♠ | 3♣² | 3. Natural. |
| 4NT³ | 6NT⁴ | 4. Accepts. |

After opener reverses and responder rebids his minor, a raise to the four-level by opener is RKB: the reason that a 4NT rebid is natural.